HIDDEN POWER

The Programming of the President

By Roland Perry
Programme for a Puppet (fiction)
L'Ordinateur du President

HIDDEN POWER

The Programming of the President

Roland Perry

Beaufort Books, Inc.
New York

ISBN 0-8253-0224-2   LC 84-9271

Published in the United States by Beaufort Books, Inc., New York.
Published in Great Britain by Aurum Press Limited.

Printed in Great Britain
First American Edition

10   9   8   7   6   5   4   3   2   1

To the Georgeff family: Diana, Michael,
Simon and Alexandra

INTRODUCTION

"Are you committed to Christ?" The question hung on the telephone line from Virginia to Ohio, inviting a stunned silence.

Mrs Mary Anne Smith had been phoned at 9 p.m., a relatively convenient time for most American households, and had been warmed up on less personal questions by the caller who claimed to be from an 'independent' survey company. Mrs Smith was unfazed. "Yes, I am committed," she replied. "My family has always been religious, and I have instilled it into my children."

The caller, a professional survey operator with Decision Making Information (DMI), sat in front of a TV computer terminal screen plying his unusual skills. He had no papers. He simply watched the questions as they came up in sequence on the terminal, then deftly typed the responses into a microprocessor. The machine listed a series of probing questions on religion. Was it important that the candidate for whom she decided to vote in a presidential election had a strong commitment to Christ? What was her faith? Did she believe in Darwin's theory of evolution or in the Biblical version of the Creation? There were more than twenty questions covering a range of current religious issues.

Mrs Smith answered honestly, sometimes articulating well, sometimes not. She had been naturally cautious at first, but soon found the questions innocuous. Was she optimistic about her future, and that of her children? What about the nation's future? What kind of President did she prefer: someone authoritarian and religious or someone intellectual and flexible? She was fascinated at times and more than a little flattered by the interest and politeness of the caller. The call itself ("I would really appreciate a few minutes of your time") lasted forty minutes and covered as many topics. It represented the visible surface of the hidden computerized campaign to elect Ronald Reagan as President of the United States.

Mrs Smith is only one of several hundred thousand Americans who answered 'attitudinal' surveys conducted by DMI and other companies before and during the Reagan Presidency. Unlike the polls made public at election time which show who is ahead or behind in a race for office (so-called 'horse race' polls), these surveys are usually kept secret. DMI's blunt questions about Jesus Christ were put to a huge number of respondents in order that the political strategists behind Reagan could, with the aid of computers, analyze the replies and uncover the importance of the religious factor in a particular county or state or across the nation. This information gave strategists vital clues for securing a majority of the religious vote. The replies to their questions told them not only where the candidate should present a more pious image but also what he should actually say to win votes. And religion was but one subject among many others ranging from defense and the environment to sex, education and welfare.

Computers can compile and link the fears, hopes, aspirations, thoughts and feelings of a nation's entire population to form a picture of its mood – like pieces of a jigsaw coming together. This in turn gives an indication of what should be said and done, and when, that will greatly increase a candidate's chances of being elected. The inclinations of each individual collectively trigger the final voting decision on election day. Knowing this, the strategist can build a framework for the candidate within which he must campaign in order to have the best chance of victory. This framework was created for Ronald Reagan long before he began his campaign in the watershed election year of 1980.

Secret polling does not stop with the broad outline of strategy. Once this is ascertained, more particular probes give tactical insights to be used during the heat of the election battle: if the image of candidate A is found by the surveys to be weakening under the mounting pressure of the campaign, it must be rounded out to appear stronger. If candidate B is seen as dangerous, he must be packaged as peaceful. If candidate C is universally considered a 'nice guy', his opponents will try to tarnish this image.

The strategists use poll after poll to monitor possible changes in public perception of a candidate. For example, they may monitor a candidate's 'dangerous image' to see if the nation's view is shifting as his image is modified to be more appealing. This so-called 'tracking' is also used to follow the views and attitudes of scores of different voting groups – blacks, Hispanics, Catholics, blue-collar, middle-income and so on. The great weight of constantly increas-ing information must be filed into categories and subcategories, cross-referenced, linked, separated, grouped and tracked. Only modern microchip computers, with their unlimited storage capacity and speed, make possible the instant manipulation of all this data by the new breed of political strategists directing their candidates toward election day. Yet the computer's power stretches far beyond its ability to file endless facts and move them around rapidly. It can be used to program entirely a candidate's bid for political office. This is no longer some science fiction dream or a possibility for the twenty-first century. It has already happened.

This book traces the power and influence of the leading exponents of the new technology and in particular the contest between the two most successful strategists of the modern political era: Richard Wirthlin and Patrick Caddell. They more than any others have learned to use modern techniques for mass manipulation far beyond the fictional scenario envisaged in 1984. In that masterpiece Orwell was issuing a warning about socialism – as practiced by Stalin in the Soviet Union – infecting Britain in the late 1940s. His 1984 was a vision of 1948. Yet now the Russians themselves want to learn from real US electoral methods, 1984-style. Early in 1981, after Ronald Reagan's election, a senior Soviet official based in Washington DC arrived unannounced and uninvited at Wirthlin's offices in McClean, near Washington DC. He wanted to meet the strategist and learn how he had managed to sell the former actor-Governor to the American people. The Russians, even more ignorant than Western Europe was about him, were amazed at the feat. They were also most interested in understanding strategic polling techniques. Not surprisingly Wirthlin refused to see the snooping Russian. Nevertheless, the Soviet Union is now copying American polling and political market research techniques.

The two brilliant political adversaries, Wirthlin and Caddell, have used the methods in a sixteeen-year battle to impose their opposite political ideologies on the United States' democratic process.

The story begins with Wirthlin and the first step in his long relationship with Ronald Reagan. When former Mexican President Lopez Portillo met Reagan on the bridge joining their two countries soon after Reagan had won the US Presidency, Portillo asked: "Mr President, who is Dick Wirthlin?"

Who, indeed?

PART ONE
1968–1976
GENESIS OF A PROGRAM

CHAPTER 1
THE RIVALS

THE MORMON AND THE MOUNTAIN LION

A chauffeur-driven limousine sped through the resplendent, rain-soaked Santa Monica Hills in the far western part of Los Angeles towards the Pacific Ocean on a late fall day, in 1968. In the back seat was Californian political operative Tom Reed and a youthful looking academic named Dr Richard Wirthlin.

"Can you tell me now?" Wirthlin asked Reed.

"Soon, soon," Reed replied, with a mischievous smile.

Wirthlin looked quizzical, but did not press him further. He had been intrigued when a fellow Mormon from Utah, Richard Richards, had said he wanted him to meet a very important contact. Now Wirthlin would have to be patient. He sat and took in the beautiful scenery, and after half an hour Reed turned to him and said:

"It's the Governor."

"Reagan?"

"He's the only one we have in California."

Wirthlin laughed nervously and looked down at his casual brown jacket, tie and slacks. He recalled reading about the Reagans' Pacific Palisades home, a place where they could get away from the official state residence in Sacramento. The Governor liked to be close to the open, rugged country where you could come across deer and the odd mountain lion. Minutes later, they pulled into the drive of a large house in a cluster of similar residences which were set apart for privacy. Before the car had stopped, the fit-looking figure of a big man loped out of the front door. It was Reagan. He was wearing an open-necked check shirt and white slacks. He greeted his visitors with the wrinkled grin which everyone knew from a thousand wet weekend afternoons of his film re-runs on TV, and with which Californians had become familiar in the two years since he had become Governor in 1966. Wirthlin was introduced to Nancy Reagan, and they all moved inside the modern, open-plan house which featured much glass and stonework. The comfortably furnished lounge boasted some Western art, and Wirthlin's eyes fell on a large, striking painting of a Mexican peasant and his wife.

Reagan ushered Wirthlin to the back of the house, and the two men sat at a small table by an outdoor swimming pool. Even though they were soon down to political business, the Governor remained informal and friendly. The conversation turned to the major issues facing California – the imminent budget and the campus riots – and Wirthlin found his opinions were listened to carefully. Besides lecturing at many top American universities, he had obtained his Ph.D. in economics from the University of California at Berkeley, the most strife-torn educational institution in the state, if not the nation.

"Enjoy yourself at Berkeley?" Reagan inquired with a grin. "Nancy thinks it's terrible there. She doesn't believe in free love."

"I pre-dated all that, Governor," Wirthlin said, smiling. "I've been at Brigham Young since 1964."

"Teaching?"

"Yes. I chaired the economics department and directed the survey research center."

"You're a Mormon?" Wirthlin nodded. "Bet there isn't any rioting at Brigham Young," Reagan said.

"It's not allowed."

Nancy Reagan appeared at the library window which over-looked the pool, and asked if they wanted drinks.

"The young man is a Mormon and they don't drink or cause campus riots," Reagan said, winking at Wirthlin. "He'll have a fruit juice and so will I."

She smiled her approval at the handsome visitor. Minutes later she brought them drinks and then left them alone again.

Reagan surprised Wirthlin by knowing more about the Mormon Welfare Program (self-help for the needy organized by the Church) than he did himself. The Governor had never been happy about state hand-outs. Life wasn't meant to be easy and to 'make it', as he had, he believed that you had to work hard. In Reagan's opinion social welfare such as he had witnessed in the UK in 1949 (while making the film *The Hasty Heart*) weakened both the state and the self-reliance of the individual.

The more their views coincided, the more Wirthlin changed his mind about Reagan and his preconceived image of him as a lucky cowboy out of the West. This was no dumb cowpoke. His articulation and sensitivity to many issues showed a more compassionate and intelligent nature. Wirthlin felt that they were relating to each other very strongly, which was not surprising for the background and roots of both men had given them similar attitudes. Wirthlin came from the Midwest. Three of his grandparents had been brought by Mormon missionaries in Europe to rural Salt Lake City, Utah, American home of the Church which, since its inception in the 1820s until well into the twentieth century, had been attacked by the Federal Government. He had been brought up on a farm and his experience through the faith, including missionary work as a youth in Europe, had given him self-reliance and individuality. Reagan, too, came from a farming district of Illinois. Many of his attitudes, such as those toward welfare and women's rights, were formed there, and he was greatly influenced by his mother who was fervently religious.

As the conversation progressed, Wirthlin was asked to assess Californian attitudes to Reagan's governorship. Wirthlin had done some polling for politicians, including subcontract work for Richard Nixon, and he had strong connections with the Republican Party. He had quickly become regarded as one of the few experts in the specialized field of survey research, which had started to interest him a few years earlier. He had designed and supervised marketing, government and political research projects. He was also one of the believers in the new computer technology. He was not a nuts and bolts computer person who could describe every little function of the latest wonder machines, but because he considered them much more than simply tools for storing and calculating data, he had quickly mastered their uses. Wirthlin had experimented in areas of 'simulation', using computers to assess marketing strategies by developing marketing models. These models were set up by converting the impressions and forecasts of managers into mathematical formulae which could be digested, linked and manipulated by computer to predict the likely effects of any changes in marketing strategies. He had also begun to consider simulating political models and using them to forecast the outcome of elections.

The kind of polling survey work Reagan wanted him to do had become popular among politicians in the mid-sixties. Nixon was interested in it, and President Lyndon Johnson would pull polls out of his pockets and show them around if they demonstrated his popularity. Pollsters had become as influential as the soothsayers of the Middle Ages, and many politicians were not making any moves without first checking with them. Yet much of the information on offer was merely the result of 'horse race' polls, which measured a politician's popularity in an election race by asking a sample of the public in a particular state for whom they would vote: candidate A, B or C. By 1968, some politicians had become more than a little skeptical. The results, often from unreliable samples, were wildly inaccurate. Politicians who thought they were going to win an election because the polls said they were twenty percentage points ahead a week before election day, were choking over their premature celebratory cigars and champagne when they found themselves beaten at the post. The pollster charlatans, out to make money fast, would soon be packing their bags and going back to advertising, or management consultancies or where ever else they had come from. Polls, it seemed, had been just another craze, like limbo-dancing or long sideburns. Some people would always like them, but they had reached their zenith and would never peak again.

There were, of course, a handful of substantial operators who understood how to poll with almost scientific precision, and how to read results and interpret them strategically in political election battles. Among the Democrats there was Joe Napolitan, who had acted as consultant to the 1968 presidential candidate Hubert Humphrey. Napolitan knew how to use surveys about the candidates' strengths and weaknesses, and could design media messages around them that would help his clients and destroy their opponents. Among the Republicans there was Robert Teeter, who would soon be well in with the Nixon crowd. And there was Richard Wirthlin. While he had links with the party and the Nixonites, Wirthlin was still at this time more of an academic than a business consultant. He certainly was not yet committed to any politician, and he had been stamped as trustworthy.

The results of any research into attitudes to Reagan's governorship were best kept secret, not just from the public, but from everyone else in politics. The reason for this was that *any* intelligence at all on his political activities and intentions, or even those of his opponents, was scarce and valuable. Primarily, the 'attitudinal' surveys that were now being contemplated would be used to reveal the state's 'mood' to the Reagan administration and thus allow the people around the Governor to build themes and strategies for his 1970 re-election bid. Yet the conversation that afternoon at Pacific Palisades indirectly revealed more than this to Wirthlin. He found it significant that the topic touched on Nixon, who had just won the Presidency.

Reagan had himself flirted with the idea of running for President earlier in the year, but had bungled it. From the general thrust of the discussion, Wirthlin got the message. He was not, at this point, being asked to poll possible support for a presidential bid by Reagan. It was not the time. For the moment, the Governor wanted to secure his job for two consecutive terms, until the end of 1974. That year would be the next opportunity for Reagan to make a better planned bid.

Wirthlin could see that the Governor was preoccupied with proving his worth in his current job, without worrying about the Presidency then. Yet the academic felt he understood Reagan's probable long-term thinking. Pat Brown had beaten Nixon for the California governorship in 1962. Just four years later, Reagan had polled a million votes more than Brown in the contest for the same office. Reagan was more popular than both Nixon and Brown in the biggest state in the nation. Wouldn't it perhaps be the same in every state if Reagan made a proper bid for the Republican nomination? Reagan had great respect for Nixon, but if Nixon could win the Presidency, Reagan, an optimist by nature, was confident he could make it too.

As dusk fell, the Governor and Wirthlin concluded their business and Tom Reed and Nancy Reagan reappeared. Wirthlin already looked forward to their next meeting; he had rarely enjoyed such stimulating company. As the limousine backed out of the drive, the Reagans waved goodbye and the Governor called, "Watch out for the mountain lions!" At first Wirthlin and Reed weren't sure if he was joking or not, but then his face creased into a waspish grin.

"I think you just met one," Reed said quietly to Wirthlin.

On the drive back to Los Angeles, Reed said: "How did you get on?"

"Very well, he's a great guy," Wirthlin replied. "Wants me to do some survey work right away."

"I think Nancy liked you too," Reed said and then added, "by the way, you never had this meeting."

Wirthlin realized that discretion was important with clients like this. He did not need either to be told that if you wanted to be 'in' with the Governor, it was important to have Nancy Reagan on your side. She was very astute as far as her husband's career was concerned. The meeting had been satisfactory all round. Reagan was backed by some of the most powerful businessmen in the state, among them Henry Salvatori, the oil man; Theodore Cummings of the supermarket chain; Justin Dart, company owner of the consumer products chain; Holmes Tuttle, the well-regarded pillar of California's financial community; and Jack Wrather, controller of a big oil, entertainment and property combine. To be an insider with that crowd, especially if they had big plans for Reagan, might just help a Wirthlin dream or two become reality. He and his wife Jeralie had planned a big family of eight or ten children, and at the age of thirty-seven, with many years of academia and research behind him, Wirthlin was keen to branch out and make his fortune. Wealth was not at all frowned upon by the Mormon Church. In fact it was encouraged, and if he wished to rise in the ranks of the Church, it was imperative that he make big money. Persecution and extreme privation a century ago had taught the Mormons that economic security was the best way of guaranteeing that trust in the Lord was not misplaced. Money was one way for an individual to ensure power and survival. To have banks full of it, in Mormon eyes, was a virtue rather than a sin. But private money also helped to swell the coffers and ranks of the five-million-strong Church: tithing, the donation of 10 per cent of members' incomes to the Church, had seen to that. People like J. Willard Marriott, the owner of the huge hotel chain, and Frank W. Gay, head of Howard Hughes's all-purpose Summa Corporation, were respected pillars of the Church. To reach the pinnacle of the faith on earth – the presidency of the Latter-Day Saints – where, according to Mormon belief, you might receive divine revelations, it would be most helpful to be rich. Not that Wirthlin was thinking he would ever have a chance of being Mormon president. It was not a position for which one lobbied. But he could be 'called' high in the Church. The wealthier you were, the better your chances of hearing such a shout.

Wirthlin's initial but important contact with Reagan was the further encouragement he needed to start his own company and capitalize on his growing experience and expertise.

THE POLLSTER MEETS THE PEANUT VENDOR

"G'night George," a chorus of voices called to Senator McGovern as he stood at the bottom of the stairs of the Georgia Governor's mansion. It was after midnight and the Democratic nominee for the Presidency was going to bed after a grueling day's campaigning in the 1972 battle against incumbent Richard Nixon. The candidate and his entourage had stopped for the night during a campaign drive through the South. McGovern looked drawn and tired, deflated even.

"He seems down," Jimmy Carter, the Georgia Governor drawled sympathetically from the doorway of the large kitchen as he watched McGovern make his way upstairs to the guests' quarters.

"Yeah, it was the TV ad the Republicans ran today," commented Patrick Caddell, McGovern's pollster. He was affectionately known as 'the chinless wonder' by others in the campaign team. His harassed expression seemed permanently clouded by some intellectual preoccupation.

"George's face was superimposed on a weathervane," Caddell added. "It swayed this way and that in the wind."

Carter nodded and walked back into the spacious kitchen where, apart from Caddell, three other members of McGovern's team were sitting talking politics and drinking beer. As the Governor went to the refrigerator for more cans, movement on the lawn outside near the closed iron gates caught his eye and he looked out through the Victorian windows where two members of McGovern's secret service detail were talking. Now that the candidate had gone to bed, it was time for a change of shift.

"It hit directly at George's perceived weaknesses," Caddell went on as he eased himself on to a seat next to Carter. "The

Republicans predictably discovered how the public saw George's inconsistency. Hence the weathervane."

"Predictably?"

"I knew it long before they did."

Carter opened a beer. He was impressed by Caddell's disarming honesty.

"It's our fault," Caddell added. "We haven't created the themes. George had nothing to fall back on."

"Themes?"

"Ideas which capture the public's mood of the moment, fire their imaginations. Look at Nixon. He's got détente with China and Russia. It's caught public attention; it's timely and well packaged. By contrast, we haven't gotten any major ideas across. We don't have a broad strategy. We play one thing and then another. It all builds this image of George as an incompetent."

"What about this Watergate business?"

"We've all pushed that to the media," Caddell said with a shrug, "but they just won't buy it."

"But if it can be proved . . .?"

"That Nixon authorized the break-in?"

"Even that he knew about it."

"Of course he knew about it."

Carter's ice-blue eyes stared searchingly. "What do you think was behind it?" he asked.

"They wanted our campaign plans."

Carter nodded and allowed a thin smile to crease his lips. This was their first meeting and Carter was forming a favorable impression of the brooding twenty-two year old. Initially, the Governor had received unflattering reports from two of his operatives, Jody Powell and Gerry Rafshoon, who had tried to see the then high-flying McGovern just before the Democratic Convention earlier that year in Miami. They had wanted to float the idea of Jimmy being McGovern's running-mate in the presidential election. But the candidate in the suite on the top floor of the Doral Hotel had been to busy to see them; they had been met and blocked by Caddell. To get rid of them he had been agreeable to recommending Carter for the ticket. But he hadn't even bothered. What an insult! He had treated them like Southern hicks . . .

This rebuff, Carter reflected later, had been a blessing. No Georgian was going to be humiliated like that again. Powell and Rafshoon had boldly suggested that he should run for the Presidency himself next time, in 1976. That same thought had been on Carter's own mind ever since he had appeared on the cover of *Time* magazine in May 1971. He had not mentioned his ambition to anyone except his mother. Carter vividly remembered sitting on the front porch of his brother Billy's home in Plains, Georgia, one hot summer's night.

"I've made a decision, Mom," he had said when they were alone. "I want to be President and I'm going to go for it."

His mother, Miss Lillian, had turned to him with a perplexed expression.

"President of what?" she had asked.

Her reaction had made him realize how implausible, even absurd, his ambition would look it he voiced it too early. A lot of work would have to be done before he could turn on a clockwork smile and say, "Hi, I'm Jimmy Carter, and I'm running for President. . ."

Certainly, he was not going to let on to McGovern or this junior master of survey interpretations. The open chat with Caddell was proving invaluable. Many of the things he was saying would give Carter indications of how he should approach his long run at 1976. The Governor felt comfortable with him, not just because of what Caddell was saying, but because of the way he was saying it. His accent was taking on more and more of a Southern drawl. The Harvard educated pollster had been brought up in Massachusetts in an Irish Catholic family, then moved to Jacksonville, Florida. Jacksonville was as deep Southern in tradition and landscape as Georgia and Alabama. The experience of these two very different environments had given the doleful, fleshy wunderkind more than a touch of the chameleon. When he was in Massachusetts, he could be the serious liberal and ease into circles in which Catholics like the Kennedys moved. In the South, he could loosen his tongue and drawl while 'shooting the breeze' with the smartest of the more pragmatic Southerners who were suspicious of Eastern intellectuals. In California, where McGovern was backed by glittering armchair liberals like Warren Beatty and his sister Shirley MacLaine, Caddell tuned up his moody persona to be more cool and chic.

Before the meeting Carter already knew vaguely of him, for five years earlier Caddell had become a local political legend. As a high school student in Jacksonville he had worked on an analysis of election returns in Florida for a math project. He had created a model for forecasting a state legislative election and astounded everyone when his predictions all proved accurate. The Speaker of the Florida House of Representatives read about him and hired him to do some polling. Caddell was just seventeen years old, and already a believer in the new faith of advanced technology and its possible applications in polling techniques. A self-avowed mechanical nincompoop who was not even interested in learning how to work a photocopier, Caddell understood only too well the value of using computer equipment to organize his data and provide him with print-outs of surveys, which he read and interpreted with brilliance and flair. The new technology of computers and polls also helped him formulate and manipulate his own theories and ideology, about which he was becoming obsessive. He passionately loved to expound on them. In Carter he found a willing listener, intelligent enough to grasp his ideas rapidly. Caddell was happy to stay up all night educating him.

Carter was intrigued by what the Watergate scandal could mean, and this allowed Caddell to launch into his obsession.

"It's nothing compared to this competence thing with George," he said, sipping his beer. "I've been tracking Watergate and it's maybe going to pull Nixon back five points at the most. But we're reading it at 60 per cent Nixon, 40 per cent for George, right now, so that five points will just help avoid the biggest landslide in history. That's all."

Caddell's face contorted and he looked more mournful than ever as he added: "I lie awake at night trying to figure out how we can change this poor image of George. It's maddening! I just don't know how! In the primaries, we had the Vietnam war issue going for us, and the alienation issue. They were problems that our opposition had to counter. But now *our* problem is at the top of the political election agenda. . ."

Carter looked sympathetic. "When you say, 'alienation issue'. . .?"

"Many voters have this anti-Washington attitude. They feel neglected and rejected by the politicians in the capital."

Caddell saw Carter's intense interest in this theme and launched into the verbal spiral which had caught the attention of many a purported liberal. "The voters are so fed up with the system and its inability to enhance their lives, that they are prepared to vote simply for change, whether it be extreme left or right."

Carter forgot about the morality of Watergate. This sort of information was pure gold which he could eventually convert into votes.

"I found this in 1968," Caddell went on, "when I did some polling in Jacksonville. Primary battles for the Democratic nomination were in full swing. Voters were looking to Wallace on the far right *or* Bobby Kennedy. Can you imagine that! A liberal like Bobby and a redneck like Wallace!"

Carter had stopped sipping his drink. His gaze had fixed on Caddell the moment he mentioned George Wallace, the beetle-browed powerful Governor of Alabama. The 'in' conversation had found a solid common ground. They both hated Wallace with a passion, albeit for different reasons. Carter knew only too well that if he was to win the Democratic nomination in 1976 he would have to be political King of the South, and to achieve that he would have to knock out Wallace, the strongest, toughest and most articulate Southern spokesman. Caddell's feelings toward him stemmed from his ideological dream of a new South, freed from racist politics.

"All this gave me my Harvard thesis," Caddell boasted, to remind Carter of his intellectual expertise. "Wallace traditionally played on the alienated and racist instincts of the South. But this big electorate he has manipulated for so long is up for grabs, if you can articulate the right theme to tap the right nerves. That's all that's needed to get their votes."

Caddell's background as a Catholic child brought up in the Florida Panhandle – a conservative Protestant area – gave him first-hand experience of the prejudice, bigotry and hatred of the South. He naturally had great empathy with blacks and saw Wallace as his nemesis. A true child of the sixties, he had been schooled in the counter-culture and had opted to tackle the established system from within, rather than attempt to tear it down from without. His vehicle for change would be a candidate who was attractive to the alienated electorate in the South and across the nation. He had no idea that his one-man audience that night might eventually be the person he was looking for.

Just as Caddell was about to expound further, Carter's wife Rosalynn padded barefoot into the kitchen and was introduced to the pollster. She put her arm around her husband.

"I'm turning in now," she said. "You going to be long?"

"Not long, honey," Carter said, and they kissed affectionately.

"Well g'night, and nice to meet you, Pat," she said warmly to Caddell, "and best of luck in your campaign."

She was not joined by her husband until almost dawn, so riveting was the discussion that followed.

CHAPTER 2

THE GOVERNOR AT THE ALTAR

Bill Roberts, the veteran Californian political consultant, tore off the print-out from the Univac computer in the 'Bomb shelter' – the secret office on Olympic Boulevard, Los Angeles, which was the nerve center for Governor Reagan's re-election campaign in 1970. He ran his fingers slowly down the columns of figures. His dour expression changed and he smiled as he turned to Richard Wirthlin.

"You're right," Roberts said, "it looks pretty damned difficult for Unruh." Wirthlin had just shown him a computer simulation of the election which put the best possible aspect on the chances of Reagan's challenger, Jesse Unruh. Mathematically at least, the computer indicated Reagan would win. The election was still six weeks away.

Roberts and his partner, Stuart Spencer, were running Reagan's campaign, and their tacit, if cautious, acceptance of Wirthlin's system meant he could confidently explain to the Governor his findings on the election, based on the simulation. It was an important moment for Wirthlin. He had been experimenting with this computer application for many years, first as an economist in simulating or modeling economic and marketing situations, and once before in politics, in 1968 during Richard Nixon's campaign for the Presidency. No part of the strategy for that campaign had been taken direct from the simulation but now, in Reagan's re-election effort, it would be. Wirthlin already firmly believed in the technique's intrinsic value in allowing better understanding of how electoral systems worked, yet he was well aware that his model was crude compared to what it could become with more experience. A big drawback was its cost, mainly because the system's lifeblood was huge amounts of survey data which had to be updated frequently. Only serious candidates for the Presidency, or the odd candidate for state elections with heavy financial backing, could afford the luxury of computers and expensive polling. In common with all large-scale scientific experimentation, success depended on money for research, and this was hard to come by in a field that was so little understood.

Simulation in science was as old as science itself – mathematical models were used to represent the physical world. Newton's laws of gravitation, Faraday's laws of electromagnetic induction and Einstein's $E=MC^2$ are all expressions which accurately reproduce and predict the behavior of many physical systems. These laws provided the basis for electronics engineers to simulate the landing of airplanes on the decks of moving carriers, or the flight of rockets at nearly the speed of light. Meteorologists were soon among the professional scientists experimenting with simulation in weather forecasting. Their skill still depended on the fundamental laws of physics, combined with inexact data such as past weather records, and early results were correspondingly mixed. Yet gradually refined simulations improved forecasting until they became standard procedure for meteorological institutions everywhere.

The big leap, which turned the technique of simulation into a hybrid science-art, was caused by the military and political scientists who began 'wargaming' – simulating war on computer – in the late fifties. There were no fixed laws here, yet war planners thought they could learn how to make conflict more systematic. Nations, people, precedents in battle, military strength and environmental conditions were all given mathematical weights and linked. Generals and political advisers in the sixties were arming themselves with computer print-outs to back their arguments about whether or not nations should enter into conflicts. The game depended on running through a myriad of 'What if?' conditions until the eyes blurred from the pattern on the computer paper. What if the Russians crossed the Rhine tomorrow with a thousand tanks? At what point could the West halt their push? What if a nuclear weapon was introduced to warn the Russians? Would it lead to retaliation? And if it did, how soon could the West introduce the weapons to make Moscow call a halt, if at all? All possible reactions from historical precedent were analyzed in an attempt to predict possible future actions.

Wargaming was a seductive sport. Generals and political scientists could wage nuclear war to their hearts' content. Frustrated warmongers could vent their feelings on the computer rather than on 'enemy' nations. Would-be Hitlers, Napoleons and Wellingtons had been forced, in the nuclear age, to 'play' at wargames, for the weapons available had reduced the real thing to insanity. By the mid-sixties, Moscow had been wiped from the face of the earth a million times in the computer room. So had Washington, London and Paris, and every military installation from Siberia to Alice Springs. It was wonderful for the rest of humanity that these battles were confined to the air-conditioned rooms housing the metal beasts. But one thing was wrong: the infinite war simulations were nudging military chiefs toward actually trying scenarios on the battlefield. Certainly by the seventies, if ever they were forced into actual combat they would be greatly guided by war scenarios already calculated and held in data banks. Despite the imprecision of wargaming, the generals, like the weather scientists, had institutionalized simulation.

Once the military and scientific communities had given the lead in using the technique of simulation to predict the future, big business began to try it. Management consultants were first, with models on sales, administrative accounting, actuarial and investment functions. Executives could simulate several hundred decisions and select the best one. Their role had in no way been usurped by machines by the late sixties, yet the technique was beginning to remove much of the guesswork from decision making. Executives of the bigger companies found simulations useful in assessing a range of marketing strategies and 'What if?' scenarios. What if we introduce brand X of toothpaste into the market next year? Is the market saturated? Can it stand another competitor if the product is brilliantly packaged and advertised? What would be the production costs? What price should the brand be in order to be competitive, and how long would it take to break even?

The first-stage marketing models were created by converting the impressions and forecasts of skilled executives into computer digestible formulae. But the business simulators found that they were limited in just the same way as the wargamers had been because there were no fixed laws to govern or predict behavior precisely. Yet the method was spreading because the new computers, like the IBM 360 series which came on the market in the US in 1964, were making it possible to experiment rapidly with any number of different equations and variables at once and calculate results instantly.

Economists, too, saw simulation as a chance to make predictions about a nation's or the world's economic outlook. Initially they fared little better than the wargamers or the marketing people, for there were again no fixed laws to govern the economy. Keynes and others had created guides to the behavior of inflation, unemployment, consumer spending, deflation and how a nation might pull out of a recession. But for every expansionist there was a monetarist and a score of adherents to other economic schools, all dependent on the background, experience, education and political persuasion of the individual. There were no fixed constants in any calculations, and the economy was subject to quirks in human behavior. Unquantifiable and unforeseeable disturbances could be amplified by speculation, loss of confidence and even panic, which would make the management of economic crises extremely difficult. Models had to be updated frequently or they would quickly diverge from reality. Still, economists continued to refine their systems in the belief that they might at least be instructive about what would be bad for the economy, and they were a way of testing alternative strategies.

Economists and marketing consultants alike also learned much about mass psychology and human behavior in the fifties and sixties, for they made incessant study of what influenced the public's decision to invest, save or purchase. They became experts in understanding how to stimulate buying, in particular, and the marketing people found more and more sophisticated ways of making people spend money.

By the time Richard Wirthlin started his company Decision Making Information (DMI) in 1969, he had gained a great deal of experience in marketing and economic simulations. He also knew more than anyone else about how to get information concerning the US population from the 38 Federal Government statistical agencies from Census to Education. This complemented DMI's own constant polling and survey work, which provided massive amounts of data for its Digital VAX and PDP computers in California. Wirthlin was perfectly equipped to experiment with simulation in political elections. Although modeling here was also restricted by the lack of fixed laws upon which to base forecasts, election simulations offered more promise than those in economics and marketing.

The 1970 model for Reagan's re-election campaign contained historical voting records and demographic data such as age, sex, income bracket, race and religion. If these records were updated and accurate, they would be reliable adjusters to the third element in the system – the data from surveys, which was the variable factor in the model. For example, if a random sample of 600 people in California was asked whether they proposed to vote for Reagan or Unruh in the election, the response would be accurate to within 3 per cent, 95 times out of every 100 samples taken. In other words, if operators telephoned 600 people at random in California, and went through the same procedure another 99 times, each time with 600 different people, on average 5 samples could be thrown away, because they would be the bad apples. The other 95 would be accurate to within plus or minus 3 per cent. If the sample said that 56 per cent of people would vote for Reagan, then there was a high degree of probability that the Governor would receive between 53 and 59 per cent of the vote in the state. This sort of accuracy could be improved with bigger samples, but the cost would become prohibitive.

More accurate and important than Withlin's ability simply to determine how much support Reagan had at any given point in the campaign was his capacity to help the Governor's team actually 'win' the election. He could use the system to 'measure' public attitudes to the candidates. Those attitudes – the feelings, reactions and thoughts – to the candidates' opposing stands on a broad spectrum of issues were far more important than any stated voting intention, because attitudes determined *how* an individual or group would vote. For instance, a voter might be wavering in his or her choice about the two main candidates. Four weeks before the election, the choice might be Reagan. It might change to Unruh in the second to last week and then back to Reagan when the voter came face to face with the ballot box. That final, irreversible decision would be based on how the voter eventually perceived Reagan or Unruh and their positions on different issues. In 1970, the simulation was not sufficiently sophisticated to be able to measure the electorate's perceptions of the candidates' image. But it could record support, opposition or indifference to certain issues. The computer could then be fed the candidates' positions, and the better these matched the attitudes of a voting majority, calculated from polls and placed in the simulation, the greater the candidate's chance of victory. For example, the simulation suggested that Reagan would win if he pushed his welfare reform proposals for the second term. Without getting into specifics, which might have diminished this support, he campaigned on the theme that welfare was "the greatest problem facing the nation today and the reason for the high cost of government". The model continually tested how well the packaged Reagan themes were being accepted by the public and compared this to acceptance of the themes of Unruh's campaign.

Wirthlin's system complemented the efforts of Spencer and Roberts, who had been hired initially in 1966 by Reagan's business friends and backers to run him for Governor. They were among the most successful political consultants in the US, with long experience of packaging candidates and ruining the campaigns of their clients' opponents. The consultants had been reluctant to represent Reagan when Holmes P. Tuttle, the financier, approached them in 1965 about a bid for the governorship. Roberts had been put off by his image of Reagan as a not terribly bright, right-wing martinet who was difficult to work with. Like Wirthlin, Roberts was pleasantly surprised on first meeting the prospective politician. "We found him to be an open and candid person," Roberts said at the time, "easy to talk with, and a good listener." However, the consultants did not hurry to take him on, despite knowing that money would be no object in the campaign.

Roberts and Spencer were concerned about Reagan's ignorance of issues facing the state. Their third meeting, at Reagan's Pacific

Palisades home, was initially tense. After speaking of some of the problems that might be encountered in any campaign, Reagan could no longer stand the indecision. "Well, what about it?" he demanded. "Are you going to do it? You've been asking me questions for three meetings now." After a moment's hesitation, Roberts nodded and said yes. At least the consultants knew they were dealing with someone who had the desire and determination to attempt a new career relatively late in life.

Reagan was fifty-four years old and his main occupation in life had been as an actor. The consultants' first task was to make sure he had some understanding of the central political issues facing the state. They employed behavioral psychologists who produced eight black books containing references to 17 main issues which Reagan could slip under his paper-thin knowledge of politics. The crash course molded his basic thinking into just enough shape to allow Spencer-Roberts to sell him to the Californian electorate. With three decades of film-making, speech-making, TV compering, radio announcing and product selling behind him, Reagan was ready for the transition to politics. His image had been carefully prepared by himself, Hollywood and the General Electric Company, for whom he had been a front man in the fifties. In films, "Ronnie always played Ronnie," his brother Neil once claimed. "He was typecast – the young American boy from the Midwest. He was always the good guy. The movies didn't really change him, they just captured the quintessential Reagan and packaged it, and presented it repeatedly on the screen." This, plus the Spencer-Roberts coaching, greatly helped Reagan to win in 1966 by a staggering one million votes.

In the 1970 re-election bid, the simulations indicated that Reagan was well on the way to another big victory, and the same day that Roberts approved this prognostication, Wirthlin made an appointment to see the Governor and to introduce him to the simulation concept. Wirthlin did not know how he would respond. Reagan had always seemed quick to learn from Wirthlin's interpretation of his poll findings, but a concept like simulation, still in its infancy in the political arena, might be a different matter.

The strategist had prepared an outline of the basic points before the meeting, and as he was led along the corridors of rich red carpet in the Governor's Sacramento building, he was still thinking about the best way to present this political breakthrough in the abstract. "This is not going to be easy," Wirthlin thought, noticing the bronze and walnut plaque on the cloth-upholstered wall above the entrance to the Governor's office. 'Observe the rules or get out', was its stark message. An aide took him through the large office to a small study where Reagan preferred to work. It was also carpeted in red, the walls paneled in wood stained dark to blend with the rugs – all courtesy of Nancy Reagan, who had created the decor, right down to the specially selected old English prints of horses which adorned the walls. The Governor took off his glasses when he saw the smiling Wirthlin and stood up from his desk to shake hands. The two men had developed a strong personal relationship in the two years since their first meeting. Reagan offered him a seat on a leather couch. "Tell me the good news and then the good news," he said, and they both laughed.

"Well, it *is* good news, Governor," Wirthlin said, opening a folder and balancing it on his knees. He ran through some of the figures from his most recent surveys in the Californian counties.

"You're running at about 54 per cent," he added, "and Unruh stands at about 44 per cent with approximately two per cent voting elsewhere."

Reagan looked pleased. "Not bad," he said. "Will that hold, Dick?"

"I think so, Governor. Even in a worst-case scenario, that gap would only close marginally. We also simulated your issue positions and Unruh's. They indicate it would be very difficult for you to lose."

"Yeah, Bill Roberts said you would explain that."

"Glad to, Governor," Wirthlin said, relieved to have been given an opening. "We make a mathematical model on the computer. Then we feed it historical voting records – how each county has traditionally voted, either Republican or Democrat, in the last four elections. It is also fed demographic data in some detail. For instance, we know how white-collar, middle-income whites between the ages of twenty-five and thirty-five think about all the main issues. In fact, we have analyzed all demographic groups the same way. To this data we can add our latest surveys on voting intentions."

"So they are linked on computer, and that gives you the vote county by county?"

"Exactly, and from that we calculate the vote across the board. Against that data in the computer, we can also set your issue positions – they are given a mathematical 'weight' or value and fed into the computer – to see how the electorate reacts."

"Whether they will support me because of my proposals?"

"Yes," Wirthlin nodded enthusiastically. He had tried to explain simulation to many politicians and few had picked up on the technical points so quickly.

"So Nancy and I can go on holiday?" Reagan asked.

"Well, Governor, we still have six weeks to go."

"But it's safe?"

"I would say so, Governor."

"Perhaps we can release some of my campaign funds to any of our guys who are in not such a good position."

"If the trend holds, yes."

A few weeks after Wirthlin's meeting, several Republicans, such as the California state comptroller, found themselves with extra funds to fight the 1970 elections, simply because of Reagan's confidence in the prediction that he was headed for another strong victory. The Governor even took campaigning easier. He felt secure in the knowledge that he was about to prove that his win in 1966 was not a fluke. He relaxed noticeably and campaigned with more style.

When pickets in Modesto showed up carrying signs that read 'Get lost, Ronnie', he walked boldly up to the fence and shook a few friendly hands. The pickets began to heckle him. "Tell us all you know, Governor," one called. "It won't take very long." The crowd laughed derisively and Reagan walked closer to the caller.

"I'll tell you what we both know, and it won't take any longer," he heckled back. The crowd roared its approval. The press in attendance scribbled in their notepads. This was a different Reagan from the stumbling, sheltered candidate that they had seen in 1966. There was a polish and confidence in the man now that had been lacking before.

Wirthlin's surveys had suggested that Reagan should campaign on the future rather than on his record as Governor. It was better and safer for a politician to look forward rather than back. In 1966 Reagan had promised to clean up "the welfare mess", which he had not bothered about too much in his first term. The emotion the Governor could project about these issues worked well enough. He made his proposed agenda the talking point each time. "Public assistance should go to the needy and not the greedy", became an easy-off-the-tongue Reagan special; he also emerged as the optimistic defender of his own generation against youthful critics of American materialism.

The polls showed Jesse Unruh closing ground on Reagan in the final weeks, and the simulation, along with all the Governor's advisers, underestimated the strength of the challenger's final efforts. They were relieved when they found that Unruh did not have enough funds for a blitz of TV commercials towards the end of his campaign. Reagan went on to win fairly comfortably, by half a million votes.

Wirthlin was not overly upset by the simulation's failure to be perfectly precise. It had been useful in guiding the campaign, but so long as it was restricted by a lack of rapidly updated information, its effectiveness would likewise remain restricted. His main aim would be to expand its capacity well beyond just measuring the electorate's response to a candidate's issue positions. Wirthlin was inspired to edge himself further into campaign strategy, rather than simply act as a pollster-adviser. He had been greatly encouraged by the way Reagan had responded, and conformed, to the computer model's guidance. The second time around, the Governor had proven that he had outstanding qualities as a campaigner. He could act out any directive with style and, if required, the right amount of passion and indignation. Wirthlin already felt Reagan would make a great presidential candidate – as long as he had an advanced simulated strategy to guide him.

CHAPTER 3
THE GISCARD CONNECTION

Joseph Napolitan nearly choked on his *crème brûlée* when a tall Frenchman walked into Les Innocents, the Paris restaurant, where he was dining. It was late one evening in the spring of 1974, during the hectic campaign for the Presidency of France, and the American consultant had no wish to see the Frenchman, a politician, with whom he had been acquainted for some time. He had just been eliminated in the first round of voting, which left Valery Giscard d'Estaing to face the Socialist candidate, François Mitterand. At the time, Napolitan was the secret adviser to Giscard. Even though Les Innocents, with its intimate and romantic setting, under low lights and cross-beamed ceiling, was designed to ensure privacy for its patrons, Napolitan was not about to hide, for he would have been spotted sooner or later. He watched the politician and his attractive young wife settle into a velvet couch at one of the fine wooden tables and then caught his attention. The politician said something to his wife and quickly moved to Napolitan's table.

"What brings you here?" the politician inquired enthusiastically.

"Vacation," the American replied in his typically laconic manner. He pushed his dessert aside, knowing that it was a safe enough answer, for he had been coming to Paris annually since the 1950s to relax and enjoy the good life.

"Sorry to see you out of it," Napolitan said, after he had introduced the politician to some American acquaintances at his table.

"Oh, well," the politician said with a Gallic pout and shrug. "You can't win them all."

"Who do you think will win?"

"Mitterand. And you? What is the opinion of America's top consultant?"

Napolitan smiled fleetingly.

"Giscard."

"Oh, why?"

"His campaign looks more professional."

The politician was suddenly more alert. "In what way?"

Napolitan shrugged and seemed to hesitate before he replied nonchalantly. "Giscard is using the media better. His advertising is sharper."

The Frenchman waved his hand dismissively. "Trust an American to mention the media and advertising," he laughed. "These things do not count so much in France."

"Maybe you're right," Napolitan conceded. He did not want to make his points too forcefully, lest the politician realize why he was really in Paris. Had the real connection been made, it would have been disastrous for Giscard. The use of an American consultant would have been strongly attacked by France's Left, who would have charged Giscard with being influenced by Yankee Imperialism.

The Franco-American link had begun a few weeks earlier when Napolitan was introduced to Giscard by a French business consultant. Giscard had not been overly confident about victory against the Union-backed François Mitterand, and he was casting around for something which would help gain the edge in the election. Giscard initially showed only mild interest when told that Napolitan was one of the most experienced politician consultants in the world, who had a deep understanding of election techniques. Giscard knew that the American had greatly helped in the campaign to re-elect President Ferdinand E. Marcos of the Philippines in 1969. But what impressed the French candidate more was Napolitan's part in a gallant failure, that of his most famous client, US Vice-President Hubert Humphrey, who fought the 1968 presidential election against Richard Nixon.

The Nixon of 1968 proved to be a far more formidable candidate than the sickly, verbose and shifty candidate of 1960 who just failed to beat John Kennedy for the Presidency. The Republican and his cohorts had learned a great deal from that defeat. They did not run him around the nation until he was exhausted. Instead they ran the most extravagant TV campaign ever staged until that point in American political history. There were no debates of the kind which had contributed to Nixon's defeats in the past, and he was pre-packaged by the most experienced communications group ever assembled for such an exercise. There was Frank Shakespeare on leave from CBS and key advertising man Harry Treleavan, to name the principals, plus H. R. Haldeman. They were determined that TV should become Nixon's greatest strength, rather than his weakness as it had been in 1960. They put him in front of the cameras to answer questions from selected citizens, and then the best of the footage was cut and edited into a dynamic advertising package. He was never shown direct-to-camera, which he had found so difficult, but in this clever, sanitized style. Nixon avoided any news conferences such as TV's 'Meet the Press'. He faced the public in staged TV studio settings, where questions were almost always worded generally enough to allow him to answer vaguely. Directed studio audiences were urged to intimidate any questioners aiming at true debate, and the candidate moved from one query to the next. This prevented any chance of a follow-up, and allowed him to punch in unchecked responses to a wide range of issues. The electorate, however, took a lot of convincing, and the Republicans were forced to run Nixon this way from February right through to the presidential election in November, with only a few changes in the script.

The Humphrey Democrats did not have the funds for such an extravaganza, and they blamed lack of money and the TV coverage of the riots at the Democratic convention in Chicago for their troubles. After Chicago, Humphrey dropped from six percentage points behind Nixon to a massive fifteen. It looked to be all over for the incumbent Vice-President – until Napolitan joined his campaign team.

At forty years of age, Napolitan had a wealth of experience in media and campaign organization. He was also one of the few men in politics who understood how to use polling data for the strategic path of a whole campaign. His outstanding judgement allowed him to 'read' them to his candidate's advantage. Coupled with this was a distinct desire to go for the opponent's jugular, a vital ingredient in American politics, especially against the Nixon team. The 1968 battle developed into a fight between the Republican ad men, who used sterile Madison Avenue techniques, and Napolitan, whose skills and techniques revolved around survey-based strategies.

Napolitan was called in by Humphrey's manager, Lawrence O'Brien, during the Chicago convention, and was appalled to find no plan, no polls to muse over, no cash and no confidence. Immediately he threw himself into the challenge. Near the end of the Chicago convention, Theodore H. White, who was working on his third *Making of the President* book, arrived unannounced at Napolitan's hotel room. White heard the chatter of a typewriter, and poked his head in the door.

"What are you doing," the inquisitive White asked, "writing a speech?"

"No, the campaign plan," Napolitan snarled.

"You're kidding. You mean that hasn't been done yet?"

"If it has, I haven't seen it, O'Brien hasn't seen it, and I don't think the candidate has seen it." Napolitan's head went down over the typewriter again, and White withdrew, amazed but happy to have stumbled on to a most telling fact about the Humphrey campaign.

Napolitan's first task was to gather information. Within days he had tried to commission five separate public opinion analysts polling in 17 different states. He had to know what kind of electorate was out there, what its moods were, and its likes and dislikes for each candidate. But because of rumors about lack of cash in the Humphrey camp, two pollsters held back data until they had been paid, and this delayed Napolitan's capacity to schedule TV or media strategy for the marketing of Humphrey. When finally all the results were in, the polls were clear on one big issue: the war in Vietnam. The mood on the lingering American entanglement in Asia was changing rapidly. Strong leadership and fresh, bold ideas were needed. Napolitan rushed out a nothing-to-lose blueprint which went straight to the center of the issue. On 14 September he gave O'Brien a memorandum which suggested that Humphrey break with Johnson and create an independent Vietnam policy that would "win back votes that should be Humphrey's, but which are now wavering." Napolitan stressed that the break with Johnson was necessary because he had escalated the American presence in the war, and was not about to back down on the involvement.

Johnson had always intimidated the less forceful Humphrey. Defying the nation's President, for whom he acted as a faithful deputy, would be agonizing.

O'Brien gave Humphrey the five-page plan the same day he received it from Napolitan, and the candidate settled back on a flight from Chicago to Washington DC to read it. Several times Humphrey let go an expletive in reaction to the bluntness of Napolitan's comments. When he came to the consultant's thoughts about a complete break with Johnson over Vietnam, he was angered by the words, ". . . it would set to rest the fears of many persons that Hubert Humphrey does not have the courage to stand up to Lyndon Johnson . . ."

Humphrey took off his glasses and turned to O'Brien. "Son-of-a-bitch!" he said. "Hasn't he ever heard of loyalty? That's what it's all about, not courage!"

O'Brien did not answer. "Don't tell me you agree with this?" Humphrey challenged him.

"It's your campaign, Hubert," O'Brien said, "not anyone else's."

The candidate went back to the plan and when he had read it thoroughly, he handed it back to O'Brien.

"There are some good ideas in there," he said. "I've underlined them, but I don't go along with the thrust. Not at all."

Napolitan turned his attention to a sustained media attack on Nixon and to urging Humphrey to debate him. The consultant was finding a direct correlation between the amount of money spent on media advertising – ads and documentaries – and Humphrey's rise in the polls. With far less money than the opposition, the Democrats had to be more innovative with their ads, and more stinging. While the new Nixon image was being molded on TV, there was more opportunity to make his running mate, Spiro Agnew, the target. Napolitan hired Tony Schwartz, an outstanding ad man, to prepare the TV and radio spots. The most controversial was called 'The twenty-second laughter spot'. It opened with the shot of a TV screen with a sign held up which read, "Agnew for Vice-President". The audio was a man laughing raucously, with the final message "This would be funny if it weren't so serious". A later Schwartz effort showed a bobbing line and continuous bleep of an oscilloscope recording a heartbeat. The message was "Muskie? Agnew. Who is *your* choice to be a heartbeat away from the Presidency?" The spot would have been meaningless to a foreigner, but it triggered an emotion in Americans who had doubts about the wisdom of the Nixon-Agnew ticket – a reservation which later proved justified. Napolitan continually tried to get Humphrey to debate Nixon on TV, but the candidate always rejected the idea. He had never fully grasped the power and importance of using television in an election.

Humphrey eventually lost to Nixon by 0.7 per cent of the national vote, and the result was in doubt until the early hours of the morning after election day. Napolitan's campaign, weakened by Humphrey's lack of cooperation on big strategy points, still whittled the 15 per cent Nixon lead down to almost nothing. The result proved how valuable was the strategic use of information, even when an opponent was using the slickest, most expensive TV packaging techniques. The Democrats had neither the resources nor a strong TV candidate, but by sharp and thoughtful planning based on comprehensive polling they came near to victory.

Napolitan's effort was brought to Giscard's attention, and at the beginning of the 1974 election battle he considered that a meeting with the American was worth a few minutes of his valuable time. The meeting could not be at his Paris apartment, nor at his country estate where he often entertained: both were liable to be prowled by the press. Nor could they meet at the Plaza Athénée, the most expensive hotel in Paris, where Napolitan stayed. Instead, a private city apartment was found. Giscard's press secretary had to lie to the media and tell them that the candidate was on his way to his country estate before the clandestine meeting could take place on Rue Varenne.

It was a strange rendezvous. The two men were like chalk and cheese, except that neither was known for loquacity, or for smiling too much. The tall, aristocratic and urbane Giscard wondered what this mustachioed American with a penchant for colored shirts and cigars could possibly know about French politics. They sat rather stiffly opposite each other in the lounge of an expensive seventeenth-century apartment, and Giscard began by discussing the differences between the French and American systems of electioneering. Napolitan listened quietly and lit a fat cigar. He offered the candidate one. Giscard declined it, somewhat disdainfully. He wasn't a smoker.

"Tell me," Napolitan said, "what kind of survey information do you use?"

"We have pollsters," Giscard replied.

"But you have not found out the nation's attitudes," the American said. "That should have been done over the last year, at least."

"Have you seen the data we are using?"

"Yes. It is not nearly comprehensive enough. You should have information on the electorate's mood and how the people feel about the candidates' strengths and weaknesses."

Giscard reached for the leather satchel at his feet and took a notepad and pen from it. He placed the pad on his knees and began to take notes as Napolitan continued. Napolitan advised the candidate to make more professional use of the limited TV and radio broadcast time, and to create more TV 'news' through staged events.

"You don't have to overdo it," the American said, casually blowing smoke away from them. "Just make sure there are more 'events' for you. Opening art galleries. Social events. Talking to ordinary people. Just let the media see you more often, and give them something to write about."

"But not today," Giscard said with a rare smile.

"No, I'm not the right kind of media event," Napolitan said with the semblance of a grin.

"What do you think of the poster ads we have?" Giscard asked.

"Your graphics have always been excellent – the best in the world," Napolitan replied. "But I don't see strong enough themes. You have time, if you can distil themes from the polls. It would be a shame if you wasted that talent for graphics. You need something sharper."

Giscard was about to ask another question.

"I take it you want me to consult for you," Napolitan interrupted.

"Well, yes," Giscard said.

Napolitan reached across and shook the candidate's hand. "Good," he said. "I think I can help you win."

Giscard's high forehead stretched and he was silent for a moment. No one had been that optimistic in recent days. Before meeting Napolitan he had been impressed by his record, but skeptical about his usefulness. The French candidate had been extremely wary about being seen with the American. Now he began to understand. It was not necessary for Napolitan to have a strong grasp of French politics. Much more important were the techniques. With certain refinements, they were universal.

After that first meeting, the two men met regularly at various secret venues. Each time Napolitan gave his advice based on polling data that was coming in daily. He did not interfere with policy, but guided the candidate on how to package his ideas, and how and when to use the media. Gradually, over the final weeks and days, Giscard saw the American's techniques working and his own fortunes changing. Victory was his.

In the euphoria of the win, the new President of the Republic managed one final chat with the consultant at the apartment in which they had first met. As they sipped champagne, they looked through the window and saw a score of media people in the street below.

"Everybody loves a winner," Napolitan said, raising his glass to Giscard.

"It perhaps would be better if you were not seen leaving together," an aide whispered in Napolitan's ear. The American gave an understanding nod, and Giscard departed quickly. Napolitan watched the media swarm around the President as he hurried to a waiting limousine, protected by security guards who outnumbered even the press. Napolitan smiled to himself. He had some satisfaction in knowing that he could apply his skills in the use of the new techniques at home and abroad. It was the first time it had been done in an important election in a leading European nation.

CHAPTER 4

THE STRATEGISTS MOVE HIGHER

"I think you can win the nomination."

Pat Caddell's words buzzed in Carter's ears as the two men sat with Rosalynn Carter in the lobby lounge of the Doral Hotel in Miami. He had heard it from his wife, from close members of the Georgia 'mafia' – Gerry Rafshoon, Jody Powell, Hamilton Jordan – and others, but never with such pragmatic conviction from an outsider of such standing in the Democratic political community. Caddell had even shown him an article he had written in *Rolling Stone* magazine that had appeared a couple of years previously when Richard Nixon was up to his ears in Watergate. It predicted that someone like Carter, with a strong Southern base, could take the Democratic nomination and even go on to win the Presidency. The candidate was aware that Caddell wanted to be his pollster, but it was February 1975 – a year before the primary elections in the 1976 battle for the Presidency. Young Caddell, a veteran of George McGovern's 1972 presidential campaign, was already trying to climb aboard the unknown Carter's bandwagon. Not only that, he had a strategy for winning that on paper, at least, looked more promising than anything the Carters had seen before. Caddell had tactics which he claimed could help Carter against the big names among the Democratic hopefuls, such as George Wallace and Henry 'Scoop' Jackson. He could see the interest in the faces of the prospective candidate and his wife.

"I always wondered how you pollsters do it," Rosalynn said.

"Just like everybody else," Caddell mumbled, and then quickly resumed his serious demeanor as he realized that both Carter and his wife had missed the line. "You mean how do we interpret the figures?"

"Yes," Rosalynn replied, "especially how you assess a candidate's strengths and weaknesses." Caddell had quickly appreciated that her intellect was not to be underestimated, and he saw her as a way of reaching Carter.

"We build profiles of the candidate and his opponent," Caddell began as he put down his glass of beer and leaned forward. He liked to gesticulate freely when articulating his business. "We ask the electorate questions about the two competitors. First, we give those we poll a card with a rating scale of one to seven. We then read a list of words, such as honest, cold, warm, trustworthy, and ask them to rate the candidate. Then we ask what the respondent likes about the candidate, and what he or she dislikes. After that sort of build-up we also tell them to rate a statement such as 'The candidate really cares about people like me."

"So you can see patterns developing?" Rosalynn asked.

Caddell nodded. "You can immediately see where the two candidates stand with, say, twenty-five to thirty year olds, or with middle-class whites, or with women. . ."

"That way you can see where you're doing well with one group and not with another," Carter interjected.

"That's right," Caddell said, stroking his newly acquired beard with its distinctive gray streak. "You can then select your campaign themes to attract the votes of specific groups. In McGovern's 1972 campaign I discovered that blue-collar workers were not solidly behind Muskie, who was the front runner at the time. I suggested that McGovern tour the factories of working-class Manchester, New Hampshire. You know, say the sort of things that would turn them on. He did, and on primary election day he scored heavily with workers. That was important because it meant he could do it nationally."

The Carters were impressed. Caddell was somebody who appeared to have the experience and techniques which could be valuable, especially in 'positioning' the candidate to appeal in a certain way in each state, and eventually, if their prayers were answered, across the nation. Image and national recognition were vital to any run for the Presidency, and Carter had always been unsure how to present himself and what issues he should choose to run on. Early in his marathon four-year bid for office he had asked his advertising man, Gerry Rafshoon, "How should I campaign? As a farmer? A non-office holder? A Georgian? A scientist? What's the best way to run?"

"As hard as you can," Rafshoon had replied, "and use everyhing you can. . ."

The Southern Governor would accept almost any image which could help. In the early stages of the campaign, Rafshoon wanted the perception of the unannounced candidate to be that of the folksy peanut farmer, as opposed to his actual career as a wealthy agricultural businessman with a peanut merchandising concern.

Carter's varied career started in 1943, when he left the family's peanut farm in Plains, Georgia, for the Annapolis Naval Academy, where he put in eleven years in the Navy as an officer on a nuclear submarine. He then returned to Georgia and in 1962 became a state senator. He ran for Governor in 1966 and lost. In the trauma of defeat, Carter became a 'born-again' Christian. He ran for Governor with new determination in 1970, and won. After less than a year in his new job, he gained some recognition by appearing on the cover of *Time* – already he was aiming higher. Carter began to cultivate the important contacts that would be necessary if he was ever to have any chance at all of making a serious bid for the Presidency. At the top of his list was David Rockefeller, chairman of the Chase Manhattan Bank, the third largest in America. He had met Rockefeller at an international trade function and had a private meeting with him over lunch at the bank on 23 November 1971. It was the first of several that were to take place over the next two years.

The two men could have come from different countries, even planets. Rockefeller, a multimillionaire, was one of the most powerful businessmen in the world. He had inherited a fortune from oil and had capitalized on this in the rarefied atmosphere of high finance and banking. He had grown up as familiar with money and power as Carter had with peanuts. The banker lived, quite literally, like a king, with his private island and planes. He kept the company of monarchs and the moneyed, presidents and the powerful. Carter, by contrast, had come from a far more egalitarian Southern background, which though not poor was always close to those who were. He was the kind of person – lay preacher, businessman-farmer, populist – whom the Eastern establishment normally eschewed or despised, unless they rose to positions which could be useful.

At the time of their first meeting, Rockefeller was organizing the secretive Trilateral Commission (TC), and Carter was anxious to know more about it. The Commission was just the sort of organization that he would like to be involved in, for it would bring the connections in both big business and politics that would give credibility to any bid for the Presidency.

In a discussion late in 1972 he boldly asked the banker about it.

"It's still early days for the Commission," Rockefeller said quietly. "But I know I can trust you not to speak about it."

"You have my word," Carter said.

"It's very sensitive. It's really a new approach to world economic affairs. You see, some of us have been concerned with our decrease in influence worldwide because of the Vietnam war. I have very high hopes that the Commission will bring new ideas to economic and foreign policy. We must have greater cooperation between Western economic powers trilaterally – the US, Western Europe and Japan."

Carter nodded. "You mean in the wake of détente?" he asked.

Rockefeller's expression changed. He smiled faintly.

"You could put it that way," he said ambiguously. "Henry Kissinger has always supported a balance-of-power approach. He and Dick Nixon have always wanted to be the brokers in a triangular alliance between the US, China and Russia." Rockefeller paused to sip his wine. "That's one way of looking at things. It involves a strategy that means these three nations would have the strength to negotiate with the underdeveloped world, particularly the oil producers."

Carter was reading between the lines. The banker seemed to be hinting that he was not altogether impressed with this approach.

"Now, this is fine for Dick," Rockefeller went on. "He is proving to be a good President, and my brother Nelson and I have a lot of time for Henry, but neither of them is a businessman, a banker. . ."

The Governor understood this to infer that détente was not necessarily the best deal for the world banking community, and its main clientele, the big multinationals like IBM, ITT and the oil giants. Because they were organized on a worldwide scale, they owned their allegiance less to the US and more to the foreign subsidiaries in Western Europe, Japan and other nations from whom they were receiving greater revenue and profit. If the US lined up with two Communist nations to deal with the Arab and Iranian oil producers, it might not be so good for the multinationals who might be asked, for example, to make concessions to please the Communists. The Russians and the Chinese might use détente as a front for expansion and the ultimate weakening of the capitalist nations. Rockefeller wanted an alternative strategy in the event of détente not working brilliantly for the banking community.

"Do you know the name Brzezinski?" Rockefeller asked.

Carter shook his head

"You should meet him," Rockefeller said. "I'll arrange it."

Fifteen months after that first meeting in New York, Rockefeller appointed Carter to the Commission, which proved to be one of the most significant events in his entire campaign. Watergate was catching up with President Nixon, and it opened up two important factors. First, Nixon's fall from grace meant his ideas and goals would collapse with him, and this provided the chance for the Commission to fill the power vacuum. As a Commission member, Carter was in the company of many influential individuals, such as the most powerful man in Italy, the chief executive officers of the world's biggest banks, the former Foreign Minister of West Germany, the Foreign Minister of Japan, the head of the world's largest oil company, several members of the world's most powerful computer company, partners of the top investment banking houses, and the heads of Japanese industry and finance. The benefits naturally worked both ways. If Carter was ever to realize his still-secret goal, the Trilateral Commission would gain from US foreign and economic policy. Rockefeller planned to have Zbigniew Brzezinski as a key foreign policy maker in a new Federal administration, and more than another twenty members of the Commission would be found top Government jobs.

The second main consequence of Nixon's troubles was that they opened up a crude theme on which Carter could plan his run. He started wearing religion, piety, morality and integrity on his sleeve. These normally private human characteristics had become marketable commodities for the potential presidential candidate. Carter decided to run against Washington DC, that Sodom of the West and center of venal corruption. Another shrewd move in terms of contacts was his assistance on the Democratic National Committee. Its chairman took him on to head the party's 1974 Congressional election campaign drive, in which he would be brought into contact with governors, senators and congressmen seeking re-election. The post provided an entrée to labor leaders, political consultants and liberal special-interest representatives in agriculture, education, consumerism and other areas. Carter played down his interest in running for President so as not to appear self-serving in his assistance to the party. Quietly his aides, Jody Powell and Hamilton Jordan, filled address books and wrote letters of thanks. There were also little touches, such as flowers and cards for birthdays, weddings, births and funerals of important Democrats. It added up to another level of recognition, if not yet with the nation, at least among key members of the party, all of whom would be unexpectedly called to account for support when Carter made his candidacy public. By 1975 Carter had developed the connections that would be essential to any credible run for the Presidency. People such as Rockefeller could pick up the phone to the heads of the TV networks and leading newspapers – some of them Commission members – and voice their approval of Carter. Far from being 'Jimmy Who?' as he had been labeled by some early in his campaign, Carter was very much a 'somebody' to the people that counted – a solid layer of the American establishment which would not allow a simple peanut farmer, as he was to be portrayed in TV commercials, to accede to the Western world's most powerful office.

By the time Caddell made his approach to Carter, just about everything was in place for a big push towards the 1976 primaries. He had the contacts, the issue specialists, and the broad moral and anti-government themes on which to run. Yet he was aware that there was no refinement to his strategy, nor were there any tactics planned for the primaries, which would be cut-throat affairs. If he could not break through and win some of them, at least, his four years of sweat and preparation would amount to nothing. Carter wondered if the serious Harvard graduate could be the person to supply the answer to his problem.

Rosalynn certainly thought so. Alone with her husband as they prepared for bed at the Doral a few hours after meeting Caddell, she said, "I think you should hire that young man."

"I've been thinking about that, honey."

"He is ever so intelligent, Jimmy, and everything he says makes sense. You need him to help beat Wallace and Jackson."

"Maybe."

"You want everything going for you here in Florida, especially. And you know how tough it is here. Goodness, how many times have you been back here now? You're haunting this state!"

"Pat certainly knows this place."

"Right, and if he was good enough for one presidential candidate. . ."

"But McGovern lost."

"Well, he *was* the Democratic nominee. He made it through the primaries against all odds. Pat helped him. You don't want to fall at the first hurdle. . ."

CHAPTER 5
PRIMARY SNIPERS

THE REPUBLICAN'S PET PIRANHA

Stu Spencer reached for the phone to call Joel Weisman at the *Washington Post*'s office in Chicago. It was a week before Reagan was to enter the 1976 race for the Republican nomination against incumbent President Gerald Ford.

"Joel, Stu Spencer here," the political consultant said. "About that story you said could destroy Ronnie Reagan."

"You mean the 'Ninety Billion Dollar' article?"

"Yeah, where he said that the Federal Government should cut its welfare program."

"The bastards buried it," the disgruntled journalist said. "It should have been page one. But it was on page twenty-three!"

"There are some real pricks around, Joel."

"They don't know a hot story when they see one."

"They missed Watergate, didn't they?"

"Yeah, until Woodward and Bernstein badgered them into believing it."

"Joel, are you sure Reagan mentioned that ninety billion figure?"

"Sure, I'm sure. He reckons he can cut the Federal budget by ninety billion. It's crazy! The figures don't add up."

"You have that in your notes?"

"No, I taped it. Doesn't everybody these days?"

"Right," Spencer laughed. "What date did he make the speech?"

"September . . . let me see . . . fifteenth."

"Thanks, Joel. I'll look into it."

"Who are you working for, Stu?"

"The President." Spencer, formerly Reagan's political coach and campaign manager in his two successful bids for the California governorship, was now fighting against him. Spencer knew better than anyone that Reagan had a tendency to be sloppy in his remarks and in the use of facts and figures. The consultant also realized that if he could expose a big error before the New Hampshire primary, it could end Reagan's presidential bid and give Ford the Republican nomination. After speaking with the journalist, Spencer immediately rang Peter Kaye, Ford's media adviser.

"Pete? Stu," he said, running his hand through his slicked-back gray hair. "I think we can nail that lazy actor who thinks he should play the President." Spencer related the Ninety Billion Dollar story and added, "Put a researcher on it right away. We want a good paper on this that we can distribute to key press guys."

"Sounds like the mistake you were after."

"Yeah, this journalist was bitching about it being on page twenty-three," Spencer laughed. "Said it should have been page one. Let's put it right for him."

A week later, Reagan officially entered the race and was asked a general question about the Ninety Billion at a press conference in Bedford, New Hampshire. "It's important," Reagan began, "that we remove the burden of welfare from the Federal Government. . ." The candidate initially had no trouble with the issue, but the following Sunday on ABC News' 'Issues and Answers', veteran TV anchorman Frank Reynolds threw him a tougher one: "Governor, you're aware that the Federal Government pays 62 per cent of New Hampshire's total outlay for welfare?" Reagan half smiled and nodded. It was the first big interview of his campaign and even the veteran of film and TV was a little uneasy. He would take a while to warm up.

"That means," Reynolds added, "that your ninety billion dollar welfare cut plan has either to be covered by the state or the state must cut its welfare. . ."

"I think that you would have to have taxes increased at state and local levels to offset this," Reagan said, "or maintain some of these programs."

"In candor," correspondent Bob Clark on the program's panel said, "wouldn't you have to tell the people of the state that you are going to have to increase their tax burden and that probably means either a sales tax or a state income tax?"

Reagan looked flustered. "But isn't that a proper decision for the people of the state to make?" he said, in a response that was unconvincing. He had not done his homework and Spencer had him.

The candidate was on the defensive for most of the run up to the primary election over the issue. Originally he had been told by his pollster, Wirthlin, that this issue was a winner in that vital state. All his surveys said consistently that the people were against burgeoning Federal welfare. The problem, however, was in the packaging. The use of the ninety billion dollar figure without the ability to substantiate it had obscured Reagan's aim of reducing the non-military Federal budget, which was a popular issue. More fundamental was the lack of communication between his closest advisers. Wirthlin, once an economics lecturer, could have told the candidate how to use the fact that the basic idea was popular. But the pollster was just one of the expanded coterie of advisers gathered around Reagan now that he was a contender for the Presidency. Wirthlin simply did not have enough power or influence in the campaign to give continuity to strategy and planning after he supplied the valuable intelligence from his surveys, which were being used to guide Reagan.

An additional problem was Reagan's 'passivity' as a candidate. This was a euphemism political operatives used to describe someone who did not brief himself well enough, or actively seek advice which would give his campaign substance. If the more competant advisers such as Wirthlin did not elbow their way forward, Reagan was inclined to accept any mediocre information at his fingertips and slip his way through press conferences, dodging the tougher questions as best he could. Inevitably, reporters became persistent, and with help from the opposition tacticians such as Spencer they began to uncover the candidate's weaknesses. There were enough 'brains' close to Reagan, but John P. Sears, the young lawyer who was in charge of Reagan's campaign, did not seem to be the coordinator he had been billed as after some successes with Richard Nixon in 1967 and 1968. Sears had organized Nixon's delegate search, and in 1969 was his political adviser until he ran afoul of Attorney-General John Mitchell, who did not like the young operative's growing influence. Sears had been the one to convince Reagan that he should run for the Presidency in 1976, despite his reluctance to tackle an incumbent Republican President for the party's nomination. Sears, however, proved most determined. He saw Reagan as a malleable and easily directed candidate who could attract the traditional Republicans and, with guidance, use rhetoric to broaden his appeal. Sears was inclined to dominate the campaign and patronize Reagan, a fact which sometimes did not please either the candidate or the Californian 'insiders' who had stayed with Reagan for the presidential campaign. Sears naturally looked to his experience with Nixon in 1968, in which the methods of running a campaign had worked. It was to be dominated by well-planned 'events' aimed at local and evening TV news coverage. A big divergence from 1968 in this campaign was the holding of news conferences, which Reagan wanted. There was no need for him to sneak off to a TV studio for staged, controlled conferences with 'the people', as Nixon had. Reagan felt comfortable in spontaneous situations. He had the old actor's sensitivity to live audiences and knew how to use them. Unlike Nixon, he loved public exposure. However, his lack of briefing on some of the tough issues was stretching even his professionalism in front of the cameras. Substantial answers were often lacking. Yet a tribute to the man's general popularity was the fact that Wirthlin's polls consistently said he was doing well in the run up to the vital New Hampshire primary, which was to be a head-on collision and the first real contest with President Ford. Reagan was optimistic, despite being plagued by the Ninety Billion Dollar issue which tended to put him on the defensive. On the drive to Los Angeles airport before the flight to New Hampshire, Reagan explained the problem to his wife.

"I'll bet Stu Spencer is behind it," Nancy remarked angrily.

"Yeah," Reagan sighed, "I'm told he is."

"That traitor!"

"Oh, he's a pro, darling. That's politics. There are plenty of piranhas around."

"Piranhas?"

"They bite the hand that once fed them."

LOST IN THE SNOW

At a special TV election center on the fifteenth floor of a new bank in Orlando, Florida, Rosalynn Carter could not stand the suspense any longer. She had to ring Caddell in Boston and find out how her husband was doing in the Massachusetts primary. Carter had surprised everyone by winning more votes than anyone in the New Hampshire primary, which had brought him into the national limelight. There had been a field of four liberal candidates, and Carter, the candidate of the center-right, had beaten them. Now the press was calling him 'Jimmy Who?', which was something. Suddenly, Carter had caught the public imagination. He had come from nowhere and was fulfilling the myth of the American dream: anyone could become President, if he tried hard enough. But could he sustain the momentum in Massachusetts, where the heavyweights, Senator Henry Jackson and Alabama Governor George Wallace, would be candidates?

"What's happening?" Rosalynn asked Caddell, and he replied, "It looks bad. My God, it's snowing like hell. This is not what we needed! It's cutting the turnout and our vote!"

Rosalynn immediately took her husband aside.

"Jimmy, prepare yourself," she said, with disarming frankness. "You look like you're being beaten."

Carter's smile evaporated. "I want to see the results," he said incredulously, and added under his breath, "I can't believe Jackson could do it!"

Minutes later, the phone was running hot for Carter as the results started coming in. The TV monitors were also telling the sorry story for the former Georgia Governor.

"Mr Carter, it looks like you are not going to take Massachusetts," one reporter said. "Where do you go from here?"

The candidate looked unhinged as he stuttered, "I . . . it seems hard to . . . it doesn't look good . . ."

"What do you think of the results?" another reporter asked. All eyes were on the candidate.

"It's too bad," was all he could mutter.

A woman TV commentator moved close with a cameraman right behind her. He was zooming in on Carter's face, looking for some flicker that might show for the first time that Carter might be cracking under the strain, as Muskie had four years ago, in similar circumstances. "Is this the end of your campaign?" she asked. It was crass and premature, but 'good' television. Tears on TV were always terrific for the ratings. But Carter, although visibly stunned, was made of sterner stuff. He bit his lip and shook his head. Excusing himself, he headed for a bank of phones at the back of the auditorium. He wanted to hear the news from Caddell.

"The paper ballots from New Bedford and Fall River aren't in yet," the pollster said. "Neither are those from the west of the state. But it's the trend, Jimmy. Your vote is so low. Well, it's lost."

"What happened?" Carter asked, his voice depressed and cracking.

"Jimmy, we just evaporated. The turnout was awful. Our vote just didn't turn out. The snow didn't help. It kept our numbers down, Jimmy. It's damned bad luck!"

A Carter aide touched the candidate on the shoulder as he put down the phone. "We must have done well in the West," he said to the candidate. Carter shook his head. "We got 14 per cent," he said flatly in a half-whisper. "When you get that low, you haven't done well anywhere."

The next forty-eight hours were the worst for the candidate and his entourage in the whole presidential battle. Everyone tried to turn their minds to the next big primary, which was Florida. It had always been their obsession. Carter knew that Henry Jackson was only planning to take part in that primary to cut into Carter's vote and prevent him from winning. The Jackson campaign was going to spend a lot of money just to stop the Southerner once and for all. Almost everyone expected George Wallace to win. Carter feared a loss, but his faith kept him hopeful, and Caddell felt a personal crisis looming for himself. He was about to test his own obsession with a theory he had nurtured for eight years. It maintained that the candidate with the right themes aimed at disgruntled Southern voters could beat Wallace in Wallace country which, to a large extent, Florida was.

SINKING IN THE SNOW

Mike Deaver, Reagan's young Californian aide, handed Wirthlin a plane ticket as he arrived at Los Angeles airport. The pollster examined it. His relaxed expression vanished. "Chicago?" he asked. "Why?"

"We're meeting the Governor there," Deaver said, as he reached down for his suitcase. Wirthlin was stunned as he watched Deaver shuffle off toward the Illinois flight.

The pollster felt a sinking feeling in his stomach. Bewildered, he began to follow. It was the Sunday before the New Hampshire primary. Reagan should still have been in that state campaigning hard! Instead, he was in Chicago and the primary was still a few weeks away. What the hell was going on? Wirthlin's latest poll showed the candidate only had a tiny lead. To be out of the state now would mean Ford could campaign unopposed and win. Hadn't Reagan seen the poll results? Even earlier surveys had not been clear-cut for Reagan. He had led on 6 February, but by 15 February Ford had made a 48-hour visit and had surged ahead. Wirthlin knew that Ford would return to the state before the primary on 24 February, and he wanted Reagan to stay in the state to combat the President. Wirthlin's polls were clear and emphatic. Whenever Reagan appeared in person, his support jumped. He was becoming one of the most predictable and popular campaigners the nation had seen. He had to keep up the momentum every time people were preparing to vote.

On the flight to Chicago, Wirthlin realized that Sears could not have given Reagan the results of that 15 February poll, because the pollster knew the candidate would have stayed in New Hampshire. Wirthlin had taken his most important poll on 18 February, six days before the primary, and the results were ominous. Reagan was four points ahead in the raw tally, but the 'undecided' vote was high. Ford's return to the state would attract more support, for on his previous visit he had swung them his way. Bearing this in mind, the pollster had made an analysis based on a 2:1 swing of the undecideds to Ford. This assumption gave Ford a tiny lead of 50.7 per cent to 49.3 per cent. Wirthlin had rung Sears to warn him.

"John, I'm sending you a memo to explain New Hampshire," he had told Sears. "The Governor must stay in the state. He may lose if he doesn't. Don't forget to please pass on the results to the Governor. . ."

Wirthlin had dictated his memo in Los Angeles to be telexed through to Sears in New Hampshire. "On February 18, it appears that Ronald Reagan enjoys a whisper of a lead. Given a confidence interval of plus-or-minus 5.2 per cent [the margin of error], it would nevertheless be folly to project a winner. Further, at least three important events will intervene between now and next Tuesday [primary election day]. First, Gerald Ford will revisit the state. While research conducted in the past indicates that second visits do not have the potency of the first, this event should not be underrated, since the foregoing data show that Ford shifted the electorate dramatically through his personal appearance. SECOND, GOVERNOR REAGAN WILL BE IN THAT STATE BETWEEN NOW AND THE ELECTION. That visit, the issues it raises, and the play received in the press can also impact the rather large bloc of undecideds. Conventional wisdom says that we can expect a voter turnout of about 100,000. That would be beneficial to the Governor. However, our DMI surveys point to a 115,000 vote, which would favor Ford. Without question, a large turnout will erode the Governor's vote margin. This is because his supporters, who are ideologically committed, will be likely to vote under any circumstances. The lower the vote, therefore, the higher percentage going to the Governor. The higher it goes over 100,000, the more likely the Governor is to lose."

In Peoria, Illinois, Wirthlin caught up with Sears and took him aside.

"Haven't you told the Governor how close it is in New Hampshire?" he asked, as they watched Reagan fielding questions from a downtown crowd.

"He's going to win there anyway, isn't he?"

"No, John, it's too close to call," Wirthlin said, keeping cool. He was not in charge of the campaign, and for the first time was regretting it. "It would have been better if he had stayed there in the snow. I think someone should tell him."

Sears gave him a rueful look. "You had better tell him," he said, "if you think it's that bad. He's going back to New Hampshire tonight. Why don't you take the flight with him?"

Sears turned and walked into the crowd to speak with Reagan's press secretary, Lyn Nofziger. Wirthlin looked up at the candidate and sighed. He had the crowd cheering and clapping, and he looked more confident than Wirthlin had ever seen him. How was the pollster going to tell his friend that he had just made the biggest blunder of his political life? If he did lose New Hampshire, it would be nearly impossible to beat Ford for the Republican nomination. The damage would be done, and Reagan would look like a loser. He was sixty-five years old and time would surely be against him running again in 1980. God, that was so far away, and by then Reagan would be sixty-nine! A further disappointment for Wirthlin was the fact that he had been using an improved simulation technique as the source of his advice to the campaign. It was proving accurate, but now he wondered how much it was being ignored. In an era when computerized information was power, he was beginning to feel more confident as a 'technician' in a world of 'gut' advisers. Wirthlin was getting more adept at handling them, for his company, DMI, had worked on scores of Republican campaigns in battles for Congress, state houses, mayoral offices and governorships across the country. Of all the candidates he had advised, he had greatest respect for the man now addressing the crowd in front of him. After a shaky start with some issues, Reagan was living up to Wirthlin's expectations of him as a great presidential candidate. As light snow began to fall, Wirthlin pulled his coat collar up, and resolved to work harder for Reagan than ever before. First, however, he had the difficult task of giving the candidate the bad news.

Wirthlin waited until they were airborne en route to Manchester, New Hampshire, before be began to tell Reagan what he could expect the next day, election day. He concentrated on explaining the 'undecided' voter position.

"If they come out in big numbers, it may be difficult to win," Wirthlin said carefully, giving Reagan the rosiest picture he could. He was cheered by the fact that the candidate took in all the possibilities and still remained optimistic.

"What do you think the turnout will be like, Dick?" Reagan asked.

"Well," the pollster began, "it could vary between 100,000 and 115,000."

Reagan looked out the window at the night lights of Manchester as they began their descent. "What happens if it's 107,500?" he asked.

"It will be very, very close, Governor."

"Perhaps we should jam a few broadcasts and tell everyone to stay indoors tomorrow because of a snowstorm."

Wirthlin grinned and nodded. "That would just about do it."

After a longish pause, Reagan said soberly, "Let's hope someone down there lights a candle for me tonight. . ."

FOUND IN THE SUN

There was something more satisfying for Jimmy Carter about campaigning in Florida. His own home town of Plains, Georgia, was only 95 miles north of the border. In the north of Florida, at least, Carter was familiar with the political climate of the rural area, particularly across the Panhandle. It was called redneck, or Wallace, country and included Caddell's home town, Jacksonville. In the last year, Carter had also familiarized himself with the politically more moderate South. Florida was to be a big showdown with Governor George Wallace and Senator Henry Jackson. Carter was in an aggressive and combative mood after his shock defeat in Massachusetts, and it was well understood by all the candidates that the winner in Florida would be the true front-runner. He would probably go on to take the Democratic nomination. Carter's instinct was to attack both Wallace and Jackson. Wallace became the prime target, and Carter set the tone in a fund-raiser letter. It read: "Please help us win a victory in Florida and allow the Democratic Party to choose its presidential candidate in an area free of demagoguery . . . I need your help now to end once and for all the threat that Wallace represents to our country."

It was the sort of election drug that made Caddell very happy. He went on to frame a basic theme, run in all the media ads, which was designed to attract the anti-central government protest vote which Wallace had played to for years. Wallace's slogan in the 1972 presidential primaries had been 'Send them a message'. The theme of Carter's campaign in 1976 was 'Send them a President'. Caddell's theory was being put to the test. Could Carter attack Wallace and at the same time take his traditional anti-Washington vote from him? It was a most complex experiment, for Carter had to run a delicate course in an attempt to attract the redneck vote in the North, and the liberal vote in the South. Caddell had to do some intense polling throughout the state to see where votes could be siphoned off for Carter. When that was established, Caddell could advise him on how the campaign's resources should be spent – questions such as how much TV advertising should be shown in one county, and what Carter should say in another, would be decided before each day's campaigning.

In the middle of the campaign Carter was in Jacksonville, and Caddell was to meet him at 6.30 a.m. at his hotel. The candidate was driving himself very hard, and trying to stay fit with a three-mile run before each day's effort. Caddell arrived late, and Carter demanded he come on the run with him.

"You've got sneakers on. You'll be fine," Carter said, limbering up in a light blue track suit. "I want to know what's going on."

The pollster was an armchair sportsman and decidedly over-weight. He stumbled into a park with Carter, a folder full of notes clutched to his heaving chest. The candidate could see he would have to stop. "OK, Pat, you've made your point," he said, indicating they should sit on a park bench. "I need you alive in this election."

"I'll show you the figures later," Caddell said, catching his breath, "but essentially we are not getting anything out of Dade County . . . but you have a sound base in central Florida and we are getting tanked in northern Florida. . ."

"Even in Jacksonville?"

"No, that's a big exception right now. Also, we could go into Tampa Bay and turn that around."

"How have we divided the vote?"

"I've divided up Wallace votes with a racial component, Wallace voters with intensity, satisfied Wallace voters, and dissatisfied Wallace voters."

"What percentage did he start with?"

"Forty-six per cent."

"And me? I was around twenty-five?"

"Right. But remember, you'll also have Jackson in there. He'll take votes away from Wallace too."

"I'm just as worried about Jackson."

"You have to be. But Wallace is the prime target."

"What are you finding that's important? I mean, what is the electorate thinking?"

Caddell scrabbled in his folder and found some handwritten notes. "We've discovered that your background is important. You can push your roots as hard as you like, and your experience. Also, just about everyone here is responding to your anti-Government theme. In the South you can go after Wallace. The liberals in all the cities – Miami, Miami Beach, Palm Beach, Ft Lauderdale, Tampa, St Petersburg – are going for it."

"The Jews like me attacking Wallace, I'll bet."

"Sure they do."

Carter stood up to continue his run. "Leave all that with me," the candidate said, pointing at Caddells' data sheets. "I'll go through it at lunchtime." The pollster gathered his folder and watched Carter jogging off, shoulders hunched and fists pumping. If ever anyone deserved to win because of determination, Caddell thought, it's him.

Later that day, at a press conference in Orlando, Caddell learned just how feisty Carter could be when he implied that Jackson had won in Massachusetts by running a racist campaign. Caddell, Jody Powell and Hamilton Jordan could hardly believe their ears. Mr 'Nice Guy' was prepared to rough it to get votes. A reporter asked Carter, "Why didn't you make an issue out of busing in Massachusetts?" His reply was, "I'm not in favor of mandatory busing, but to run my campaign on an anti-busing issue is contrary to my nature. If I had to win by appealing to a basically negative, emotional issue which has connotations of racism, I don't intend to do it myself. I don't want to win that kind of race."

At the end of the conference, he walked over to his campaign team. "I want to cut some anti-Jackson commercials right now," he said firmly. Late in the afternoon, the candidate, Rafshoon, Caddell, Powell and Jordan met at a studio back in Jacksonville for a TV and radio taping session. As Carter, Rafshoon and Caddell went over some scripts, the candidate started scribbling. "What are you doing?" Rafshoon asked, and without saying anything, Carter handed him his changes, which were marked in red. He had toughened up all his references to Jackson. Caddell was intrigued. When they were alone in the studio, he asked Carter, "Why did you do it?"

Carter, who was drawn and pale, shrugged and shook his head. "I just don't know how to put it in words. I just wanted to say it. I know I can get away with it up here. We need those votes."

Essentially, Caddell realized later, Carter's instincts were running ahead of his ability to verbalize. He was doing naturally what Caddell was doing with his razor-sharp polling and analysis: attempting to attract votes wherever he could. The liberal vote in the state was measured at a modest 10 per cent. But Carter needed every point he could get, and he was going after it. Attacking Jackson on specific liberal issues would take a few points away from him.

On election day, 9 March, Carter flew into North Carolina to begin campaigning for that state's primary, which was still two weeks away. By late that night the results were coming in, indicating a Carter victory in Florida. The final count was Carter 34 per cent, Wallace 31 and Jackson 24. Temporarily derailed in Massachusetts, the Carter train was back on track.

TACTICS IN THE NIGHT

Reagan lost to Ford in New Hampshire by 1317 votes out of 108,000 ballots cast, yet despite the closeness of the race, the psychological factors were vital to both candidates. The result was a morale booster for the shaky incumbent President who had needed some sort of mandate to suggest he was not just a caretaker. On the other hand, it was Reagan's first election defeat ever, and while the candidate looked on the bright side, his campaign team, which had expected to win, received a shock. Wirthlin, more frustrated than surprised, took the moment to inject some of his own strategy ideas into the flagging campaign.

As soon as the loss was certain, he met Sears in the latter's room at the New Hampshire Highway Hotel to review the polling data on the next contested primary, and to work out some kind of strong strategy. The question was, what should Reagan do to regain lost momentum? Should he campaign more on domestic issues or attack Ford on foreign policy? Wirthlin went painstakingly through all the issues with Sears until the early hours. The pollster had employed his simulation technique, which had come up with at least one possible solution. The simulation and surveys showed that Republicans were not especially concerned about foreign policy. Only 12 per cent of those asked said they were. Yet Wirthlin had discovered one important factor. If the Governor took a hard line in foreign policy, it could contrast noticeably with the Ford-Kissinger line, and also Ford's leadership style, which was not regarded as powerful or forthright.

"You sure about this?" Sears asked, examining a print-out.

"I did polling for Ford before Reagan entered the race," Wirthlin said. "The surveys check through over two years. If there is an opening, it is in how Republicans perceive Ford. Reagan is well known because of his background, but he is not known well. People are not certain where he stands yet. This means his slate is clean. He can write anything he likes on it. If he gets tough with Ford and Kissinger over foreign policy, this will make headlines and give Republican voters a clear choice."

"It's the only way he can stand out as different?"

Wirthlin nodded. "With a tough line on the Panama Canal, for example."

Sears looked at his watch. It was after 5 a.m.

"I think it's worth a try," he said.

"OK, John," Wirthlin said, "but remember, the Governor will have to attack Ford and Kissinger by name. He'll really have to open up the differences to make this approach work."

NO LANGUAGE BARRIER

Carter had just finished speaking to workers in a Pennsylvania steel foundry when an aide handed him the clippings from the leading morning papers. On the ride back to his hotel in Philadelphia, an article by the *Washington Post*'s David Broder riveted his attention. It was entitled, 'Carter: Some Paradoxes'.

"There are few people who can match Carter when it comes to, weaving a spell with words," Broder wrote. "He had been called 'fuzzy' by his critics, but the truth is he uses language with extraordinary precision of effect – but not to clarify meaning. His intricate sentences weave in and out of an issue, each strand of words spelling reassurances to part of the audience. A student of psychology and learning techniques, Carter employs the principles of selective perception and reinforcement. For example, he lets critics of abortion focus on his statement that 'I think abortions are wrong,' but nourishes their opponents' hopes by adding a few phrases later, 'I am opposed to any constitutional amendment in this area.' "

Carter had been following a thematic approach suggested by his own instincts and reinforced by Caddell's polls, which were showing how to be very precise in the use of the themes. Now, at an important juncture in the primary battles, the perception of him as unclear on issues had caught up with his campaign. It had to be rectified quickly because Carter hoped to knock his main rival, Henry Jackson, out of the race in the Pennsylvania primary. The candidate waited for an expected phone call from Caddell at his hotel and immediately raised the problem.

"It's OK, Jimmy," Caddell reassured him. "We have been picking up this 'fuzziness' thing for a few days now. Jackson will know of it too, and I hear he plans to hit you with it."

"Have you spoken to Gerry?"

"Yeah, all the tag lines at the end of your commercials will be changed. They will all be very specific: Jimmy Carter on tax reform . . . Jimmy Carter on inflation . . . Jimmy Carter on welfare. They will be the same ads as we have been running in Pennsylvania, but we will label them with issues."

"Will that be enough?"

"Should think so. What more could we do? You're now going to be very clear on all the issues. If Jackson goes after you on that, he'll be on a loser."

The temporary change in the campaign approach was enough to defuse the 'fuzziness' issue, and Carter went on to win Pennsylvania. He collected 37 per cent of the vote, with Jackson getting 25 per cent, Morris Udall 19, and Wallace only 11. By routing Jackson in a big-labor Northern industrial state, whose major city was controlled by a machine solidly behind Jackson, Carter had delivered a finishing blow to the Senator. Celebrating his victory, Carter was confident enough to say that his candidacy was "in good shape to get a first ballot victory" in the looming Democratic convention. And it was. Carter went on to take the nomination without any further strong resistance. He was now one step away from his main goal.

SAVING FACE – DIRECT TO CAMERA

While Carter and Caddell were sniping their way through the primary battles, Reagan was losing each fight with Ford and fast running out of money to sustain his campaign. Despite the vigor he applied in attacking Ford on foreign policy, it was only enough to give Reagan respectability in each primary. The overall strategy and the packaging of Reagan was simply not strong enough to lift the candidate into the lead. Wirthlin's advice was still being largely ignored, although sporadically he was getting his points across, sometimes with Sears, and on the rare occasion he could get close to him, the candidate himself. Before the North Carolina primary, he had a chance to brief Reagan on board a commercial airplane on the way to the state capital. Their campaign was now about two million dollars in the red, and they could not afford to run a private campaign plane.

In a quick review of polling data, Wirthlin told Reagan, "Your movie connection is a big plus with voters."

Reagan winced. "Then why aren't we seeing it in our ads?" he asked. "I just don't understand it."

Nancy Reagan, who was wrapped in a blanket with her head resting on her husband's shoulder, looked up. "Why is that, Dick?" she asked Wirthlin. "If Ronnie's film career is useful, they should be using it."

"It goes back to the way Harry Treleaven ran Dick Nixon's ads in 1968," Wirthlin replied. "He used a *cinema vérité* technique then, and he's doing it with our ads now. The idea is to make a candidate look like a politician on the campaign trail. It avoids the problem of using a candidate straight to camera. Very few people can hold an audience that way. Harry is worried that if we use that method it will remind the electorate of your acting background."

"Ronnie can hold any audience," Nancy said, sitting up and rubbing her eyes.

Wirthlin nodded. "Eighty per cent of any audience for thirty minutes," he said. "I've run surveys on it. No one has ever matched that."

"Then why can't we change all these silly *cinema vérité* things," she said. "Throw them all out. . ."

"We haven't got the money," Reagan said bluntly. Nancy frowned her disapproval and nuzzled close to her husband again as the candidate's press secretary, Lyn Nofziger, eased into the seat next to Wirthlin and joined the conversation.

"Everyone has always wanted to try their own style with you," he said to Reagan. "Harry's way was right for Nixon. The less he had to do direct to camera, the better. But it's wrong for you."

"Dick always was a third-rate actor," Reagan said.

Two days later, during the North Carolina primary campaign, Nofziger dug out a thirty-minute tape that had been made at a Miami TV station studio in the last week of the Florida primary. Nofziger edited out references to Florida and sent it off to the state's TV stations for prime-time viewing. It was vintage Reagan, straight to camera all the way, and the conservative North Carolina audience loved it. In a shock victory, Reagan went on to take the state 52 to 46. That success prompted the campaign to use the no-frills technique for a national address by the candidate. It was a beggar – an appeal for funds – which raised a remarkable $1.5 million, and this saved the campaign from financial embarrassment. The new approach helped give the campaign a second wind, and Reagan had his biggest breakthrough in the Texas primary, where he took all 96 delegates on 1 May. Three days later he took 130 of the 139 delegates in the Alabama, Georgia and Indiana primaries. On 11 May he won Nebraska, while Ford took West Virginia. Ford was still ahead in the overall delegate count, but Reagan was causing him trouble right up until California. It seemed unlikely that Reagan could win the nomination, but he at least wanted victory in his home state, where he had never lost an election. Reagan campaigned vigorously. He held several press conferences and media events, which were closely monitored by his own people and the Californians in the Ford camp, Stu Spencer and media man Peter Kaye. Answering questions before the Sacramento Press Club, Reagan said he would provide a token contingent of US troops as part of a United Nations Command, if Rhodesia requested it to fight guerrillas. When Spencer read the transcript of this conference, he immediately rang Kaye and suggested they do something about it in Ford's media advertising.

"It's made the headlines everywere," Spencer said. "It'll bring back all the old fears about Reagan being a 'dangerous' right-winger."

"Could you come up with something, Stu?" Kaye asked. "You know, just a punchy tag-line?"

Three days later, Spencer and Kaye ran a TV commercial with a punchline that said, "When you vote Tuesday, remember: Governor Ronald Reagan couldn't start a war. President Ronald Reagan could." The next morning, Nofziger drove to the Los Angeles offices of DMI and found Wirthlin in the computer room examining printouts. Chomping on a large cigar, the pot-bellied press secretary asked Wirthlin if he had seen the Ford campaign ad.

"Yes," the pollster said, "and we've already run a survey on it. Most people simply don't believe the commercial. They don't believe the Governor would ever start a war."

Nofziger examined some of the results. "Stu has gone over the top this time," he said with a smile, "way over the top."

"Lyn," Wirthlin said, handing him more data sheets, "the reaction is so bad to this ad, you could almost run it completely as a Reagan ad."

"You mean people are seeing it as a smear against him?"

"Absolutely."

Nofziger's eyes widened and he stood staring at the data. "I've got an idea," he said. "Just keep your eye on our commercials."

Nofziger rang Kaye's agency. He purchased several copies of the Ford ad and had them rerun entirely as a Reagan spot. At midnight on primary election night, Wirthlin rang the candidate to tell him of the likely outcome of voting.

"It's a terrific win, Governor," Wirthlin said. "You are going to take the state by a 2 to 1 margin."

"That's great, Dick," Reagan said. "Maybe Stu Spencer was working for us all along!"

Despite Reagan's late surge, it was just too little and too late to save his bid for the Republican nomination. He ended up supported by 1070 delegates, while Ford collected just 180 more, which won him the right to contest the national battle against Carter.

Reagan took his loss well, and in a speech in a crowded ballroom of the Alameda Plaza in Kansas City after the convention, he had all his supporters weeping. Many thought it might be Ronnie's last hurrah. But Reagan gave a hint that he had other ideas when he quoted a line from an English ballad by Dryden: "'Lay me down and bleed a while,'" he said, his voice husky. "'Though I am wounded, I am not slain. I shall rise and fight again.'"

Amid the clapping and cheering, Nofziger turned to Wirthlin and said, "There may be life in the old dog yet."

Wiping away a tear, the pollster replied, "Sure, there is. He's going to live until he's one hundred."

CHAPTER 6

OPERATION 270

THORNS IN THE ROSE GARDEN

Robert M. Teeter, President Ford's pollster, had discovered a clear pattern in his surveys: when the incumbent campaigned in the primaries in person, he lost ground in national polls. Teeter, of the Detroit-based survey group Market Opinion Research, had written a report for Stu Spencer, who was in charge of Ford's campaign strategy for the election. Teeter had emphasized the fact that the President stood a much stronger chance of beating Carter by staying home in the White House and acting 'presidential'. The pollster had also found that Ford was not well received as a speaker, so the suggestion was that his every performance for the cameras be strictly controlled and produced by professionals. Teeter's implication was that Ford should be handled just as President Nixon had been when he was a candidate in 1968 and 1972, and during his six years in office. Spontaneity was a greater enemy than Jimmy Carter, and if this was not avoided the polls suggested that Ford would be sure to lose his job.

Teeter's report also included the pros and cons in the public's perceptions of both Ford and Carter. It wasn't flattering material for the President. He was seen as dithering, and as a puppet of his Secretary of State, Henry Kissinger. The public did not like the way he seemed to spend a great deal of time worrying about politics. They preferred that he get on with governing the nation. He was seen as boring. On the other hand he was generally considered trustworthy, with the one exception that many did not like his decision to pardon President Nixon after Watergate. This had tarnished his image. However, he was liked, for he was seen as a good, honest man who tried hard, and who was "safe and would do the right thing".

Armed with this, and with data interpreted by other strategists, Spencer prepared to produce a strategy for Ford which would spell out the methods that had to be used to save his Presidency. In a breakfast meeting at a downtown Washington restaurant, Spencer met with Teeter before putting the finishing touches to a book of tactics.

"All we have, really, is a used Ford that some *might* buy," Spencer said ruefully.

Teeter was more hopeful: "There is a chance if you can firm up the public's feelings about his personality and character," he said.

Spencer shook his head. "Not easy," he replied. "At the

moment, he is seen as an OK nice guy caretaker President who bumps his head a lot. The people still seem to think LBJ was right when he said that Gerry can't chew gum and fart at the same time."

"All the more reason to have him campaign from inside the White House," Teeter said.

"I saw the figures. But great! A candidate who doesn't really get out on the campaign trail!"

"He should let Carter do all the campaigning," Teeter said, sipping coffee. "He'll make mistakes. That will gradually reduce his vote. Also, the public is not sure about him. They like the President's character more at the moment. He should be able to close the gap, if he doesn't make any big mistakes."

"Trouble is, Gerry thinks he is a good campaigner."

"That's because he has been a successful candidate in Senate elections."

"I'll have to convince him to stay in the Rose Garden."

Spencer spent several days composing a 124-page book for Ford and then made an appointment to see him at the Oval Office. After greeting Spencer with his usual friendliness, Ford lit his pipe and settled back in his swivel chair behind the Oval Office desk to hear the battle plan. Spencer sat forward on the edge of his chair with one hand on the desk. "Mr President," he said. "As a campaigner, you're no fucking good!'"

SMILE, YOU'RE ON VOTE-CATCHING CAMERA

"Remember Watergate," Caddell said as he handed Jordan detailed polling results state by state. They showed where Carter was strongest and weakest, and where he needed to campaign earliest and most often to win the magic number of 270 electoral college votes necessary for election victory. Carter's two key strategists had met in the Situation Room at the Atlanta headquarters of the campaign. "If this gets into the Ford camp, they'll derive our battle plans," Caddell added. "We should also keep it secret from Democrats."

Jordan eyed him quizzically. "They won't like it?" he asked. "We don't want to ruffle feathers. Some state leaders are going to be upset enough about us giving them a complete miss. No need to upset them in advance."

The Caddell data was used to guide a strategy developed by him and Jordan where a 'per cent of effort' of the whole campaign was computed and assigned to each state. This was based on the size and importance of the state and the Democrats' chances in it. California, for instance, weighed in with 5.9 per cent of effort because it was the biggest state. Wyoming and Alaska, on the other end of the scale, scored just 0.6 per cent. The figures were also applied to a master scheduling formula for Carter, his running mate, Senator Mondale, and their families. Parallel to this overall plan, Caddell and the other advisers had to concentrate on a three-part debate in October. Ford had little choice but to take part, because he was so far behind in the polls. Carter, on the other hand, saw it as a chance to break clear of his opponent and secure the election. But after the first debate on domestic affairs, in which Carter only managed to hold his own, he was forced to work harder for the next bout, which was on foreign affairs. A rehearsal was staged and Caddell, Jordan, Powell, Rafshoon, Stu Eizenstat, Representative Les Aspin of Wisconsin, and foreign affairs advisers Brzezinski and Richard Holbrooke, fired questions at him in a San Francisco hotel ballroom. Brzezinski dominated the preparation. He expected to get a key government post along with 25 or so members of David Rockefeller's Trilateral Commission, if Carter won the Presidency. Brzezinski had been educating Carter on all matters foreign for three years since the candidate had joined the Commission.

Caddell joined in the quizzing, but was more concerned about Carter's mannerisms than what he had learned from Brzezinski. Caddell had been polling the candidate's strengths and weaknesses for two years, and he felt he knew some of them even better than Carter himself. At one point when Holbrooke and Brzezinski were arguing how Carter should respond to a question, Caddell said to the candidate, "Better to smile more, when you can."

Carter, who was standing quietly behind a lectern, replied, "Foreign affairs are not always laughing matters."

"I'm going on your first debate," Caddell said. "Some groups saw you as fierce and cold. They don't trust you because of it."

"Like who?"

"Young mothers."

"Gotta turn on all those young mothers," Jordan quipped.

"With lust in my heart?" Carter said, and everyone laughed. A few days earlier, *Playboy* magazine had published an interview with Carter in which he had said, "I've looked on a lot of women with lust. I've committed adultery in my heart many times."

A few hours later, during the actual debate in San Francisco's Palace of the Fine Arts, Carter looked more confident, and in just the right mood to take advantage of the biggest blunder of the campaign.

In answer to a question on US relations with the Soviet Union, Ford said, "There is no domination of Eastern Europe, and there will never be, under a Ford administration."

After Ford had stunned the panel of questioning journalists by expanding on this theme, it was Carter's turn to reply. The Democrat seized the moment: "I would like to see Mr Ford convince the Polish-Americans, and the Czech-Americans, and the Hungarian-Americans in this country that those countries don't live under the domination and the supervision of the Soviet Union behind the Iron Curtain." It was a good vote-catching response. Instead of trying to give a knowledgeable answer based on his coaching from Brzezinski, Carter had in mind all the political points he could score. Caddell's influence in dividing up the nation geographically, ethnically and in a score of other ways seemed to have paid off. Before the debates, he had advised the candidate to respond with every voting group in mind at all possible times. While Carter was not a good performer in front of the cameras, he had a retentive memory and presence of mind which allowed him to spray out his messages everywhere. At one point, he referred not simply to "the Pope", but to "his Holiness, the Pope", as if he was a Catholic. Blacks, Hispanics and women were mentioned repeatedly, as were just about every other group in the nation that Caddells' polls had dissected. At times the sheer volume of the words and statistics that Carter spewed out gave the impression that he had been programmed.

When Ford made his mistake on Soviet Union domination and Carter responded comprehensively, his team was ecstatic. Ford's strategist, Stu Spencer, was also in the audience. Not being a foreign affairs expert himself, he was unsure initially if the President had blown it or not. He looked at Ford's adviser, Brent Scowcroft, who was sitting next to him. The foreign affairs expert had gone white, and Spencer was aware that there was going to be trouble.

At the end of the debate, Caddell rushed to the dressing room. He shook hands with Carter and said, "That's probably the most decisive presidential debate in history!"

The happy candidate replied cockily, "Wait until you see the next one." Moments later, while his makeup was being removed, he asked his pollster, "Pat, did I smile enough?"

"Oh, yeah," Caddell said. "You won them all tonight."

The press and media post-debate analysis focused on Ford's 'mis-speak', as the White House called it in true Orwellian style, and this, far more than the President's ignorance, made Carter the second debate winner. Yet rather than the expected breakthrough by the challenger, Caddell's surveys were most sobering. Ford was gradually closing a large gap and could even win the election if Carter did anything glaringly or consistently wrong in the last two weeks. Carter's lead was down to 6 points. He led 47 to Ford's 41, with 2 per cent for Eugene McCarthy, who was running an independent race, and 10 per cent for others or undecideds. A crisis meeting was called on Monday 18 October at the Atlanta headquarters, and all Carter's key people attended. With the election close, Caddell and his hot data were beginning to influence the direction of the campaign more and more. Jordan, who was managing Carter's effort, asked Caddell to give the team a run-down on the race to that point. In a room resembling a military briefing room, with charts, maps, and boards covered with statistical analyses, the pollster gave the assembled squad the somber news.

"We are seeing serious slides in all the big states," he began, using a pointer to indicate them on a large map. "And we are virtually even everywhere – Pennsylvania, Texas, Illinois, Ohio, New Jersey, Florida, Mississippi, and Oklahoma are tightening up for us. But there is slippage in South Carolina and we are losing Louisiana."

Gone was the elation over Carter's combative effort in the debate. Some in the team had not realized how close the race had become. Even the normally cocky Jordan was anxious. "What effect will the voter turnout have?" he asked hopefully. He had been briefed the day before about the preparations that both parties were making in their efforts to get supporters to the polls.

"If we predict voter intentions on a low voter turnout," Caddell replied with a shrug, "then Jimmy Carter is behind." This was pollster parlance that all could grasp quickly. From the euphoric hopes and expectations of victory, the sober facts were that Carter could very well lose after all.

"Which group is he doing worst with?" Powell asked. "Is it still women?"

Caddell nodded. "Particularly housewives." There were no more jokes about seducing the female vote. It was a real problem, and several of the squad wanted to know why.

"Women are supporting us on issues," Caddell said with a characteristic frown, "but on personality questions they feel far safer with Ford."

One of two openly protested that this seemed wrong. Jimmy was a nicer guy than Gerry any day. Caddell was forced to reel off supporting facts and figures to the stunned group.

"How do we combat this?" Rafshoon asked.

"The fact of the matter is," Caddell said, dropping a favorite Bostonian phrase, "women feel Jimmy is a risk and that Ford is safer. We must break through that concern by not giving them any excuse to say they don't trust Jimmy. Then they are left with voting on the issues. That's what we want. Then we do better."

"So any negative advertising attacking Ford is dangerous?" Rafshoon asked.

"Deadly," Caddell said adamantly.

"And Jimmy attacking Ford in person?" Jordan asked.

"That's just as bad. Every time Jimmy rounds on Ford or refers to a Nixon-Ford administration, or something like that, we lose ground."

Rafshoon wasted no time in calling New York to restrain the creative Tony Schwartz from making his brilliant, but potentially negative advertising for the Democrats.

Even when the Republicans went on the attack with authentic man-in-the-street ads which denigrated Carter, Rafshoon vetoed Schwartz's commercials using actors in New York streets doing much the same thing against Ford. However painfully, the Democrats were turning the other cheek in an effort to avoid a backlash from women and other doubting groups. Carter, who had been tough and precise in attacking Ford, also restrained himself on the strength of Caddell's advice. The candidate even attempted to make some political capital out of this in the third debate.

"The American people will not see the Carter campaign running TV advertisements and newspaper advertisements based on a personal attack on President Ford's character," he said. "I believe that the opposite is true with President Ford's campaign . . ."

As the weeks dwindled down to days, the President continued to carry the election to his challenger right until the final day before the actual deciding vote when opposing pollsters could not be drawn on a solid prediction. The Ford-Carter battle had become too close to call.

MARATHON WINNER

On election day President Ford was joined in the Oval Office by Richard Cheney, his chief of staff, James Baker, his campaign manager, and Teeter and Spencer all of whom carried news of polls taken as people left the booths in key precincts around the country.

"It's too early to tell," Spencer kept saying, as early results showed Ford trailing badly.

The President did not react, for he had been forewarned by Teeter that Carter could be expected to build up an early lead in the South. As the news continued to be grim, despite the hopeful atmosphere in the White House, Ford kept repeating with added determination, "We are still going to win."

After briefing Carter for the third time on exit polls around the nation, Caddell settled in with others in the campaign team in the

Capital Suite on the fifteenth floor of the Omni International Hotel in Atlanta to watch the predictions on TV. All three networks were geared for quick computer analyses of the actual results and for sound predictions. The game was to be first to bring the nation news of a winner. At 6.30 a.m. all three networks called Kentucky for Carter, who sat in front of three sets. He squeezed his wife's hand and kissed her affectionately.

"Well, we got one," Jordan said, which brought a nervous titter from the rest of the Carter family and his closest advisers. Seconds later, when Indiana went to Ford, there were some boos. Then Ford took Kansas, Nebraska and Connecticut. But then it began to happen for the peanut farmer from Plains, as a small avalanche of states in the East and South went his way: Massachusetts and Rhode Island to East Virginia, North Carolina and Tennessee, down to Florida and over to Alabama. Caddell could not stand it any longer. He got up from an armchair and paced around the room, hands in pockets. His obsession and beloved alienation theory was beginning to come true. Southern blacks especially had come out in big numbers for Jimmy Carter, and the pollster felt a deep surge of satisfaction. But he tempered it, for it meant nothing if Carter could not win those 270 electoral college votes.

"Ford has to win five or six of the big eight," Caddell said to Powell and Jordan. With the South in Carter's column, the election battleground was now the Northern industrial belt running from New York west through New Jersey, Pennsylvania, Ohio, Michigan and Illinois.

At midnight, all eyes turned to the TV set carrying CBS's coverage. Walter Cronkite appeared. "Carter is the winner in Oregon," he said dramatically. "I repeat. Governor Carter has taken the state of Oregon." A big cheer went up in the suite. An aide checked it with the other two networks, but they would not concede it to Carter. One suggested Ford was more likely to take it. Several people groaned. Carter, cool but unsmiling, said to Jordan, "Ham, get me Daley in Chicago."

The mayor came on the line and Carter asked him pleasantly, "How we doin'?"

Daley, one of the most influential politicians in the history of the Democrat Party, gave Carter some cheer. "I think you'll do it," he said excitedly in his rapid-fire way. "We've got a good vote here in Chicago, and if you do as well downstate, it's ours."

Caddell went into a bedroom and began making calls around the country. After several minutes, he let go some expletives under his breath, and hurried to Carter's side.

"You're going to lose New Jersey," he said quietly, "and it looks confused in New York. The vote's all over the damned place!"

"Get me Beame in New York," Carter snapped.

When that city's Mayor came on the line, he said, "Well, I don't know what's happening everywhere, but you're going to take the city easily. I reckon enough to take the state."

"Now, you're sure, Abraham?"

The mayor paused on the other end of the line. "Yeah, I'd bet on it," he said confidently.

Carter took in a sharp, nervous breath and gave a thumbs up sign to Caddell, who had heard the conversation while taking another call.

"Pennsylvania's yours!" said Caddell, and Carter was smiling again.

"What's the margin in Philly?" he asked Caddell.

"About 260,000," Caddell replied, shuffling some notes.

"Well, Rizzo promised us 300,000," the candidate said with a laugh, "but I guess 260,000 will have to do. Wish these mayors would keep their promises."

Even Caddell gave a semblance of a smile at that. He could see that Carter was sensing victory. At 2 a.m. all the networks seemed set to give him the election, but another half-hour went by before Hawaii was predicted as his. He was now five electoral college votes away from 270. But then the results slowed to a crawl and the clock ticked on for nearly another hour before NBC gave Carter Mississippi, and the Presidency. Everyone in the suite embraced each other wildly and there were tears in many eyes, including Carter's as he held his wife. Caddell hugged and kissed Carter's mother and yelled, "He's done it! He's President!"

"President of what?" Miss Lillian said with a wide grin, but she was hardly heard above the din.

THE LAST DRY RUN

The Sunday after Carter's victory, Wirthlin met with his company's top market researcher, Vince Breglio, after a service at their local Latter-Day Saints church in Los Angeles. Wirthlin had invited him home for a Sunday lunch, and during the drive back in his gold-colored Mercedes, the discussion turned quickly to the presidential election.

"I don't think he could ever have beaten Reagan," Wirthlin said, "if we could have used the simulation. He had a whole new world of populist support. It would have come through strongly in a national campaign."

Breglio agreed. "Do you think he'll run again?"

"Don't know yet, "Wirthlin said. "I've spoken to him at his ranch. He's enjoying it out there. All he would say was that he had had his last dry run."

"Sounds promising."

"I'm sure he feels he could have beaten Carter." Wirthlin pulled a piece of paper from his inside coat pocket. "Take a look at that," he said, passing it to Breglio. It was a Ford White House internal memorandum.

"Just read the bits I've underlined," Wirthlin continued, seeing his partner's intrigued look. It was about Caddell's part in Carter's campaign. It read:

The close connection between the candidate and his pollster has had important tactical results. Caddell always has polls in the field on a basis sufficient to disaggregate key states and constituencies from a national sample. Hence there is the possibility of a quick response to any new shifts in their opinion and their immediate communication to the candidate. The Ford operation by contrast, as befits a presidential staff operation, had double or triple the reaction time to new voter moods – a real disadvantage in a short campaign. On an institutional basis, Caddell is a generation ahead of most other techniques. No one has yet devised a system for protecting a Republican candidate from the Caddell-style alienation attack.

"Who wrote this?" Breglio asked.

"Don't know," Wirthlin replied with a mysterious grin, "but we can develop a computer system to protect Republicans, particularly the Governor."

"The simulation could have done it this year."

"True, but we need to have a greater say in strategy," Wirthlin said, pulling into the driveway of his large home. Three of his sons were playing touch football on the front lawns. "I want an updated simulation like nothing seen before," he added, as the car stopped. "A computerized strategy is the only one that can win."

PART TWO
1979–1980
PROGRAM FOR A CANDIDATE

CHAPTER 7

CRISIS FOR A LEADER

CARTER'S CATHARSIS

Pat Caddell was frustrated and worried. It was well into the third year of the Carter Presidency and his polls were telling him that America was heading toward some sort of moral or spiritual crisis. The pollster knew that if he confronted the President directly with his findings, he would not get a good hearing. Carter had trouble enough with the economy, inflation running high, and his own popularity which had slipped to an all-time low for any president. He would not be receptive to information indicating he was also in power during a period when a malaise of pessimism was sweeping the nation. Caddell had tried explaining the problem to Jody Powell, Carter's closest adviser in the White House, but did not get far. In desperation, the pollster rang the one Carter 'insider' who had never failed to give the President brutal advice – his wife. Caddell had used her often to reach the President, but never on a matter he considered so vital.

"I really would like to come and see you," Caddell told her. "It's very important. And I would like several hours." Rosalynn hesitated. She had a tight schedule and it was rare for anyone to request block time like this. Yet the urgency in Caddell's voice prompted her to agree.

"I'll schedule breakfast next Monday," she said. Three days later, on 9 April 1979, he was ushered into the White House living-quarters at 7 a.m. Caddell knew that as the non-resident intellectual of the President's close circle of advisers he had the reputation of being somewhat of a doom-and-gloom merchant. It made him nervous, for he was concerned about making the First Lady understand the gravity of his findings.

Rosalynn Carter had already been up working for more than two hours when Caddell arrived and was busy going over that Monday's pressing appointments with an aide in a small dining-room used for working breakfasts. She greeted Caddell with a handshake and a warm smile as the aide slipped away. The pollster, awkward and frowning, was immediately put at ease as breakfast was ordered. But he could not relax completely. He wasn't sure he could get his points across in a couple of hours – points that had taken him months to analyze and articulate.

"Since the end of last year," he began, laying out his folders on the large, polished oak table, "we have been detecting some very alarming trends in the way people think about themselves and their own futures." He slipped two sheets from a pile and handed them to her. "There has been an enormous growth in pessimism," he added. Rosalynn's eyes searched his, but she said nothing.

"We tested this with detailed questions designed to measure a person's feelings about the future of the nation, and about themselves. We also asked them to compare the present with five years ago, and five years into the future. By the end of 1978, pessimism about the nation's future was up from 30 per cent during the worst crises of the early 1970s, to 48 per cent – nearly half the American public. Also during 1978, the percentage of people pessimistic about their long-term personal futures rose from 20 per cent at the beginning of the year, to 32 per cent at the end."

The First Lady had been concentrating hard, occasionally glancing down at the figures and summaries on the sheets in front of her. "Couldn't that all be due to the state of the economy?" she asked.

"That's true to some extent," Caddell replied. "But we faced a serious recession and an oil embargo in 1973, and people were not nearly as pessimistic."

"Are you saying that it's Jimmy's leadership?"

Caddell shook his head dismissively. "These figures have hardly anything to do with Jimmy," he said. "In fact, when the pessimism curve started going up, his personal ratings were going up. . ."

He was interrupted by a member of the kitchen staff who poured coffee, and hovered for a moment ready to serve them.

"Jimmy's ratings went up after the Camp David Accords between Sadat and Begin. At the time, inflation had slowed down and the economy was not looking in bad shape. Yet the pessimism about America's future was much higher than in, say, late 1974 and early 1975, when we had high inflation, a massive recession, Nixon's resignation and the crumbling in Vietnam."

Rosalynn nibbled thoughtfully on her toast. "So, from what you've said," she began hesitantly, "Jimmy's in control during some kind of transition period, after all the worries of the early 1970s?"

"That's exactly what it is," he replied, encouraged by the speed of her understanding. "The Presidency is weakened, Congress is stronger than since before Roosevelt. The special interest groups who lobby Congress are stronger than ever. People see government – the political process – as more isolated than ever."

Seeing that Rosalynn looked confused, he added, "I honestly believe that Jimmy has a great opportunity. He can try something bold. To paraphrase Napoleon, every crisis brings a new opportunity – 'Glory comes only in great danger'. . ."

"What do you suggest he could do?"

"It really needs a grand gesture from him. As President it is his duty to alert the nation and lead. Set an example. He can focus the nation on its goals. For instance, he could call a constitutional convention. . ."

Caddell's ideas worried Rosalynn Carter enough for her to convince her husband that he should listen and take action on the pollster's advice. But the President needed an understanding of the intangible problems now posed, and Caddell began gathering literature from the nation's leading sociologists and government scholars. There was James McGregor Burns's book, *Leadership*, which suggested that leaders could shape and elevate the motives, values and goals of followers through the vital teaching role of leadership, which the author called 'transforming leadership'. Another heavy tome was Christopher Lasch's *The Culture of Narcissism*, which touched on Caddell's beloved alienation theory. There was also Daniel Bell's *The Cultural Contradictions of Capitalism*. Alexis de Tocqueville's classic *Democracy in America* was in there too. Caddell's concern was to make the President aware of a sociological phenomenon in the US where people (the 'alienated') were dropping out of the political process. In the big states of California, New York and Pennsylvania many people had not voted in the 1978 mid-term elections and had stayed away from polling booths in their millions at a time when there were population increases in these states. The pollster wanted the President to see an opportunity for capitalizing on the fact that national interest appeared to have given way to special, and individual, interests.

Caddell was inspired by the thought that if the President understood the problem he could reach out for the increasing number of 'rejected' voters – those who had opted out of the process – and create a realigned national coalition of support which would save the nation from its spiritual and moral malaise, and vote Carter back into office in 1980. The alternative, Caddell believed, was potential national chaos, and he quoted de Tocqueville's analysis of society's breakdown to the President: that when self-interest dominated national interest, it would lead to the disintegration of the conditions of freedom. In short, if there was no national will to hold the attention and loyalty of the people, self-interest groups would compete and eventually destroy each other.

Caddell passed on all these works to the President, and thus began a reading and education program for both men. For Caddell, this was a personal period of graduation from his obsession with the problem of the alienated voter, which he had exploited so successfully during the 1976 election. For Carter it was an interlude of intellectual learning on the job. Caddell moved methodically, and many of the authors whose works had occupied their thinking were invited to dinner at the White House with the President. Ideas about the mental state of the nation were further articulated and emphasized in a rarefied atmosphere of scholarly endeavor. Outside in the real world, however, a gasoline shortage had people grappling each other at the gas pumps. Carter's popularity continued to plummet to below 25 per cent, which was lower than Nixon at his worst. It seemed to be a very large hint that part of the nation's problem might be found in the lack of leadership at the very center of government. The President was moved to take some kind of initiative, but he wasn't sure what it should be. Vice-President Fritz Mondale, supported by Stuart Eizenstat, the Domestic Affairs adviser, did not care much for Caddell's intellectual arguments about issues of national confidence. These two took a more pragmatic approach and wanted Carter to be politically conventional. The President decided to call a domestic summit at his Camp David retreat to thrash out all the problems. He cancelled a speech which would have tackled the energy crisis, and invited all his leading advisers to join him.

Soon after the Camp David deliberations had begun, Caddell received a phone call from Jordan.

"Pat, Jimmy's reading your 107-page 'memo'," Jordan said, and added cynically, "You sure know how to keep things brief."

"Yeah, well, it's a complex topic, Ham," Caddell said a little defensively.

"I know," Jordan said. "I read it."

"What did you think?"

"I've got some reservations," Jordan replied, "but basically I agree with it. It's strong. I think Jimmy's gonna go for it."

"You do?" Caddell said, as he moved behind his desk to sit down.

"Yeah, he's reading it right now. Seems pretty damned impressed so far."

Caddell swallowed. "My God!" he said in a whisper.

"What?" Jordan said.

"Nothing, Ham," the pollster said, composing himself. "So what's going to happen? He has canceled his speech and – "

"He wants you to come to Camp David."

"Today?"

"Tomorrow."

"For how long?"

"A day," Jordan said. "See you all."

The receiver went down and Caddell sat stunned, unconsciously stroking his beard. He stood up and shut his office door, a sign to his staff that he did not want to be disturbed. The pollster was momentarily struck with terror. He stared down through his window at the busy rush of people along Washington's Pennsylvania Avenue, and wondered if he had done the right thing. Had he gone too far this time and over-exercised his influence with the President? Caddell had always been a worrier. Events in his recent past had happened so fast that he did not feel he could always cope. He had greatly helped in giving the nation Jimmy Carter and gained working challenges and rewards such as the $250,000 annual contract with the Democratic Party. There had also been an expansion of his private business. The quarterly reports of his polling company on American public attitudes, with subscriptions costing $20,000 a year, were being taken by many of the nation's top companies as well as governments of other nations, such as Saudi Arabia. All this had helped make him a rich man, while his proximity to the Oval Office gave him enormous public influence. And he was still only twenty-nine years old. At times like this Caddell felt his rise was really just a dream (or was it a nightmare?). Any moment he would surely wake up to find himself back at Harvard toiling with his thesis.

He looked over at the mess of papers, books, files and folders on his desk and spied the tip of the blue binder which held his long memo to the President. He reached for it and began to read it through, not once but three times. Two hours later, when he had finished, he was fortified by his own analysis. He would follow through his arguments. To hell with anyone who could not understand the crisis and what had to be done. He had done his research. Let those who opposed him come up with stronger ideas and hard evidence to support them.

Caddell's one day at Camp David ended up being six, as the pros and cons of alternatives were tossed back and forth among Carter's inner circle of Jordan, Powell, Rafshoon, Caddell, Mondale and Eizenstat. Initially the news media and the rest of the nation feared that Carter was experiencing some sort of personal crisis. After a few days the President's trouble seemed contrived, especially when nearly 150 other people were invited to the retreat. Mayors, members of Congress, governors, labor leaders, businessmen, state legislators, county officials and media people dropped in to give their advice to the listening President. Many were flattered to be asked, but some, usually the politically more astute, were disturbed by the sense of urgency about the meetings and Carter's self-deprecatory manner. Some wondered why it was all necessary. Even if Caddell's fears about a national malaise had been explained to them, many would have had their doubts about the President's reaction. Could he not have learned all the things they were telling him in the two years he had been in office, some asked. Didn't he read editorials? The visitors appreciated that the oil crisis was causing shortages and anger at the gas pumps, but that wasn't the end of the world. Perhaps this President needed a crisis in order to govern.

Carter presided over the final meeting of all his top advisers. There was an informal atmosphere in the lounge of the cabin retreat as the extended Georgia 'mafia' sat around on couches and chairs. Everyone was dressed casually – the President wore an open-neck shirt, slacks and sneakers. The discussion was free-flowing but tended to be one-sided. Caddell's arguments were forceful, well articulated and always backed by his weighty statistical analysis. Carter sat impassively during the meeting, taking frequent notes. He occasionally asked questions, and effectively presided by making certain all opposing views were aired fully. But by contributing so little the President did not let on which way he was leaning.

Caddell suggested that Carter should re-establish his connections with the voter, otherwise the consequences would be dire for his Presidency – especially with the next election only sixteen months away. Eizenstat opposed Caddell's argument, saying he thought it better that Carter deliver a strong speech on energy. Caddell protested that there had been four already, and pointed out that Carter had had eighty million viewers when he made the first one, and only thirty million on the last one. The strategist used this to endorse his view that something stronger and more significant should be said in a speech. He also wanted the public to see executive action that would meet the wider problem of the nation's feelings and spirit.

Carter pulled the Vice-President into the discussion. Mondale sided with Eizenstat and made sure everyone realized that he totally opposed a constitutional convention, which had been put forward by Caddell as a possible grand gesture by Carter. He saw danger in this because 'everyone' would be tempted to put forward their ideas on how a constitution could be framed. Mondale thought this would put the country in real peril. He indirectly criticized Caddell by suggesting it would be a bad thing for the nation to be made aware of some of the "social psychology stuff that had been floating around". Caddell protested that there was nothing necessarily negative about the President explaining the problem and indicating how the nation together could avoid a crisis. Rafshoon suggested that Carter was forced to do something at this stage, because the nation had been expecting an energy speech. The President, to everyone's surprise, blithely replied that they (the nation) might be disappointed. Several of the advisers looked at each other. Hadn't the boss realized how unsettling his delay had been, especially with the nation waiting for him at least to appear as if he was taking action concerning the gas shortages?

The opposing views became vehement before Jody Powell suggested that they try to incorporate Caddell's big theme *and* energy in an all-encompassing speech. The energy problem and its solution could be seen as a specific instance of how the administration should tackle the broader crisis articulated by Caddell. In the end a big speech for 15 July was planned following this suggestion, which, in effect, was a victory for Caddell. His input was by far the greatest, and his views, by virtue of their fundamental and complex nature, had to be expounded upon in greater depth.

In the actual address, which Carter had rehearsed harder than any other he had ever given for television, the President hammered his fist on the Oval Office desk to emphasize points. Carter's advisers had urged him to be forceful because they were painfully aware that he was proving to be one of the least vivid figures in American politics. He chided Americans for their narcissism and borrowed heavily from a 1975 Caddell speech on alienation.

"It is a crisis of confidence," Carter said. "It is a crisis that strikes at the very heart, soul and spirit of our national will. We can see this crisis in the growing doubt about the meaning of our own lives, and in the loss of unity of purpose of our nation. The erosion of our confidence in the future is threatening to destroy the social and political fabric of America." The people had looked to Washington, he said, "and found it isolated from the main-stream of our nation's life". Looking for honest answers, they were given "easy answers"; seeking leadership, they were given "false claims and evasiveness, and politics as usual". The "special interests" were prospering while the country was afflicted with "paralysis, stagnation and drift". After describing the general moral crisis of will, the President then admitted to some of the blame by quoting several of the critics invited to Camp David: "This from a Southern Governor. 'Mr President, you are not leading this nation – you're just managing the Government.' 'You don't see the people enough any more.' 'Some of your cabinet members don't seem loyal. There is not enough discipline among your disciples'." Finally, Carter went on to mention the energy problem and outlined the specifics of a new energy policy.

Immediately the address was over, Caddell rushed to poll the electorate. Not surprisingly, he found that 79.6 per cent of the nation agreed with what the President had said about the moral and spiritual crisis in the country. Carter's popularity, according to an independent Gallup Poll, went up 11 per cent, and Caddell's further polls found that Carter's support on certain issues had jumped up to 30 per cent.

Lifted by this, Carter soon after went through with the firing of several members of his cabinet, but he erred badly in taking the national focus away from his televised message. The timing seemed to be wrong. However, the cumulative events at Camp David were of brain-spinning inspiration to a handful of men in the country. These were all the Republicans thinking about being candidates for the Presidency. If they had been unsure about their candidacy before the domestic summit, they had certainly changed their minds by the time it was over.

THE PERENNIAL CANDIDATE

The rough, asphalt trail up the mountain was so steep and winding that it seemed much longer than seven miles to Richard Wirthlin as he drove up it one day late in the summer of 1979. His destination was Rancho del Cielo, the Reagans' hideaway home on a saddle ridge 2400 feet up in the Santa Ynez mountains. Wirthlin had driven from the fog-shrouded Refugio State Beach on the Pacific Ocean, and at times wondered if he had taken the right track, so rugged were the surrounds. Yet just like Reagan, who was already on another tortuous trail to the US Presidency, Wirthlin had come so far there was no turning back. It was Reagan's third and last attempt, and although there were going to be plenty of obstacles along the way, Wirthlin firmly believed that the permanent candidate – Reagan had been running for office since 1965 – could reach the pinnacle this time. Unlike the 1976 run against incumbent President Gerald Ford, there did not now seem to be any unpassable boulder to block Reagan's advance. There was no air of defeatism in his camp in 1979, as there had been in the heady and ill-planned days of 1975 when the candidate had been a most hesitant starter. Reagan himself was also now more confident of reaching his goal, despite his sixty-eight years.

Wirthlin, too, was feeling better about his own aims and dreams. His company, DMI, had expanded into one of the most successful survey organizations in the world. Apart from its many political clients, DMI, like Caddell's company, Cambridge Research, had a fat and formidable list of business clients, large and small, public and private. DMI's lists had also boasted the Departments of Labor, US Postal Services, Health and Human Services, and the Office of Education. Wirthlin and his burgeoning group had cultivated important connections, and were able to reach for information into all the 38 Federal Government statistical agencies. People such as Vincent Barabba (an original DMI associate director who had become Director of the Bureau of Census in the Carter administration) were well disposed toward DMI and other similar firms. In the mid-1970s, this link had become most useful. The Census, a subdivision of the Department of Commerce, then began developing a service especially for DMI and other survey groups which sold data on how and where to sell market products, and candidates. A quick-to-serve baby food, for instance, should be aimed at areas with many working mothers, and census figures showed exactly where they were. This was also invaluable in pinpointing target groups – young mothers would be one of the scores – for political candidates wanting to refine and hone their messages in order to garner votes. This sort of access to vote-catching data complemented DMI's own incessant polling and survey work, which provided massive amounts of information for its big storage and Digital VAX and PDP computers in Los Angeles and the company's new offices in McClean, near Washington DC. The American population had been sub-categorized into 108 groups by DMI's computers, and the company had about 300 trained operatives for its survey and analysis work. With each successful marketing venture and election of a DMI-backed candidate, more doors were opening to the company's shrewd and thoughtful principal.

Despite this development in all areas of marketing and research, however, the pollster's mind was now firmly fixed on a rendezvous with former Governor Reagan, not just on a sunny mountain top but in the highest political office in the Western world. Wirthlin was determined in his own methodical, unassuming way to help Reagan reach his goal over the next eighteen months. Not that Wirthlin was unaware of the rewards his company would receive as a winning candidate's adviser; he had only to look at Pat Caddell to see that. But there was far more to it than this, for all American political strategists agreed that this was the most critical US presidential election in history. The winner would influence world events at a time when nuclear confrontation was at its most precarious, and when international economic chaos would be a strong possibility. Like his rival Caddell, Wirthlin had an ideological commitment in getting his choice elected. They both firmly believed their man was the right one for the most difficult and dangerous job in the 1980s. Just as Caddell had risked much by going with Carter long before the primaries of 1976, Wirthlin was taking a big gamble by placing all his chips on Reagan when the 'smarter' money seemed to be going elsewhere. There was a large field of Republicans shaping up for 1980, not to mention the possibility that Ford might be drawn in. The pundits were pointing to Reagan's age and image as a two-time loser in the presidential stakes. Some of the other top party operatives, such as Howard Baker and pollster Robert Teeter, had joined George Bush. He was handsome, experienced and relatively young at fifty-six. Bush was already running on the slogan that he was 'Up for the eighties', a dig at the old man on the mountain. The former CIA director was a fresh patrician face acceptable to the Northeast, the power brokers of which were hoping for a Republican challenger who did not come from the Midwest, West or South. Yet Wirthlin's gamble was based neither on a whim nor on blind loyalty. He was backing his judgement, a judgement which was constantly being modified, expanded and changed by an increasingly sophisticated and accurate computer simulation system. This had been experimented with for a decade, and more recently had come through a big test during the 1978 mid-term election. In all the hundreds of elections for Congress it had about a one per cent error rate in predicting winners. With this and DMI's bulging computer data banks, Wirthlin believed that if ever a computerized system was ready for a presidential candidate's election it was now, and vice versa. No matter how the pollster experimented with his system, it always indicated one thing: Ronald Reagan was the best candidate for the electronic media and computer age. The one important proviso was that he should have his tortuous path programmed every inch of the way to the Oval Office. Only a highly disciplined, flexible system could guide Reagan and show him how to slide his way past the traps which would be set by Carter's powerful pollster Caddell, whom Republicans feared and respected for his tough and often brilliant tactics.

Wirthlin felt the key to Reagan's chances lay in the use of the system which was secretly code-named PINS, Political Information System. If guidance was used piecemeal or as infrequently as it was in 1976, then Reagan would most likely be a three-time loser. PINS had to be the backbone of the campaign strategy, and whether this was so would depend on Wirthlin's position in the campaign hierarchy. He was already far better placed than in 1976, and had become a key member of the team which formed the nucleus for running the candidate. John Sears was back as campaign director, and was in charge of the political strategy, while Edwin Meese was chief of staff and in control of briefing the candidate on issues. Others in the team were Michael Deaver, Peter Hannaford, Jim Lake, Charles Black, Paul Laxalt and Lyn Nofziger, who was running the early front operations for Reagan's campaign. Essentially only Sears stood between Wirthlin and control of strategy, and the New York-born, Notre Dameeducated lawyer was not about to stand aside when there was another chance of electing the candidate. Sears felt he had done well in 1976. He regarded himself as a better operator than the Californians. He intimidated many of them, including the candidate, because of his connections in the East. It was generally conceded that he had the links there that they did not have, and they knew that Reagan could not hope to win the Republican nomination without doing well in the big Northeastern states, such as New York and Pennsylvania. He would probably score heavily in the Midwest and South, but it would not be enough. There had to be a strategy that was realistic in key Northeastern states, and Sears claimed that he was the only person who could concoct the vote-winning methods in that vital region. In fact, the only person among the coterie of advisers in Campaign '80 who felt truly confident about running Reagan anywhere was Wirthlin, such was his conviction about the candidate and PINS. Like Sears, he had the strategist's mentality: any problem could be broken down to its elements and tackled. Unlike Sears, Wirthlin had PINS, which was totally dispassionate about Reagan's chances anywhere, and he felt it had the capacity to integrate any number of strategic operations into one overall plan which would first see Reagan take the Republican nomination, and later the Presidency.

But Sears, besides having superior knowledge of the Northeast, also considered himself to be a more pragmatic operator than the ideological Californians surrounding the candidate. To him, they lacked shrewdness. Under pressure he thought they would fall back defensively on ideology, which would be a losing position. This was how it had been for Goldwater, who was of the same thinking school as Reagan, and Sears feared that unless Reagan moved closer to the center and appeased the moderate wing of the party, he would be in trouble. The strategist had learned from watching Richard Nixon, who had left ideology behind to become a master of political maneuver. Nixonian politics was about winning and losing, not about rigid ideas. America had countless might-have-been politicians, both left and right, who had failed because they had never learned the expediency of either apparent or real compromise. Sears was challenged by the opportunity of directing Reagan more toward a centrist position. Wirthlin, however, felt more comfortable with Reagan's ideology; he believed in packaging that ideology rather than in trying to change the candidate. He was more concerned with the public's perception of the candidate's character than its perception of his ideology. What was said was less important than how it was said. Whereas Sears saw himself as the dominant figure who stage-managed the candidate, Wirthlin was intent on directing an overall campaign strategy of which the candidate was the dominant figure. Under Sears, there would be a new Reagan. Under Wirthlin, true Reaganism would be given an acceptable face.

The purpose of Wirthlin's visit to the ranch that late summer's day was to brief Reagan, not only on his own position and image, but also on his rivals for the Republican nomination, and Carter. The strategist turned off the mountain road and along a gravel lane through a forest of oaks until he was looking down across a sloping meadow toward the ranch buildings. These overlooked the ocean on one side and the Santa Ynez valley on the other. As he came to a stop, he saw Nancy Reagan striding toward him. She greeted him with a hug.

"Ronnie's fixing the fence," she said. "He was planning to keep working until you arrived. Why don't you go get him?" Wirthlin nodded and strolled to the back of the house and could see Reagan, stripped to the waist, struggling with a sawn-off telegraph pole which was being lowered into the ground by him and his ranch foreman, 'Barney' Barnett. Reagan looked tanned and remarkably fit for his years, if a bit fleshy around the chest and middle. He had kept in good shape by doing ranch chores, and the complete fence of 123 poles was his handiwork. He and Barnett had sawed the bottom six feet from each pole and they had been set in the ground as posts. Fifteen foot lengths had been cut from the remainder of the poles, and the ends had been notched and fitted to the posts.

Reagan wiped the sweat from his brow and shook hands with his visitor.

"Just doing a little fence-mending," he said with a smile. "Now you're not going to tell me I've got more to do with the party, are you?"

"Not just yet, Governor," Wirthlin grinned. "I think you'll eventually have more support from the party than anyone."

Reagan donned a shirt, told his foreman he would help him again later, and then led the pollster to a stone patio – one of the additions made by the Reagans to their Mexican-style house. They sat on benches at a wooden trestle table and Nancy brought them fruit juice. Wirthlin began by discussing a leading issue, Reagan's age. "We have approached this from at least ten different ways," the strategist began. "We probed on whether you were seen as too old, too tired, too out of touch, or simply if you were seen as not up to the demands of the Presidency. There wasn't anything definitive."

"You know, Dick, I feel fifty," Reagan said. "That's the age when a man is surprised when he doesn't get a rejection, and relieved when he does."

Wirthlin laughed. "Well you look fine, Governor," he said, "and I really believe this issue will blow over as our campaign gets under way. For instance, we found that people over sixty-five, conscious of their own age and frailties, say they are worried about age, but it doesn't show in their voting. Once you are seen on the move in the primaries, I can't see it as any problem at all."

"I can joke about it?"

"I don't see why not."

"I'll use the old one – 'the reason I keep looking younger is because I keep riding older and older horses'."

Wirthlin smiled. "That's fine," he said. "The key point is that when you campaign in person your voter support goes up, sometimes dramatically, and that is important. More important than anything is the way you are perceived. Your personality, your character."

"What about Carter?" Reagan asked. "How is his popularity right now?"

"It's marginally better than two months ago when he fired those cabinet members," Wirthlin said, "but he is not perceived as a strong leader. Not at all. In fact, I'm doing some research on this. Leadership looks like looming as a key issue for 1980."

CHAPTER 8
THE MUDDYING OF CAMELOT

The September morning that Wirthlin briefed Reagan, Senator Edward Kennedy of Massachusetts had unofficially decided to run for the Democratic nomination against the incumbent President. The news had transformed Kennedy's busy office in the Old Senate Office Building into a jungle, from the reception festooned with larger-than-life shots of the brothers and the family, to the Senator's own study, which also had its share of legendary mementoes, from framed personal letters to photos. Volunteers were lingering in the corridors and the Kennedy Senate staff were inside the cramped open office trying to answer the phones which were running non-stop. There were a lot of smiles on the faces of Kennedy people, perhaps out of relief that the speculation had ceased. The last of the brothers was in the race. Dreams of Camelot had returned. Long-time staffer, attractive Melody Miller, who had first worked for Robert Kennedy in 1964, was confidently telling a caller over the phone: "Carter's approval rating is down to 19 per cent. Ted leads him two to one in the polls. The Senator has to have a chance. . ."

Leaning against his office door, the Senator's speech-writer Bob Shrum was more voluble and bouncy than ever. Unwrapping a large cigar, he was laughing derisively at a reporter who had asked him: "What does the Senator think of the President's comment that he would 'whip the Senator's ass' if he entered the race?"

"Well the whips are out now," Shrum said, "they're cracking. We'll see whose ass gets whipped!"

Everyone from Kennedy down seemed to think that if ever he was going to run, this was the time. There had been talk about him running for the Presidency ever since 1968, the year his brother Robert was assassinated. The tragic Chappaquiddick incident dampened speculation and made the Senator cautious in 1972 and 1976, but advisers now felt that the years had erased the problem. Kennedy had weighed up the consequences of challenging someone from his own party, which could be split by such a move. He had thought through the possibility of his run causing a Republican to eventually beat a weakened, battle-scarred Democrat. He had listened to Democrats both sycophantic and serious who had all urged him to go for it. On balance, Kennedy had convinced himself the effort was worth it. He would justify his actions by proving Carter was not good enough for a second term, and that his lack of leadership was damaging to both party and nation.

The handsome, if overweight, new candidate emerged from his study, smiling and ebullient. "Good to see you," he said, enthusiastically shaking a visitor's hand. It was clear from his demeanor that he found the prospects of election battle exciting, even heady. This was tempered by the physical dangers of his candidature. With two brothers slain in politics it had taken a great deal of courage to join the race for the Presidency. Yet Kennedy's adrenalin was flowing. This was it. He pumped hands, touched shoulders and kissed the cheeks of his supporters who had rushed to the aid of the cause. In the midst of it all, he felt his elbow being tugged persistently. It was his young press secretary, Tom Southwick. Kennedy moved to one side for a moment.

"I've scheduled an interview with Roger Mudd for 29 September," Southwick said. "That OK?"

Kennedy looked relaxed and shrugged. "Yeah, why not," he said. "Best to get it out of the way before the real campaigning fun starts."

The TV interview at Kennedy's home in Cape Cod went smoothly enough for the first half-hour. Roger Mudd, dressed casually in a sports jacket and blue jeans, sat on a lawn chair opposite the Senator, who wore a double-breasted blue blazer, slacks and dark open-neck shirt. They were near a cliff overlooking the ocean, and behind them was the Kennedy's gray shingled house. Mudd, a star of CBS, had proceeded gently enough but knew he could not afford to be timorous or lenient. Other reporters, with lesser reputations, and without links to the Kennedys, were certain to be rough with the Senator.

"What's the present state of your marriage, Senator?" he asked.

"It's – I would say that it's – it's – it's – I'm delighted that we're able to – to share the time and the relationship that we – that we do share," Kennedy said. He fumbled his way all through the response, adding that he and his wife "had had some difficult times", but had "been able to make some very good progress".

Mudd, too, felt the pressure of the moment as he went on to a follow up. "Are – are you separated, or are you just – what – how do you describe the – the situation?"

"Well I don't know whether there's a single word that should – have a description for it. Joan's involved in a continuing program to deal with the problems of alcoholism, and – and she's doing magnificently well, and I'm immensely proud of the fact that she's faced up to it and made the progress that she's made. And I'm – but that – that process continues, and that – it's the type of disease that one has to continue to – to work on, and she continues to work on, and the program that's been devised is – is in Boston."

Mudd soon went on to Chappaquiddick, and initially fed Kennedy with the opportunity to give a strong answer, but the Senator became defiant and kept challenging the interviewer with – "If you have any questions, I'll answer them." This left Mudd little choice. He asked some important questions of detail about that fateful night a decade earlier in which Kennedy had driven a car off a bridge and had caused the death of a young female assistant, Mary Jo Kopechne.

"Do you think anybody will ever fully believe your explanation?" Mudd asked, following up with, "What guarantee is there that you would not again act, as you said, irresponsibly or inexplicably when your own career came in conflict with the public's right to know?"

Kennedy groped his way again, and finally stone-walled by referring Mudd to the transcripts of the public inquest into the incident, in which the judge had concluded that Kennedy had been guilty of criminal conduct. Mudd then inquired whether the Kennedy children were church-going Catholics; and whether the Senator as a parent had had problems with his children over drugs. He also asked how Kennedy would handle the present generation 'phenomenon' of young people living together. The interviewer had been tough but fair in couching his questions generally enough to give the Senator a chance of answering without getting embroiled in specific responses about his own family. But Kennedy was totally unprepared. He continued to reply unconvincingly and often incoherently. As soon as the ordeal was over, he shook hands with Mudd perfunctorily and walked back to the house. He rang his press secretary.

"What the hell did the guy want," he said to Southwick angrily, "coming in here like that and asking me – in my godamned house – if my nephew David was a drug addict! Do you love your wife? . . . That sort of thing!" "We thought it was going to be a sort. . .," Southwick began, "you know, what the Cape had meant to the Kennedys. . ."

"Well, it wasn't!" Kennedy said, distressed.

"None of it went well?"

"Not really. It was a mess! Disastrous!"

"Do you think we should try for another chance, another interview, to do better?"

Kennedy took a deep breath. "I don't know about that now," he said, still seething. "I'm going to have to change and take Patrick and the other kids out in the boat. The film crew want more footage."

The CBS documentary of Kennedy was not to be broadcast until some time in November, but the candidate's closest staff were beginning to think that the campaign might have some problems even before it had officially begun. There was a need to counter any adverse media attention that could build from the Mudd interview. Campaign manager Stephen Smith, Kennedy's brother-in-law, began to cast around for a top media consultant. High on his list was New Yorker David Garth, a Runyonesque, straight-talking media specialist whose clientele included New York Mayor Ed Koch, New York Governor Hugh Carey, Connecticut Governor Ella Grasso, New Jersey Governor Brendan Bryne, US Senators Adlai Stevenson and John Henry, and Los Angeles Mayor Tom Bradley. Outside the US, Garth had worked with Luis Herrera, the President of Venezuela, and he expected to work in Israel with Begin for the re-election of the Lukid Coalition. Garth did not have a reputation for genuflexion. If he was to represent a candidate it meant he or she was a person of strong character with a clear political direction. The consultant had to have faith in people he worked with and claimed to have rejected five in every six people who wanted his services. Garth always investigated a potential client and when the feelers came out from the Kennedy camp the consultant called two of his key staff into his Fifth Avenue office.

"I want you to talk with Kennedy's strategists," Garth said. "Find out what they know, what sort of strategy they have. I don't want to get involved unless we have their full cooperation."

Kennedy was given a chance to redeem himself in a second interview with Roger Mudd on 12 October in Kennedy's Senate office. There was a far more tense atmosphere this time, mainly because about fifteen people including the film crew were crowded into the Senator's study. Several of his staff were on hand, obviously hoping for better responses from him. Kennedy had concentrated his mind more on Chappaquiddick and Mudd began by asking supplementary questions on the topic. Yet still Kennedy played safe and referred him to the record of the inquest.

Mudd's style was not sensationalist or sharply inquisitorial, but, it was quietly probing, and when Kennedy continued to stone-wall, the interviewer suddenly switched away from Chappaquiddick. Frustrated, he asked a question which he had not prepared.

"Why do you want to be President?"

Kennedy had defended his way through the toughest session, and now looked a little stunned. At first he was caught in a dilemma. He had not formally announced his candidacy. How could he answer that one without making it into a premature announcement? Worse still, he had not ever been asked that before, at least not in such a direct way.

"Well, I'm – were I to – to make the announcement and – to run," the Senator began uneasily. "The reason that I would run is because I have a great belief in this country, that it is – has more natural resources than any nation in the world, has the greatest educated population in the world, the greatest technology of any country in the world, the greatest capacity for innovation in the world. And yet, I see at the current time that most of the industrial nations of the world are exceeding us in terms of productivity, are doing better than us in terms of meeting the problems of inflation, and they're dealing with their problems of energy and their problems of unemployment. And it just seems to me that this nation can cope and deal with its problems in a way that it has in the past." Kennedy looked as impressive as ever with his voice booming. But he was not answering the question. Mudd was astonished and wondered whether he should ask him again. The Senator was so wound up that Mudd let him continue.

"We're facing complex issues and problems in this nation at this time, but we have faced similar challenges at other times. And the energies and resourcefulness of this nation, I think should be focused on these problems in a way that brings a sense of restoration by its people to – in dealing with the problems that we face – primarily the issues on the economy, the problems of inflation, and the problems of energy. And I would basically feel that – that it's imperative for this country to either move forward, that it can't stand still, or otherwise it moves back."

"What would you do different than Carter?" Mudd said, again feeding the candidate an opportunity.

"Well, in what particular areas?" Kennedy replied, as if this was a trick question. Mudd, like every senior political reporter in Washington, was aware of the ramifications of Carter's recent Camp David retreat and his subsequent 'malaise' speech.

"Well, just take the – question of – of leadership," Mudd said.

"Well, it's a – on – on what – on – you know, you have to come to grips with the – the different issues that we're – we're facing. I mean, we can – we have to deal with each of the various questions that we're – we're talking about, whether it's in the questions of the economy, whether its in – in the areas of energy."

Everyone in the room was relieved at the end of the interview and there were polite, if formal, thank yous and goodbyes. As the CBS crew carried its equipment down the Old Senate Building corridors, the sound man said to Mudd, "Boy! That question, Why do you want to be President? . . . he really struggled. At the end his answer was just meaningless."

Mudd rolled his eyes back in his head. "I want to be President because the sea is so deep and the sky is so blue," he said ruefully. "It was embarrassing to even ask!"

"Sure, it always sounds so simple," the sound man replied, "but it tells you so much about his campaign."

Mudd nodded and said, "And the person."

That afternoon Garth's people returned to New York to report what they had learned from Kennedy's staff.

"They think that you can get away with avoiding TV reporters' questions," Garth's media researcher said, "and now they've apparently run into a mess with Mudd at CBS."

"When's that aired?" Garth asked, scribbling on a note pad.

"They don't know exactly. But they suddenly realize they've got troubles with the media they didn't anticipate. Mudd's questions sort of shocked them. They didn't think reporters could get that tough."

Garth lit a cigar. "They seem to have just opened their doors and said 'We're in business . . . '" he said.

"That's right. One day it was Kennedy of the Senate. Now it's Kennedy of the presidental campaign."

"What about their media plans?" Garth said, puffing thoughtfully.

"They just haven't got a strategy."

"You're kidding!"

"No. Nothing. They must have thought that because he's a Kennedy that was enough."

"They have no idea about polls either," Garth's key pollster said.

"Jesus!" Garth said, and the pollster added: "They kept asking us why they needed to spend money on polling if they could get hold of a TV network poll early."

Garth look incredulous as his media researcher went on: "The problem is fundamental. The staff is senatorial, and they are good at specific issue areas, but they have no idea how to use them in a big presidential campaign."

"They're very defensive about it too," the pollster said. "They regard modern campaign tactics of media events as kind of slick. They're out of touch. They think it's 1960, Kennedy versus Nixon. City Hall speeches, non-stop tours and maybe some TV . . ."

"Plenty of the advisers from that campaign are around again," Garth acknowledged with a shrug. "Let's back off for a while and see what happens. I want to see this Mudd interview for a start . . ."

News of the Mudd interview swept through media circles, and before it was aired early in November, rival network ABC rushed to put something on before CBS. Kennedy was placed in front of the cameras again and ABC news correspondent Tom Jarriel interviewed him. Jarriel had heard that Mudd had been tough, so he tried to outdo him.

"Senator Kennedy," he said, "you cheated in college, you panicked at Chappaquiddick. Do you have what it takes to be President of the United States?"

Kennedy was better prepared. He half-smiled and replied as if he had been asked, do you think you'll get big-voter support around the country. "Well that will be a question that will be decided by people all over this country during the course of the primaries and the caucuses, and hopefully it will be decided after that were I to gain the nomination of the Democratic Party . . ."

The interviewer went on in ruthless style, but Kennedy stayed cool, if defensive, and this time he was coherent. The problem, his campaign manager now realized, was the relentlessness of the media screening. This was not just another Massachusetts Senate election. It was the testing ground for the toughest job in the world. No one in the campaign team could handle it or develop a counter-strategy. They had to hire the best media specialist available, and fast. Smith's feelings seemed justified when just three days later the Mudd interview was aired on a Sunday night at 10 p.m. The rival networks ran the movies *Jaws* and *MacArthur* against the interviewer and it held only 15 per cent of the national audience. Yet researchers found that the nation's most influential people watched it. Also the opinion shapers in the press, who had all been carefully prepared by CBS, editorialized heavily and were mostly highly critical of Kennedy's performance. The general reaction prompted Smith and Kennedy to fly to New York a few days later in an effort to persuade the reluctant Garth to work for them. Over lunch, when it appeared that the two parties were not going to reach an arrangement, the topic inevitably turned to the interview.

"I watched *Jaws* instead," Kennedy said. "It was nice to see someone else being chewed up."

Garth was sympathtic. "You have to prepare a stronger response to Chappaquiddick," he said, "that will kill the issue as far as the press is concerned. If you respond the right way, you'll even get public opinion on your side. Once it's dead, Carter will have to be very careful how he attacks you on the character thing." Garth was certain that Kennedy would make a strong media candidate with guidance and a clearly defined strategy. But the consultant was still concerned with the Senator's middle-level staff who were naturally guarding their own positions jealously. On the one hand he liked Kennedy and Smith, and because of his affinity to the candidate was inclined seriously to consider taking on this difficult, if not delicate, project. On the other hand, he did not want to get deeply involved.

"I'll tell you what I'm prepared to do," he said. "Even though we won't work on your whole campaign, I'll get my people to prepare something on Chappaquiddick. When's your next TV interview?"

"Next Sunday on 'Meet the Press'," Smith said. "It's vital that he comes through that well."

"Right," Garth said, "we'll have a firm set of replies ready for it."

Kennedy rehearsed his answers for the NBC program as if he was making an important speech, and although nervous, he was better prepared than he had been over the past decade. The 'Meet the Press' panel opened with a barrage of questions on Chappaquiddick. Kennedy did not forget, and he remained calm.

"There is no information to be uncovered," he said categorically in response to one probe. "If there was, there would be absolutely no reason for me remaining in public life, let alone run for the Presidency of the United States. Absolutely none." This was not a new Kennedy but a more confident one. He reminded the interviewer of all the tragedies of his life, including the loss of his brothers and the impact of a son who was a cancer victim. "I have responded to those challenges by one, acting responsibly, and two, by the continuing commitment that I have to public service. I would not run for the Presidency unless I was completely satisfied that I could deal with any of the pressures that would come to that particular position."

The media had done their worst, but Kennedy was still in the race. The next big battle would be with the President. What would be Carter's strategy in attacking the Senator?

Late in the month Kennedy and his staff were in Boston for the dedication of the John F. Kennedy Memorial Library. Some of Carter's people, including Pat Caddell, were there. The young pollster felt apprehensive about the upcoming battle between the President and Kennedy for the Democratic nomination. Caddell was a great admirer of the Senator, and they had much in common. Both were Irish Catholic Bostonians who had gone to Harvard, where they even had the same room in the freshman dormitory, Wigglsworth C-21. They were both politically liberal. In his student days Caddell had worked briefly for Kennedy and had done some polling for him in the Senate races.

"Why don't you hire this man?" Kennedy said mischieviously to Bob Shrum, as Caddell came over and shook hands with them. "He doesn't look like he would be fuzzy on issues." Kennedy had often kidded Shrum about the fact that he had left Carter's 1976 campaign because Shrum believed Carter was too 'fuzzy' on important issues. Caddell had originally hired Shrum for that campaign.

"I wish I didn't have to choose sides," Caddell said. He feared that the Carter-Kennedy contest could end up with both candidates destroying each other, which would leave the way open for a Republican President. "It's like 1861," Caddell added, "and I'm saying goodbye to all my Northern friends before putting on the Confederate uniform in the Civil War. Except that this time I'm defending the Federal Government."

"That's fine," Kennedy said with a smile. "Just remember who won the war!"

CHAPTER 9

CAPTIVES OF TECHNOLOGY

INSPIRATION

"Do you think strong presidential leadership could lead the nation out of its troubled period?" The question gave Mrs Mary Anne Smith pause. She had just been asked a series of definitive questions over the phone about her reaction to major crises, such as the Vietnam war, Watergate, President Ford's pardon of Richard Nixon, the fall of Saigon to the Communists, and the oil and energy problems of the mid-1970s. Yes, they had been depressing. Yes, such a consequence of events had shaken her faith about the future of the nation and what sort of a world her two children would grow up in.

"I don't know," she said. "We certainly have not had really strong leadership for some time. President Carter seems a nice man, but he is not a great leader."

"Who do you feel was a strong leader?"

"Well, I'm forty-three and I don't remember Roosevelt or Truman," she said hesitantly, "but they were both regarded as being strong."

"Suppose Roosevelt, or someone like him, was in power," the caller persisted, "do you think he could lift the nation's spirit, lead iit out of its difficulties, and make you more confident about the future for the nation and your children?"

Mrs Smith thought hard again. "Yes," she said firmly, "I really do believe that. But there don't seem to be any great men like that around anymore, do there?"

"Thank you, Mrs Smith," the caller said, "you have been most helpful. Would you mind if we called again to see if you had perhaps changed your opinion on a few things?"

"No," she said, still a little intrigued after thirty-eight questions. "What do you want it for again?"

"You could say we were taking the nation's pulse, seeing how people feel about a whole range of issues."

"That's very interesting. Who did you say you were from again?"

"DMI," the caller said. "We're an independent survey organization."

For most of 1978 and 1979, DMI, under the direction of Wirthlin's deputy, Vincent Breglio, had carried out one of the most extensive probes of public attitudes ever held in the US. Tens of thousands of people like Mary Anne Smith in Ohio, a working mother of two, married to a chemical engineer, had been quizzed over the phone by 300 trained DMI operators for up to 45 minutes, usually between 8 and 9 at night. There was no mention of Carter or Reagan or any of the other candidates about to compete for the 1980 Presidency.

DMI, under Breglio's expert handling, was probing the psyche of the nation and feeding the results into the company's computers for further collation and analysis. The themes that were emerging were remarkably clear and well defined on one major issue, among many, that would be invaluable to the company's most important political client, Ronald Reagan. That key issue was leadership. Carter was not providing leadership when the country most needed it. The candidate who was able to convince the nation that he could provide good leadership would be the one a majority would be inclined to support. Yet this was not just the amorphous ill-defined concept that the media had been demanding in its editorials. DMI had categorized and subcategorized every aspect of a strong leader's ideal image. A powerful President had to be compassionate. He had to be quick and decisive. He must not be a tyrant or inclined to lead America into conflict to prove a point. Yet he had to stand up to the Russians. He should not be bellicose or belligerent, but he should be bold and credible to Americans, allies and foes alike. He had to make the world respect America. This was even more important than being liked. He had to make America militarily strong, unquestionably the number one power on earth. The President must not be a bully or imperial, but tough if national interest was ever threatened. He should believe in peace, but not peace at any price – it must be peace through strength. The man should look like a president and be a good family man. He should also pay homage to the important symbols of the nation, which would be proof that he truly loved it.

All this and much more added up to a clear picture of what sort of person the nation wanted in the Oval Office in the 1980s. Wirthlin firmly believed that Reagan embodied many of the qualities demanded. When the strategist placed the candidate's profile next to the ideal, any characteristic that did not match could be made to do so. Reagan could act it out on the campaign trail until it became accepted as a feature of his image. Yet it was not simply the fact that he had a long career of acting behind him which allowed him to deliver the right line, mood or expression when required. He had also been a governor for eight years, a candidate four times (five if his 1968 bid for the Presidency was counted) in state and national elections over fifteen years. Reagan's six years as a front man with General Electric, in which he had visited 150 plants in 38 states, had made him responsive to and experienced with live audiences so that he was equally at home in front of a camera or a crowd. A combination of acquired skills as a film and TV actor, politician, PR man, candidate, journalist and radio announcer over forty years had made him the most nearly perfect person for programming in the history of politics.

Wirthlin with his deep understanding of systems and strategy realized this, but he did not have control over the campaign. Sears was in charge and he had a different approach, which Wirthlin thought would not take advantage of the major themes that he was distiling for the candidate by late November 1979. Sears basically wanted Reagan to run as the Elder Statesman among the large field of Republican candidates. The candidate was to act as if he was above all the hard campaigning in which the Republicans mauled each other. Wirthlin, by contrast, wanted him to compete. He thought Reagan should take every opportunity to spell out what he stood for and demonstrate that he was a potential president. The public had to feel and see and hear him . . . sense his leadership qualities. Sears's softly, softly approach of keeping the candidate under wraps would be disadvantageous, Wirthlin considered, because although the surveys showed that Reagan was better known than any of the other candidates, he was not known well. The public knew about his film star background and that he had been California's Governor, but they had little idea of what he stood for. History had shown that the nation would not vote for a leader they did not think they understood or trusted. If they never saw the candidate, how could they learn about his beliefs and character, Wirthlin argued.

Getting the candidate to take advantage of all outlets in the primaries would also provide the chance for him to start running early against Carter, and not simply the other Republicans. Wirthlin had calculated that it would take the best part of a year to sell Reagan to the American people and implant in the nation's collective mind the picture of a leader . . . in direct contrast to Carter. Wirthlin's strategy was also to destroy the notion that Americans were pessimistic about the nation's, and their own, future. That was only true, Wirthlin claimed, if the nation was given weak leadership. Powerful leadership could galvanize the national will and push it toward a great future. These would be the key thoughts behind the selling, packaging and computerizing of Ronald Reagan's 1980 campaign.

By late November, Wirthlin was beginning to worry that it would soon be too late to save the candidate. But the pollster's frustration became his inspiration. At 3 a.m. one morning, in a rare moment of insomnia, Wirthlin left his bed in his large

McClean home and went downstairs to his study. There he began writing like a man possessed. The six pages that he had written by dawn were the basis for his computerized strategy. Even if Sears took no notice of it, Wirthlin was determined, in his quiet way, to make his views known at every opportunity. If Sears would not listen, maybe the candidate would.

A month later, near Christmas, Reagan was still being hidden and protected. Wirthlin felt compelled to brief him in a way that would make him aware there was a sound alternative strategy, should the campaign run into trouble. At a further meeting at the Reagan ranch, he did not directly contradict Sears but instead methodically set forth his ideas on the best way of campaigning.

"Whenever you campaign in person," he told the candidate, "your popularity goes up. Remember what happened in the New Hampshire primary in 1976." Reagan nodded, his head tilted to one side, frowning in concentration.

"Being seen really makes all that much difference?" he asked.

"Oh, unquestionably," Wirthlin said and then pulled out figures and quoted them. "Also, there are some worrying preconceptions and misconceptions about you. These have to be rectified or we help our opponents paint an unfavorable picture of you."

"What are the major problems?"

"Governor, you are seen as dangerous and uncaring, and a potential warmonger."

Reagan was bemused. "Oh, a gift that God could give us, to see ourselves as others see us," he said ruefully.

"To an extent we have that gift," Wirthlin said, "and that image must be changed for you to have a good chance of winning the Presidency."

"How are we doing against Bush?"

"Your lead nationally is 57 to 13. You are ahead in every state we have polled. Bush is still so little known that 40 per cent of Republicans who were asked about him said they did not know enough about him to even rank him among the contenders."

"That's pretty encouraging for us," Reagan smiled.

"Yes and no," Wirthlin replied. "While it's bad for him, it could mean that if he grabs media attention by doing well in Iowa – by winning – he could fast become your only formidable opponent."

"You mean because he has a clean slate?"

"Exactly, Governor. There are no negative perceptions about him, yet."

VOTE PRESIDENT, NOT PROTEST

Shortly after it was know that Kennedy was definitely a presidential candidate, the Georgia 'mafia' met at the Georgetown home of

Pat Caddell to plot the tactical destruction of the Senator's campaign. Apart from the strategist, the group – which had been meeting since the beginning of fall 1978 – consisted of Tim Kraft, the President's appointments secretary and now his national campaign manager, Hamilton Jordan, Jody Powell and Gerry Rafshoon.

Caddell's ideas were beginning to dominate proceedings as the crucial primary contest between Kennedy and Carter loomed, for only he had the facts at hand. The strategist had also, after twelve years in countless elections, developed sharp tactical methods for disposing of opposition candidates. If Caddell had at times during the year been ostracized by his White House colleagues, all was forgotten now as he laid out the plan for the battle with Kennedy.

"We have to make the primary voter feel that in deciding to vote for Kennedy or Carter," he told them, "he or she will be deciding which one they prefer as a protest vote in the primaries. We can't let that happen in this campaign. It's too dangerous. Kennedy could challenge us strongly on the protest vote."

The media campaign for Carter was devised by Rafshoon to fit this strategy. Early in 1980, the TV commercials began appearing in the run up to the primaries. The main one, on the surface, seemed harmless enough. In it the President said: "I don't think there is any way you can separate the responsibility of being a husband, or a father or a basic human being, from that of being a good president . . . What I do in the White House is to maintain a good family life, which I consider crucial to being a good president." Another ad showed him in serious conference with foreign statesmen. "President Carter is always cool in a crisis," the narrator said. All this was vintage Caddell. His surveys had found that, despite having passed the first barrier of press attacks, Kennedy was still carrying a lot of 'negative baggage' on the character issue. There were questions about the Senator's lifestyle and background and what sort of person he was under the mask of legend. The positive ads about Carter were meant to remind the viewer that Kennedy's marriage was in trouble, despite the fact that his wife Joan courageously trotted alongside him and campaigned stoically under tremendous pressure. The inverse message aimed at the nation's subconscious was that Carter was a better human being – someone more fit to be president. The 'crisis' reference, which was not quite as subtle, was meant to trigger the electorate's mind on Kennedy's behavior at Chappaquiddick. There were doubts about his reasons for leaving the scene of the accident. Had he panicked in that crisis? Caddell was careful not to be too unsubtle, for Kennedy had already quashed the direct questioning on the incident and the character issue. To harp on it directly could cause a backlash and hurt Carter, who was busy preserving his carefully nurtured 'nice guy' image – one of the very few firm assets he had left early in 1980. The ads used were to work both ways. Carter's packaged humanity was polished and presented to the nation again, while at the same time the messages reinforced prejudices and doubts about Kennedy. This cunning method had its impact. Despite the fact Caddell was picking up in his polls that Kennedy was seen as a better leader than Carter, the character perceptions, being reinforced by the Carter campaign, were still troubling voters. The tactic of influencing people to make a decision on who they would like as President when they voted in the primary, also looked like being successful. Caddell had found that people in 1980 had lower expectations of a president than they did a decade ago. The electorate had begun to accept that there could be many things outside a president's control. It followed that people also felt they had switched presidents too often. There did not seem to be enough compelling reasons for dumping Carter in favor of Kennedy.

The Senator's campaign fell into a trap when it started off by suggesting that if the nation substituted him for Carter things would be better. People began taking a closer look at Kennedy and the media put him and his stand on issues under the microscope. Caddell began to notice a dramatic shift toward Carter, who was further helped greatly by the Iranians taking fifty Americans hostage early in November 1979. People were wary of siding against the President at a time of crisis. As the primary season began, Jimmy Carter was again the front-runner.

BURNING BUSH

Wirthlin's warning about how Reagan should campaign, and the possibility of a front-running break by George Bush, came true when Bush picked up a small victory against Reagan in the Iowa caucus vote. Nightmares of Reagan's failure in the first real test of 1976 – the New Hampshire primary – came back to haunt the campaign. Reagan called a special meeting in a Chicago Holiday Inn suite before the New Hampshire primary to announce a complete change in tactics.

In a defiant mood, he told the somber inner circle of Sears, Jim Lake, the press secretary, Charlie Black, the national political adviser, Edwin Meese, Paul Laxalt, Lyn Nofziger and Wirthlin: "I did not debate in Iowa, but I will debate every chance I can from now on in. We are going to campaign like hell in New Hampshire come snow, snow and more snow."

"Governor, I don't think . . . ." Sears began, but was interrupted by the candidate: "We are going to make news with statements on issues every day if we can . . ."

After his experience in 1976, Wirthlin made doubly sure everyone in the inner circle was aware of the polling position when the Reagan entourage hit New Hampshire. The candidate was more than 10 per cent behind Bush and slipping in the state, and the reversal was reflecting itself nationally. Reagan stuck to his word and campaigned like a man half his sixty-nine years as the snow floated down and the temperatures dipped below zero. He stood outside factories and shook hands with countless workers, always in time for the evening TV network news. He gave several press conferences, and used every chance to address voters in cities and towns across the state.

A week before the primary, Reagan was at a local TV station about to go on camera in a debate with the six other Republicans candidates, including Bush, when Wirthlin took his candidate aside.

"You're essentially even with Bush," he told him, "which is a strong comeback, Governor. I think you'll pull ahead after tonight's debate." Reagan was buoyed by the news and winked at his pollster as he filed out on to the studio floor with the others. They all sat on stools in front of an excited live audience, the members of which would be invited to ask questions of the candidates. As the evening progressed there did not seem to be much between the candidates in a crowded forum. Bush, if anything, was not living up to expectations and seemed to be on the defensive, rather than being a confident front-runner. At one point a young man stood up and said, "Governor Reagan, a few days ago you made an ethnic joke and you were caught. You issued some kind of abject apology and explanation. Do you think that this kind of ethnic humor has any place in the campaign for the highest office in the land?"

Reagan shifted on his stool and looked embarrassed by the question. "I'm glad you asked that question," he said, "because I don't think my apology was abject. It was sincere . . ." The candidate then went on to give a lame, humble and questionable response, and ended up by saying, ". . . from now on, I'm going to look over both shoulders and then I'm going to tell stories about Irishmen, because I'm Irish."

A combination of luck and showmanship had seen him slide through it, but it turned out to be the only memorable part of the whole evening, except for Reagan's strong closing statement about his 'vision' of America. His explanation of the joke had high-lighted several characteristics. He was suitably indignant about the fact that he had told the joke in private and that a reporter had 'stiffed' him by reporting it. The old actor showed humility by couching his response in a partly apologetic manner, and then added a little touch of humor at the end. People watching squirmed a bit with Reagan because he came across as being very fallible and human. But it was good acting, and left the other six looking robotic by comparison. Crane had seemed plastic, Connolly grim, Bush defensive, Dole unremarkable, Baker ordinary and Anderson boring. None, except for Reagan, had a chance to expound on views, issues and topics which would have given the audience some feeling of true familiarity. In a country where character was the most important basic issue, only one of the contenders had shown he had any, even if his answer had made him appear a little foolish. Early the next morning Wirthlin phoned Reagan at his hotel. Nancy answered the phone. "He's still asleep, Dick," she said. "I'll tell him any news as soon as he wakes up."

"He was a clear winner last night in the debate," Wirthlin said gleefully.

"That's fantastic!"

"Nancy, do you have a pen? I want you to pass the figures on to the Governor."

Nancy was ready.

"OK," the pollster said. "First, 37 per cent of the state's Republicans watched the debate. Second, 86 per cent of them identified a clear winner. Third, the Governor had 33 per cent, Bush 17, Anderson 14 and Baker 12."

"Twice as many as Bush! Oh, Dick, do you think he'll win the primary now?"

"If a trend develops from here, yes," Wirthlin said. "And Nancy, there was another thing. The Governor scored highest on 'strength of leadership' and 'competency'."

After scribbling for a moment, Nancy said, "Dick, what was this Polish joke that got Ronnie into so much hot water?"

"Wouldn't he tell you?"

"Guess it must have been dirty," she said. "He said he never wants to tell it again."

"Well, it was clean."

"Please, Dick . . ."

"OK, Nancy," Wirthlin said with a laugh. "How do you tell the Polish guy at a cockfight? He brings a duck. How do you tell the Italian guy? He bets on the duck. How do you know the Mafia was there? The duck wins."

"Oh, that's just silly," Nancy said. "Why do men think these things are so funny?"

A second debate was organized by the *Nashua Telegraph*, but this was originally meant to be a one-to-one affair between Reagan and Bush. Sears was not confident that his candidate would cope well, so he engineered the debate at Nashua High School to include four more Republican candidates at the Reagan campaign's expense. When all six turned up, the people from the *Telegraph* were not happy. They had wanted the original Reagan-Bush contest. At one point the *Telegraph*'s editor and the debate's moderator, Jon Breen, said to the sound technician, "Turn Mr Reagan's microphone off."

Reagan looked angry. He quickly leaned forward and said, "I'm paying for this microphone, Mr Green." Reagan had gotten the moderator's name wrong, but that didn't matter. The audience broke into cheers.

The TV cameras had not been there to cover the whole debate, but now the networks had a news item of high drama to run for the next forty-eight hours. The debate had been held on a Saturday night. Because of the conflict, the story ran into Sunday and then Monday, as the significance of events at Nashua became apparent. Bush had been made to look churlish and aloof in all the TV clips of the event. He had never agreed to hold other than a direct encounter with Reagan, but Bush's reaction did not endear him to the other candidates or the media. Instead of making light of the incident, Bush became defiant, then frozen and silent. When the untelevised debate finally went ahead between the two candidates, Bush's confidence had dropped. He was defensive and lost the contest. It was the beginning of the end of his campaign. By Sunday night Wirthlin began to pick up voter reaction to the affair which again highlighted character perceptions. Reagan had moved from 8 to 14 points clear of his opponent. Bush campaigned hard for the next few days, but then quit the state a few days before the election.

Two days before the vote in New Hampshire, all the networks showed shots of a fit, lean Bush jogging in the sun in his home state of Texas. They contrasted this with shots of Reagan in a thick overcoat shaking hands with workers in the snow and extreme cold outside a factory.

Wirthlin rang Reagan the same day. "It's a landslide," he told him. "You're going to win big, perhaps by up to 25 to 30 points."

"Looks like George made my 1976 mistake," Reagan said.

"That was part of it, Governor," Wirthlin said. "Anyway, we've got him now. He's lost support right across the nation."

ADJUSTING THE FIGURES
After a resounding victory against Kennedy in Iowa, most of the Carter camp were confident that they would be able to end the

Senator's campaign early. All the independent 'horse race' polls indicated that Carter was up to twenty points ahead of Kennedy in the run up to the New Hampshire primary. Yet if that caused complacency in some quarters it did not do so with Caddell. He had discovered an underlying trend which suggested that the candidates were much closer together. The trend revolved around the issue dubbed 'war talk'. The world beyond America's shores looked decidedly hostile with the Iranian hostage crisis and the Soviet Union's occupation of Afghanistan. The electorate was wary, and frightened of bellicosity. There was, the feeling ran, enough to contend with, without fuelling the possibility of more conflict with angry words.

Caddell had discovered the 'war talk' issue by asking respondents to his surveys a series of questions designed to reveal issues which might force them to reconsider their voting preference. Queries such as, if Carter attacks Kennedy because he wants to cut the defense budget, would that make you re-think your vote? And, do you think Carter has done the right thing in handling the Afghanistan crisis? Has he gone too far? If he keeps up current tactics, would you be inclined to vote against him? Caddell found a big problem with a large core of voters he called 'soft' on Carter. They had kept supporting the President because of the way he handled the Middle East crisis and brought about the Camp David Middle East Peace Treaty between Egypt and Israel in the previous year. Voters were forgetting about this with all the 'war talk', and they were perhaps looking to register a protest vote against Carter if he continued talking too tough unnecessarily. This was exactly the opposite to the way Caddell wished the vote to go, for he was still nervous about a sudden groundswell lifting Kennedy on a protest vote. The pollster had a higher regard than any of the Carter people for the Senator, for he appreciated that underneath Kennedy's benign visage was a very proud member of a fighting Irish clan. Kennedy had faced much deeper emotional setbacks in his life than election defeats. Unless he was really stopped early, Caddell feared the Senator would hang on. If he sensed victory anywhere, Carter might be in trouble. Kennedy was a far better speaker than Carter. So far the Senator had not been really inspired, but if he did have something to fire him, there might be no stopping him.

Caddell saw the chance to thwart the challenger early. Kennedy's campaign was already running out of money and his confidence had been low since the Mudd interview. Carter's victory in the caucus vote in Iowa had not been quite enough, and Caddell's surveys were showing that in February the gap was not 20 per cent, but nearer 5 per cent, if the figures were adjusted to follow through on potential trends.

Caddell as usual sounded the alarm bells and this time the members of the Carter campaign were fully attentive. Carter had scheduled a press conference. On his pollster's advice, he prepared political responses to every question on foreign affairs, which were designed to influence the New Hampshire 'soft' voters worried about 'war talk'.

"What is your next move as regards the Soviet Union's invasion of Afghanistan?" one reporter asked.

"We must convince the Soviet Union, through peaceful means, *peaceful* means, that they cannot invade an innocent country without impunity," Carter replied.

Reporters counted seven mentions of peace in a follow-up question. A CBS newsman asked, "Are you going to call for a draft, Mr President?"

Carter was wound up on the peace theme now, and instead of 'war talk' there was conciliatory language on any topic relating to the military. "I categorically did not call for, and do not anticipate calling for, a draft," he said. (The target here was 'soft' voters.)

In answer to one question about new moves on Iran, Carter began with, "My whole approach, and the approach of my administration, as the record shows clearly from the Middle East Agreement . . ." (Again, 'soft' voters.)

Another reporter challenged him about Kennedy.

"Is the Senator correct when he claims that your administration has stolen the idea to establish a United Nations commission on Iran?"

Caddell had been finding that Kennedy was unpopular for attacking the President on his approach to Iran. Many voters polled were saying that American lives were in danger and therefore everyone should pull together and rally around the flag. There certainly should not be any attack on the nation's leader at such a critical moment. With this in mind, Carter had been nicely primed to act tough. He could even afford to appear angry. He answered: "His statements have not been true [the aim here was to draw attention to Kennedy's character and imply that he cannot be trusted], they've not been accurate, and they've not been responsible [don't ever forget his irresponsibility at Chappaquiddick], and they've not helped our country [this was code for lack of patriotism]."

Caddell polled a day later in New Hampshire and rang Carter immediately. There was no need to approach Rosalynn. This was pick-your-way-through-the-primaries time and no one remotely near the President had anything like Caddell's tactical brain.

"Mr. President," he said, "the Senator's negatives went up."

"Which ones, Pat?" Carter asked.

"His credibility and dependability."

"How do you think the conference went?"

"Quite well," Caddell replied cautiously, "but everyone must keep up the pressure still. You must go for a knockout in New Hampshire. Gerry's got to change the advertising there too. It's too negative and it will raise the 'war talk' issue."

With Carter's backing, Caddell directed that one radio spot be pulled off the air immediately. It charged that Kennedy was saying one thing and doing another on several issues, including defense. The ad said that Kennedy had often supported defense cuts in the past, and implied that Carter was against this. Caddell had calculated that it could upset the 'soft' voters, so it had to go. Rafshoon was asked to make two more TV ads designed to focus the voters on Carter and Kennedy as a presidential choice to avoid the dreaded 'protest' vote. In the meantime, an older 'peace' TV ad was run. It showed Carter at a town meeting in Elk City, Oklahoma, in March 1979. A woman stood up and said emotionally, "I want to say something. I am the mother of three teenage boys . . ." the camera zoomed in on her tearful face ". . . and I want to say thank you, Mr President, for your role as a peacemaker." The camera pulled out and the crowd was shown wild with enthusiasm. A cut to Carter caught a lingering glimpse of the man's humble pride. The narrator hammered home the 'peace maker' theme, as did the two new ads which followed days later, putting the presidential choice before the voters. In one, the narrator said: "A man brings two things to a presidential campaign. He brings his record and he brings himself. In the voting booth, the voter must weigh both record and character before deciding. Often it's not easy, and the voter winds up asking, 'Is this the person I really want in the White House for the next four years?' " The final visual was a hand ticking off Carter's name on a ballot paper.

Caddell ran a final poll a week before the New Hampshire primary and found, in common with many of the 'horse race' polls, that Carter was between 17 and 20 points ahead. But Caddell was more interested in the disguised figure based on the 'will-you-change-your-preference-if' adjustment. It showed an 11-point lead for Carter. The pollster would have like a far healthier margin, but he took some satisfaction from knowing that he had lifted the adjusted vote from 5 to 11. The actual vote was a Carter victory of 49 to 38. The adjusted figure had been accurate and Kennedy's better showing surprised all except those in the President's campaign. It was not the knock-out blow they had hoped for.

SEARING SEARS

Reagan jumped from his chair and lunged at Sears, both fists clenched. "I know what's happening," he said furiously, "you're trying to get Ed out of the campaign!" Nancy, Charlie Black and Jim Lake restrained the candidate, as Sears sat stunned by the outburst. They were in a suite in a hotel at Andover, Massachusetts, just over the state line from New Hampshire. The meeting between the five a few days before the primary had come to a head after Sears had gone over familiar territory regarding the competence of Ed Meese, Reagan's issues man. Sears felt Reagan was not being briefed well enough, which implied he wanted Meese to leave the campaign. Sears had already seen off another of the Californian clique, Michael Deaver, in a previous disagreement. Deaver had left rather than cause further disruption by battling with the dominant campaign manager.

"Now we're not going to get anywhere by fighting," Nancy said to her husband as he sat down angrily. "The one thing that counts is what's best for the campaign, and that means a win for you, Ronnie."

Nancy had remained neutral until that moment as she watched the bickering around her husband. She saw both the value of Sears and the importance of Meese, for whom Reagan had great respect. When Black, Lake and Sears left the Reagans alone after the meeting broke up without resolution, she said: "You're going to have to make a choice, and soon."

"I know, honey," Reagan said, "but they sure as hell aren't going to stab Ed."

"Then John, Jim and Charlie will have to leave and you can replace them," Nancy said. "You're doing pretty well here campaigning differently from the way John wanted anyway."

"Yeah, Dick says we are going to win big."

"Think about it, Ronnie – it's too important not to make a decision soon."

Wirthlin's assurances that Reagan was heading for a strong victory in New Hampshire which would virtually finish Bush as a challenger had given Reagan renewed confidence to make changes. He now felt that the Republican nomination was his if he followed the same strategy adopted in New Hampshire – a combination of his own instincts about campaigning plus the strategy of his pollster. In a series of fast moves and with impeccable timing, Reagan waited until the afternoon of the primary before asking Sears, Black and Lake to meet him at his suite on the third floor of the Holiday Inn just across the Amoskeag Bridge.

Sears arrived to find his two partners waiting for him. "What's it all about?" he asked. The others shrugged.

"Don't know," Black said. "Wonder who else is up there?"

In the suite were the Reagans and William Casey, who had recently joined the campaign's management in order to keep the peace between Meese and Sears. The Governor greeted them with cool politeness and all three men were suddenly aware what was happening. Sears sat on the couch next to Reagan, who said stonily: "We have to solve a few problems," and handed Sears a piece of paper. It was a letter of resignation for all three political operatives. When they all knew its contents, only Lake wanted to protest.

"Governor," he said emotionally, "you don't realize this, but Ed Meese manipulates you."

Reagan stood up and shook his head. "That's just not true," he said huskily. The three stunned and disappointed men filed out silently, leaving the candidate with his wife and new campaign director.

"Bill," Reagan said with a sigh, "can you call Ed in here? I want to complete the restructuring of the campaign right now. See if you can find Lyn and Mike. They will have to be told quickly."

Deaver and Lyn Nofziger, who had also been dumped by Sears for Jim Lake as press secretary, were to return to the staff. Ed Meese would become chief of staff and maintain his role in briefing Reagan about the campaign issues.

"What about the press?" Casey said.

Reagan looked at his watch. It was 2.20 p.m. "They'll learn it soon enough," he said. "It's too late to affect the vote, and too early to look as if the victory precipitated it."

Two hours later, Wirthlin was sitting at a desk in his hotel room examining exit polls when the phone rang. It was Reagan. "Dick, there have been a few changes," he told him. "I have had to fire John, Jim and Charlie. I would like to know if you would consider taking over strategy and planning."

"That sounds very interesting, Governor," Wirthlin said, "but I'd like to discuss it with Jeralie first."

"Sure, Dick," Reagan said. "Just call us back when you have made a decision." Wirthlin phoned his wife and explained the sudden offer, telling her how it would mean him being away from the family many nights until November. Realizing the offer was a great opportunity for Wirthlin to achieve certain ambitions, she gave him her blessing.

Wirthlin rang Reagan and accepted. Then he reached for the phone again to ring his senior colleague at DMI, Vince Breglio, and Richard Beal, a consultant for the company who was lecturing at Brigham Young University in Utah. They were both told to start concentrating on the fine-tuning of PINS.

"We have a free hand," he told Beal. "It can be totally PINS-based strategy, but it's going to mean a hell of a lot of work." He organized a meeting at Brigham Young for the following week and when that was done, sat down alone to contemplate the opportunity that had opened up for him. The experiment to computerize a candidate's bid for the most important political office in the Western world now had a chance of being carried out. It was an exciting and almost overwhelming prospect – so much so that the strategist was prompted to give thanks to God in his Mormon heaven.

CHAPTER 10
PINS – PROGRAM FOR A PRESIDENT

In a crowded computer room at the Mormon university of Brigham Young in Provo, Utah, Dr Richard Smith Beal was discussing a project with his best International Relations students. At the end of his short lecture Beal, who at times seemed like a young Mickey Rooney, took aside a tall Hawaiian in his early twenties named Grayling Achui.

"How'd you like to work for us through the summer?" Beal asked. "I have a very special project."

Achui touched his glasses in surprise. "Sure, Dr Beal," he said. "I was going to ask you about summer projects."

"This one starts like yesterday," Beal said mysteriously, "and you are going to have to learn how to program quickly."

"Well, I wanted some computer experience," Achui replied. "Count me in."

"Good," Beal said, handing him a brochure. "That's a manual showing you how to instruct a computer so you can make calculations on it. The instructions are the program, or 'software'." Beal led Achui over to a PDP 10 computer. "You know what this is?" Beal asked, and then tapped him on the forehead. "You have this, the manual, and the machine. I want you to learn how to program a little exercise in the manual and bring me the results on Friday."

"Friday?" Achui said, startled. "Next week?"

"No, this week."

"But that's only forty-eight hours!"

"You're quick, Grayling, very quick."

"What's the big deal?"

"It took me forty-eight hours to do the same exercise when I was a post-graduate at USC. If I could do it in 1970, you can do it in 1980. Besides, we have this project."

"Aren't you going to tell me what it's about?"

"Nope," Beal said. "But have I ever given you a bum steer?"

"No . . ."

"This could be the chance of a lifetime."

Beal shook hands with the student, wished him luck and marched out of the computer room. Achui sat down and began to study the manual. He looked at his watch. It was 5 p.m. "Why not start now," he thought. Fourteen hours later, as the first gray light of dawn bathed the campus, Achui was still working. He realized that it would take him the better part of those forty-eight hours to complete the project on time, so he soldiered on through the day with small breaks to rest and eat. The following morning he successfully ran a program on the computer, and was ready to join a squad of eight other Mormon undergraduates and graduates on Beal's mission for Wirthlin. This entailed setting up and fine-tuning the advanced Political Information System – PINS – for use in Reagan's national campaign for the Presidency that fall. There were also other programs to be developed for building a campaign strategy, which would be continually tested and analyzed for effectiveness by the PINS simulation network. Essentially the strategy would have one overriding and dominant role: victories in enough states to take Reagan over the 270 electoral college votes needed to win the Presidency.

Beal, a man in his mid-thirties, had hand-picked his assistants for speed and intelligence. They had first to be specialists in political science – researchers, economists, statisticians – who could handle computers intelligently enough to be proficient under pressure. Neither Beal nor Wirthlin could afford to have incompetents around them in the heat of election battle, where the misunderstanding of an order would have PINS spewing out nonsense. The people selected had to be knowledgeable enough to spot anomalies in the system's results and be able to correct them immediately.

The team's temperament was also vitally important to success or failure. Wirthlin and Beal did not want frustrated power-mongers who would lead their candidate along paths that satisfied their own lust for power. They sought an academic approach based on profound respect for PINS. They needed people prepared to put their reliance, confidence and trust in the technology they had created. Just like the new generation of technologically minded children growing into a different world from their computer-illiterate parents, Wirthlin and Beal wanted their squad to be a world away from those who did not have access to, or did not understand, the modern methods of electing politicians. In the same way that children of the 1980s had become aficionados of computers by using them for everything from video games to homework in unlimited mind-stretching exercises, this election team was to use PINS to broaden and deepen their own political perceptions. The system would be designed continually to test, reject or verify their experience, knowledge, gut instincts and intuitive thoughts. And again, like the infants of the automated eighties, the political scientists engineering Reagan's run would grow comfortable with the technology and become ingenious in experimenting with it.

Another notable aspect of the team's temperament was the fact that every one of them was also a believer in a more heavenly faith. They were all Mormons – members of the Church of Jesus Christ of Latter-Day Saints. This peculiarly American ecclesiastical invention, along with several other churches, believes in God the Father, Jesus Christ the Son and the Holy Ghost. Hereafter its beliefs differ from the others. A unique doctrine of the Mormon orthodoxy is the belief that God has a wife in heaven; this leads to the emphasis on the family that pervades every corner of the Church's life. Mormons, for instance, are virulently opposed to the Equal Rights Amendment which they believe would take mothers away from the family structure.

The gulf between Mormonism and other Judeo-Christian faiths widens and becomes important in the context of contemporary America thanks to Joseph Smith who in 1820, at the age of seventeen, claimed that he had been visited by an angel called Moroni. Other visions followed and he is said to have been given directions which enabled him to translate sacred records on gold plates, written by Moroni's father, the ancient historian, Mormon. These records became the Book of Mormon, which tells of a lost tribe of Israel that crossed the Pacific and settled in the Americas in about 600 BC. According to the Book the US became engulfed in darkness during the three days from Christ's death to His resurrection; it claims that Christ later visited the New World, and that around AD 420 the Lamanites – the Antichrists of the New World – rose up against Christ's followers and obliterated their civilization.

In 1829 Smith claimed to have received divine authority to the office of priesthood, thought to be lost to the world since early New Testament times. In 1830 he and an associate, Oliver Cowdery, founded the Mormon sect, and at once began making converts. Because America is the home of the Church of Latter-Day Saints, Mormons are intensely patriotic and regard the country as a divine land. This is why they are today committed to strong military defence in order to preserve it.

Wirthlin's team in 1980 adapted effortlessly to the use of computers. These machines were tailor-made for the modern, clean-cut Mormons, who became disciplined and systematic in the execution of the PINS' mission to program Reagan's path to election victory. Their minds had been trained, indeed indoctrinated, to be ordered and structured. They eschewed what they saw as the common vices of our society – alcohol, drugs, sex before marriage – and anything else which they felt could possibly mar their efficiency in their private or working lives. To the Mormons of the 1980s, computers were objects of utter perfection, machines of infallible logic and discipline. If used properly, they promised to speed the march of Mormon progress in life and business, and thus expand Mormonism. Its members, for example, have built a vast computerized genealogical library in the side of a Utah mountain to enable them to trace dead ancestors whom they can baptize into the Church.

Not surprisingly, the two faiths – in the PINS technology and the Mormon Church – became inextricably bound in 1980, because Ronald Reagan, described by a senior Latter-Day Saint as a 'Mormon in heart and mind', believed in the same political doctrines as they did. They wanted America to be right-wing and conservative in most matters, particularly military. So did the candidate. They wanted a limited welfare state based on 'self-help". So did the candidate. On every possible major issue, the Mormons lined up behind the real Reagan. If he was elected it would be a great boon for the Mormon Church and its members, who would certainly receive big dividends. If Reagan was anything, he was incredibly loyal to friends and supporters. His victory would be sure to see a flood of Mormons into the new administration. Many would receive key positions in running the country. Some could even aspire to unprecedented opportunities, power, money and connections in the world's most important political capital.

All this was enough incentive for Wirthlin, Beal and Breglio to drive their team hard to extract from PINS the clues and answers on how, when and where candidate Reagan would campaign to win.

Beal's initial task was to adjust PINS for the special demands of 1980 after the simulation had been developed over thirteen years by Wirthlin. It had five main elements. First there was the dynamic up to the minute survey data on how the candidates' votes were progressing in each county and state, and nationally. DMI carried out the polling and used the standard sample of 1500 people to gauge national opinion (just 600 for one state) which in each case was accurate to within plus or minus 3 per cent, ninety-five times out of a hundred. When operators phoned the random sample, they would always ask for demographic data from all the respondents, such as occupation, sex, religion, income, race, number of children, cars and so on. This told the operator and the computer what sort of sample had been contacted, and this information could be mathematically adjusted to make the sample more truly representative of the nation, state or county.

Fixed demographic information in the computer, the second element of PINS, adjusted the data. For example, if 600 people were phoned in the state of Hawaii, and it was found that they included 500 females, 400 Republicans, and 250 people in the low-income bracket earning 15,000 dollars or less a year, then the computer would compare this with the census and DMI's incessant research and sampling of Hawaii which gave the true demographic make-up of the state. For example, that state would have 308 females, 190 Republicans and 69 in the low-income bracket in every 600 people on average. The accuracy of this basic data depended on keeping abreast of changing population and demographics from year to year.

The third element in PINS, which had to be programmed into the 1980 updated system, was DMI and official government historical voting information, which went back as far as fifteen years. This data varied. Some states' records were longer and more reliable than others, and in certain cases voting records had only been kept for twelve years. Blacks in some states, for example, had only had the vote since 1968. These historical records showed the patterns which had developed in different states and counties. They showed how a state had traditionally voted and whether it had been Republican or Democrat oriented. The records also showed how the state or county had voted for individual candidates. For instance, the computer could quickly indicate how a certain county in New York had voted for Reagan in the primaries of 1976, and how another county in his home state of California had voted in the 1966 and 1970 elections for Governor, and in the presidential primaries of 1976 (and soon, of 1980 also). This highlighted key indicator areas. Carter, for example, had run far better in Ohio than any previous Democrat in presidential election history. It would be a key barometer in 1980. If a strong base of support for the President was seen to be eroding, it would be a good sign for Reagan. Again, as with the demographic data, the historical patterns could act as an adjuster and indicator for the other elements, to make PINS increasingly accurate.

Element number four was the assessment of the Republican campaign's strength in each state. Did the state have a strong or weak chairperson? Was there a healthy cadre of volunteers to man the telephones, distribute written propaganda and, most vital, flush out the voters on election day? Each state's party organizational power had been carefully calibrated to adjust the figures of the other three elements. For instance, if the other three factors indicated that Carter would win 51 per cent of the vote in New York, but it was found that Carter's vote-motivating set-up was marginally stronger than Reagan's in that state, then that 51 per cent might be adjusted upward to, say, 52.5 per cent on election day.

Finally, element number five was a collective subjective judgement by political experts. This was the 'human factor' in the system which acted as a 'control' over the rest of PINS. At regular intervals, Beal, Wirthlin and Breglio – themselves part of the team of experts – would consult with others inside and outside the campaign who had great political savvy. They ranged from Nofziger and Spencer to Kissinger and Laxalt. In addition, there might be some person with special knowledge in a county who might, for example, claim that if Reagan visited a certain area and spoke about defense it would change the vote dramatically in the county and swing the state to Reagan. The campaign director might ask the candidate to make a brief extra stop accordingly. Factor five actually gave a mathematical 'weight' to the 'gut' instincts of all the observers, so that the system was calibrated to be as foolproof as possible.

Individually, each element of PINS had long been used by modern political analysts. Each was a 'snapshot' of an election at one particular point in time. It was like a Polaroid photograph. You knew what something looked like at one instant. If it was a poll on how a sample of the electorate thought they would vote – for Candidate A or B – this would be a very rough indicator indeed without the link with the other four elements. In fact, a single element could be wildly wrong in what it predicted, especially if the election was close and there was a high percentage of swinging voters or 'undecideds'. Yet combined with the other four, it allowed PINS to give a much larger, better defined, and therefore more accurate picture. And if voting intentions were 'tracked' – followed and updated – daily, as Wirthlin intended, then a moving picture could be made of the whole campaign to determine how the candidate and his opponent were progressing.

The Wirthlin-inspired development which could have turned this hybrid science-art into more science than art was the capacity to ask 'What if' questions of the PINS simulation. He had started doing this with Reagan in 1970, but then had been restricted to 'asking' the system how the vote would go if the opposing candidates persisted with their stated positions on issues. The main set of issues in 1970, when Reagan opposed Jesse Unruh, was concerned with welfare. By polling and asking Californians a variety of questions on welfare, and whether they intended to be influenced by the candidates' positions on other major issues, Wirthlin discovered that Governor Reagan was in for a comfortable win if he continued with his welfare themes. A decade later, Wirthlin planned to take this 'What if' capacity into a new dimension and incorporate a far greater range of subjects, from how the electorate would react to certain character perceptions, right through to how best to allocate campaign resources, and what the impact of a third candidate (as John Anderson was promising to be) in the national election would be. For instance, in considering the image of the President, Wirthlin planned to diminish Carter's 'nice guy' image, one of the few character perceptions that was strongly positive for him. If Carter was seen to be vicious during the campaign, even a liar, how would that affect the vote in Alaska, or Texas, or Nebraska, and right across the nation? Now it was not only 'issues' that were to be tested against the system but every imaginable important question.

Another instance would concern campaign scheduling. The strategist would say to the PINS system: suppose in certain states, John Anderson, the third candidate, runs a strong campaign. How will that affect the Reagan vote in Massachusetts, or New Jersey, or Connecticut? How will it affect the Carter vote? Should the Reagan campaign add another stop in each of these states to prevent his advance, or would it be better to let it go on, especially if it is taking votes away from Carter? When considering the undecided votes, what if they were to break against Reagan? For instance, if the undecideds went 60 per cent for Carter and only 35 per cent for Reagan, how would that affect the situation? What would the position look like if the Reagan team could improve his position 2 or 3 per cent? Would that tip the state his way?

Such fine measurement could be vitall if Reagan and his opponent were both approaching the winning target of 270 electoral college votes. The knowledge of how to pick up a few percentage points, even in the last hours of the campaign, could mean the difference between winning and losing. To obtain those extra supporters, Wirthlin would tailor Reagan's message to change the minds of some of the wavering voters in this county or that. He might be flown to Kansas City in the morning and the Bronx in the afternoon, where Hispanics in one county and upper income whites in another would receive a different message through TV, radio, press and speeches by Reagan and his surrogates. Wirthlin desired flexibility, especially as the election battle reached the final days. He wanted to be able to test and take action when and where he saw the opportunity to move the vote Reagan's way. Once the research had been done, a question could be asked of PINS, by programming in the appropriate figures, and the result would appear on the screen in a few seconds.

Worrying about very small increments in the vote was to become an obsession of the Mormon squad. No source was left untapped. In advertising, Wirthlin tested the various ways of presenting Reagan to find the commercial that did most to boost his support. The strategist decided to use two test counties in

Texas and California, and in a costly exercise his 300 operatives rang homes in those counties until they found a statistically reliable sample of viewers' reactions. ("Were you watching '60 Minutes' tonight? If so did you see the ad for candidate Reagan? What did you think of it? Was it better than the others you've seen? Would it influence you to vote for him rather than his opponents? What factors did you like/dislike about the ad?") One type of ad might influence only 4 per cent more voters to support Reagan. But 4 per cent across the board could win an election.

While Wirthlin was keeping an open mind, he had learned from experience that using Reagan 'direct to camera', without special frills and technical tricks, was the best way to lift support for him. Now, as campaign director, Wirthlin would have overall control of who made the ads, how they looked, and what they said. It was a far cry from the frustrating days of 1976, and even the early months of the 1980 campaign, when he saw the same mistakes that had ruined Reagan's other bids being repeated. The strategist now relished the thought of backing his own judgement, always tested against PINS.

The system's greatly enhanced capacity, since 1970, to 'war-game' and extract answers to any number of 'What if' questions, gave the Mormons a moving picture of the campaign in progress in 1980 which allowed the director to see how strategy, or any individual tactic, was affecting the candidate's chances. If the method was building his support it could be amplified (more of ad type 'X' in state 'Y' at time 'Z'). If a tactic proved a failure, it could be spotted quickly and dropped. As Director of Planning and Strategy, Wirthlin would control the allocation of resources for the whole campaign, which meant he would make sure his system was never starved of 'live' data daily for his system. In 1980 he could tap huge dollar resources and also use much improved, faster computers and peripheral equipment on which to run the PINS programs. No longer compeled to be near cumbersome machines to obtain printouts (hardcopy) of the latest calculations, the Mormon team now planned to link computers in Utah, McClean and Los Angeles by terminals. So-called 'smart', or intelligent, terminals, no bigger than TV sets, could access all the big computers necessary. Data would be easily displayed graphically on terminal screens. If a printout 'hardcopy' was required, there were also graphical plotters – mechanical arms – which could trace out on paper anything coming up on the screen.

With all the data and technology available for programming Reagan's run, Wirthlin and his Mormon team still had to maintain their control of the campaign for their experiment to have a chance of success. All the computer sophistication in the world would be useless unless the program was followed closely. This meant that Wirthlin, Beal and Breglio had to construct an easily digestible strategy which the candidate would follow from March to November.

CHAPTER 11

PLANNING FOR THE MAIN EVENT

THE FIGHTER *V.* THE BOXER

Senator Kennedy, like some lumbering bar brawler who had never boxed in the ring, just kept coming out round after round when the bell sounded. No matter what tactics Caddell tried he could not bring the Senator down for the full count. In language reminiscent of another Irish fighter named Reagan four years earlier in the battle against President Ford, Kennedy went on saying, "I'm not going to quit." The press kept baying for him to throw in the towel but, like Reagan, he refused. And gradually he began to connect against his opponent. Carter would not involve himself in any real infighting such as that which a debate would provide, so Kennedy concentrated his energies on thrilling the big crowds he drew.

Previously overshadowed by the memory of his impressive brothers, the Senator began to find that he too had something special to offer – something truly individual – as he used his barrel-chest to boom out and at times grip his audiences. Seventeen years in the Senate had given him more political experience in some areas than brothers John and Bobby put together, and because he came from a more clear liberal tradition than Carter, he often seemed more substantial on issues than the President.

Kennedy's comeback started with a speech at Georgetown University. He attacked Carter with well-directed jabs: "The 1980 election should not be a plebiscite on the Ayatollah or Afghanistan. The real question is whether America can risk four more years of uncertain policy and certain crisis – of an administration that tells us to rally around their failures – of an inconsistant non-policy that may confront us with a stark choice between retreat and war. These issues must be debated in this campaign. The silence that has descended across foreign policy has stifled the debate on other essential issues. The political process has been held hostage at home as surely as our diplomats abroad."

On the stump, too, his deliveries began to have more articulation, direction and punch. Shortly after Georgetown he was in Des Moines, Iowa, before a crowd of a thousand who gave him his most enthusiastic welcome in the campaign to that point. With their cheers ringing out Kennedy walked slowly to the stage, one fist raised in the air, Sylvester Stallone-style. He spoke with confidence and humor, and when he was stopped by applause, he would chuckle, clear his throat and jab the air before making his next point. "Mr Carter suggests that there's a malaaaaaise in the spirit of the American people," Kennedy said, mocking the President. "Well, I tell you I have not found that to be true, in talking to farmers, in talking to working people, in talking to the elderly, in talking to the young . . ." At the end of the speech the applause and whistling would not stop, so instead of taking his seat, Kennedy strutted around the stage, that fist defiantly puncturing the air. He was now acting like a champ.

The Senator's gradual improvement began to worry Caddell as his polls showed some alarming shifts away from the President. These were accentuated just before the Massachusetts primary which Kennedy was certain to win, when the United Nations took up a resolution which called on Israel to dismantle civilian settlements in occupied Arab territories, including Jerusalem. The US shocked Israel by voting *for* the resolution, making it unanimous. Forty-eight hours later Carter explained that this had been a "mistake" and a "failure to communicate" between the AAmerican mission to the UN and the White House.

At the time, Caddell made an appointment to see Jody Powell in his basement office in the West Wing of the White House. "The focus is going off Kennedy and on to the President," Caddell told Carter's closest adviser. "Attitudes are softening to Kennedy and hardening against Jimmy. The voters are concentrating less on Iran and Afghanistan. The focus must be kept on Iran especially, otherwise, if it shifts too much to the Administration's record and Jimmy's leadership, we're in trouble."

"How does it look for the New York primary?"

"Bad with this UN vote. Jewish support has slipped markedly. Kennedy will win Massachusetts easily and he could cut us in New York."

"Jesus!" Powell said. "Just hope Jimmy isn't a hemophiliac."

THE MORMON ARCHITECTS

Grayling Achui arrived at the cheap hotel in Provo, Utah, late one night and went straight to Room 31. He knocked and was called in by Beal, Wirthlin and Breglio. The unpreposssessing suite was a mess of papers, charts, computer print-outs, books and folders, some of which the three men were poring over. Beal gave him a list of things to calculate and retrieve from the Brigham Young computer. Like the rest of the Mormon squad who had been refining the 1980 PINS system, Achui was being called day and night to research facts for the strategist. Achui looked down the list. It read:

Require voting patterns and current polling data on the

following groups: 1. Clerical/sales workers. 2. Craftsmen and foremen. 3. Union households. 4. Veterans. 5. Working women. 6. Catholics. 7. Born-Again Christians.

Achui scratched his head. "Wish I knew what this was all about," he mumbled quietly to Beal, who replied, "Don't worry, Grayling. You don't have to know yet. Just do it."

"OK, Rich," Achui said, turning to leave. "That's what you're paying me for."

Achui drove to the university campus early the next morning, and after searching out the data he bumped into another member of the squad, Mario Hegewald, a twenty-two year old who had made his specialist field survey work. The two students had breakfast together in the science department's cafeteria.

"It's all so damned secretive," Achui complained. "They won't give us any clues."

"It has to be pretty important for Wirthlin to be flying in so often. He is one of Reagan's top advisers."

Achui frowned. "But they're staying in that rinky-dink little hotel!" he said.

The two began to compare notes. Hegewald had been carrying out research on Republican traditional voters, and Achui had done work on non-traditional voters such as the list Beal had given him the night before. The researchers agreed that their findings had to be part of an important project, which was probably a strategy to be tested against PINS which had just been set up. But a strategy for what, they wondered? Wirthlin and Breglio had returned several times from the primary campaign, but none of the data was directly connected to that, which was sewn up for Reagan anyway. This seemed to leave just one option, which surprised both reseachers. The Mormon architects were creating a full-blown strategy for the national campaign of October and November, which was still half a year away. As far as they knew, this was the earliest such detailed preparation ever for a presidential election. If nothing else, Reagan was going to have the best prepared campaign of any candidate in political history.

FOCUS ON IRAN

"Jimmy's been bleeding a little since we lost in New York," Caddell told Powell over the phone on 31 March. "Tomorrow's Wisconsin primary is going to be a big test to see if he is hemorrhaging or not. People are beginning to take a harder look at the economy. They're talking more about the inflation rate, and unemployment."

"Will we win tomorrow?"

"It's looking fairly good. But we wouldn't want anything bad to break before the vote, like it did with the UN resolution before New York."

Powell sighed. "Well, we can't do much about Iran," he said.

"Except keep the focus on it if you get any good news."

Several hours later, in the middle of the night, the news came in from Tehran that the President of Iran, Bani-Sadr, was about to meet the Iranian Revolutionary Council and get them to agree to release the American hostages. At 3.48 a.m. Carter and his key aides met in the Oval Office to discuss developments. After about two hours, the President, sitting on a couch, looked at the clock on the wall. "They should have some news by now," he said. He turned to Powell and asked him to get some further confirmation. While the President and the Secretary of State, Cyrus Vance, went over the latest information with the Deputy Secretary, Christopher Warren, Powell and Jordan worked the phones trying to discover more details on events in the Iranian capital. A half hour later, Powell reported back: "Nothing to add to the fact that Bani-Sadr claims to have a majority for the transfer of the hostages. He has to meet with the Council, discuss it formally, and then he plans to make an announcement." Carter sighed wearily, and sitting forward said, "Guess there's nothing more we can do. We'd better release something on it."

"Do you want me to do it?" Powell asked.

Carter stared back for a moment. "No, I had better hold a press conference," he said and looking at the clock again, asked, "What's the best time to catch the morning news programs?"

"Around seven," Powell said. "That'll ensure nationwide network coverage."

"Think we have time to do that?"

"Yeah," Powell said, getting to his feet. "I'll have to move fast though. Where are you going to do it from?"

"Here," Carter said. "It's the news we've been waiting three months for, isn't it?"

At 7.13 a.m. Carter made a brief speech from behind his desk in the Oval Office. He claimed that Bani-Sadr's statement was a positive step which meant the American Government would not have to impose economic sanctions against Iran. Reporters were cautious.

"Mr President," one said, "what assurances do you have that the hostages will be transferred to neutral territory?"

"We have no assurances that this will be done except that the President of Iran has said it will be done."

Several other reporters wanted to ask a follow up, and one picked out by Carter said: "Do you know when they will actually be released and brought home?"

There was a hushed silence before the President replied: "I presume we will know more about that as the circumstances develop. We do not know the exact time scheduled at this moment."

Democrats went to the polls in the primaries that day in Wisconsin and Kansas. They voted overwhelmingly for the President over Kennedy, and virtually ended any real chance of the challenger winning the Democratic nomination. A few days later Tehran announced that Bani-Sadr had not been able to secure his majority in the Revolutionary Council and the fifty Americans remained in Iranian custody without any immediate prospects of release.

CHANGING THE IMAGE

While the Carter campaign team struggled to throw off the Kennedy challenge, the Mormon squad were putting the finishing touches to their first strategy document in the plan to program Reagan's election bid. Not the least problem at that early stage was an internal difference between Reagan and the rest of the party. A concerted effort would have to be made to have everyone, including former President Ford, close ranks behind the candidate, especially during the convention. There were also problems of scheduling, handling the press, and calculating the voter groups to be aimed at. Yet by far the greatest focus of the team's analysis was on the images of the two opposing candidates. They found little to work on with Carter, for the electorate saw him as a nice, hardworking man. Until PINS highlighted some glaring weakness in Carter's character, which had not become apparent in his battle with Kennedy, the Republican attack would have to center on the President's lack of leadership, which would be linked to an implication of incompetence, and on the administration's failures in foreign and domestic affairs. Wirthlin, Beal and Breglio had learned much by closely following and analyzing the Carter-Kennedy battle. The aim was to take Kennedy's valiant effort one step further. He had successfully attacked Carter's record and his style of leadership, but he had failed to establish himself as a credible alternative. This now became the key task of the whole Reagan campaign, and the Mormon team spent many days and nights dissecting just how it should be achieved. Finally, at a meeting in Beal's office on the Brigham Young University campus, they examined the major weaknesses in Reagan's image as perceived by the voting groups that had to be attracted in order to win the Presidency.

Wirthlin, speaking into a tape recorder, said: "We must make the Governor appear less dangerous in the foreign affairs area, more competent in the the economic area, more compassionate on the domestic issues, and less of a conservative zealot than his opponents and the press now paint him to be . . ." Wirthlin switched off the tape to discuss further how they should make Reagan look.

"I've got an idea that should solve all our problems," the round-faced Breglio said drily. "Let's get a completely different candidate."

The others laughed, for after the years of analysis and preparation the absurdity of the suggestion seemed momentarily funny. Yet it also highlighted the task in front of them. While a complete overhaul of the Reagan image was out of the question, there would have to be some carefully designed changes if he was to appeal to moderate voters in the center of the political spectrum.

"What should I say here?" Wirthlin said, setting the tape down. "Basically, I guess, we have to make him look a more warm, human, approachable individual."

"That's the way we see him," Breglio agreed. "But we have to make the nation see him this way, too."

The strategists knew they would be greatly helped by Reagan's acting experience. Whatever character they settled for at any one time, the candidate would be able to adjust his appearance, manner, speech and comments to fit the demands of the program. In most cases it would not be so very different from the nice, warm, guy-next-door part he played in most of his Hollywood B-movies.

Once the Reagan strategy was created, Beal and his team began testing it against PINS to search for ways to improve the candidate's chances of winning. By June, they had already highlighted a tactic which would go a long way toward giving Reagan the Presidency: former President Gerald R. Ford should be chosen as his running-mate. Surveys had found Ford greatly respected by the national electorate, and particularly among Republicans. When this information was fed into PINS – "If Gerald R. Ford, former US President, was to be Ronald Reagan's Vice-Presidential running mate, would you vote for the ticket?" – the results astonished Beal. He immediately phoned Wirthlin at his McClean office near Washington DC. "It's amazing," he said excitedly. "No matter which way you look at it, a Reagan-Ford ticket could even build to a landslide! Ford would strengthen the Midwest and make sure Reagan took California."

"If only Gerry wants it!" Wirthlin said. "I'll have to get Bill Casey to try to speak with him soon. Gerry and the Governor have not exactly been buddies since 1976."

"Gerry really wants to see Carter out," Beal said. "Maybe that will be enough incentive to woo him."

"That will be part of it," Wirthlin agreed. "We must try to draw him into the campaign. Perhaps we can offer him the chairmanship of the National Agenda Council . . ."

"Well, he's the only running-mate who makes the Governor a clear winner. Bush doesn't appear a bad choice, especially among the Northern industrial states and New York and Texas. He appeals to the moderates, but he isn't known as well as Gerry and he doesn't guarantee a strong combination."

"I'll see what can be done," Wirthlin said. "We must do our best to get that dream ticket!"

SHIFTING THE FOCUS

Toward the end of the primary season in early June, Caddell was ushered into President Carter's hideaway study next to the Oval Office. These meetings were sometimes an ordeal for Caddell, and no less so for Carter, for the pollster was compelled to bring the President his survey results, however unpleasant. Unlike Reagan, who left all interpretations to Wirthlin, Carter liked to check some of the detail himself because he felt it gave him greater understanding of the situation. Occasionally, such was his attention to the fine print, he would find something extra in the figures which he felt could be significant.

"I don't like those cracks in our traditional party support," Carter said as he pored over Caddell's computer sheets and succinct reports. Catholic Democrats, blue-collar workers, male Northern Democrats and upper-income Democrats were all wavering. The cold facts furrowed Carter's brow, for he knew that it would be hard to protect those voters from the Republicans. Reagan's team would be seeing the same thing, and would be attempting to woo these groups.

"If Reagan succeeds in focusing national attention on the administration's record," Caddell said, "then you'll be in trouble." Carter looked up and stared icily at his pollster. He had heard this several times during the year in the primary battle against Kennedy, and was not yet fully resigned to it. He felt his Government had achieved much. But his pragmatic side also recognized that the economic indicators were worrying many. Inflation had been at a crippling 18 per cent, as had the bank rate. Unemployment figures were moving up too. No matter what Carter's good performances, he saw the importance of Caddell's arguments. The unpalatable fact was that the Iranians had saved Carter from having attention placed more on the administration's record, the economy and the President's leadership. The miserable state of affairs was blatantly clear from Caddell's analysis. The end of the hostages crisis could be disastrous for Carter. Ironically he was doing everything he could to end it, especially since his abortive attempt to bring the hostages back by military force. But timing was now critical. If the hostages were brought back long before the presidential election in November, there might be time for Reagan to place the focus on the administration's record. If the hostages could be brought back sometime in October this would be perfect, for there probably would be an outpouring of thanks to Carter which would translate into enough votes to win a second term in office. However, a failure to bring them home at all by November could bring other imponderables. If the administration could at least look as if it was trying hard and there was some chance of success, this would possibly maintain support for the incumbent. On the other hand, Caddell feared, public frustration about inaction and America's impotence could create a backlash. In anticipation of the worst, Caddell was urging for an alternative major strategy to be tried to avoid campaigning on the record.

"Our options are closing," Caddell said, when Carter had finished reading.

"The bottom line is that we have to make Reagan the issue. We are going to have to go after him."

Shortly after issuing this warning Caddell turned his mind to writing a detailed strategy that would give Carter some hope of winning. It wasn't an easy task and Caddell found himself with the lonely prospect of working into the early hours at his penthouse office in the National Permanent Federal Savings and Loan Building at 1775 Pennysylvannia Avenue, just two blocks from the White House. Surrounded by photos of his own political career – from his clean-shaven days with George McGovern's 1972 presidential campaign, to more recent shots of him with Carter and the Pope – Caddell crouched over his desk and scribbled on.

He started by bemoaning the fact that he lacked vital tactical information. "We have no general election data on Carter, Reagan, Anderson issues, general attitudes, states, etc., except that gleaned from public polls," he complained. "There is a great urgency to correct this deficiency. Therefore much of this memorandum is premised on hunch, experience and theory." The strategist then spelt out the painful truth. Carter was not a popular leader. He was perceived by the nation as unable to cope with worsening economic conditions. The President also seemed overwhelmed by problems in foreign affairs, notably those with

Iran and the Soviet Union. Consequently, the coalition of groups that had backed him in 1976 looked like deserting him this time around. Yet there was hope if Carter followed a strategy to hold the Southern states, which had been very good to him in the past, and if he went after Northern blue collars, liberals and suburbanites. "Blacks and Catholics become essential," Caddell pointed out. "Jews and browns are important." (By 'browns' he meant Hispanics.) If the strategist had his way, these groups would suddenly find themselves most popular with the President. Caddell suggested a political zigzag to seduce them. "We have to vigorously seize the center back from Reagan," he wrote, "particularly in foreign policy. We must push him back out to the right and away from the center, particularly in the North. While not abandoning the general positions on domestic issues, we have to find several 'safe' issues so that the President can move hard left in the North and Midwest. This also requires wooing back Kennedy and party liberals."

Having described positive actions, he then set out the plan for destroying the Reagan campaign, which had some similarities to the way Kennedy had been outpointed in the primaries. The basic idea was to highlight Reagan's incapacity for the Presidency. However, there was some difficulty in this because the electorate saw Carter himself as incapable of handling the job. So Caddell had to be content with suggesting that the President and his team develop themes about how tough the Presidency was. The aim was to make those dissatisfied with Carter compare him with the alternative in terms of the qualities needed for such a demanding role. "We want to send a number of subtle and not so subtle messages," Caddell commented, ". . . that is the hardest job in the world . . . a place that needed a cool head . . . that it needed someone smart, who could handle complex issues . . . also it demanded a person with incredible stamina and energy . . ."

"We can force all the concerns about Reagan – age, impulsiveness, rigidity, simplicity, intelligence and experience – to center stage," he went on. Finally, after his umpteenth cup of black coffee, he commented on the opposition strategists: "Since Sears's dismissal there has been a question of whether anyone around Reagan has the ability to formulate a first class political strategy. They are inexperienced in general election politics."

CHAPTER 12
CONVENTION WISDOM

DREAM TICKET TO NOWHERE

"If Ford had made an impassioned 'your country needs you' plea to you in 1976," Wirthlin asked Reagan, "would you have joined his ticket?"

"Dick, I would have accepted," Reagan replied.

"Governor, can you afford not to give Gerald Ford the same opportunity?" Wirthlin asked, pressing his point. He had subtly backed Reagan into a corner at a meeting in the candidate's suite at the Detroit Plaza.

"No, I guess not," Reagan said. "Why don't you discuss the idea with Ed and Bill? But keep it secret."

Wirthlin was elated. It was the beginning of the Republican convention and he had set in motion the 'dream ticket'. Now he planned to head the negotiations with Ford's aides, with whom he had already had discussions in the past month since the PINS analysis had made the idea irresistible. Wirthlin saw it as a chance of speeding his own strategy, first of building Reagan as being 'presidential', and secondly, much later in the campaign, of attacking Carter. So far, Wirthlin had made judicious use of his powerful position. Through quiet persuasion he had managed to get his way at the convention, which was the second stage in his computer-programmed strategy to get Reagan elected, following the successful effort in the primaries. The convention speeches would pump the basic themes which Wirthlin had identified from his polling.

Carter's 'malaise' speech of a year ago, for instance, was to be attacked repeatedly and contrasted to the positive way Reagan would run the nation. Speeches in general would be peppered with conclusions drawn from DMI surveys which showed broadly that Americans wanted to enter 'a period of stability', and that they were worried about their economic future. Reagan's address, written by Californian aide and public relations man, Peter Hannaford, after close consultation with the strategist, was to stress five words: family, work, neighborhood, peace, freedom. Emphasis as always was to be put on open-ended themes rather than clearly defined policies.

Another Wirthlin directive was that there should be a grand display of unity at the convention. There was even to be the quaint touch of having entertainment by the nation's best known Mormons, Donnie and Marie Osmond. These clean-cut Midwesterners would gush into living-rooms of the huge audience and attract the youth vote. They were firm supporters of Reagan and planned to sing a song called 'Go Ronnie, Go'. But what the strategist wanted most of all from the convention was real excitement, and this he hoped to generate by bringing Ford to the ticket.

The first step was a courtesy call by the Reagans to the Fords at their suite in the Detroit Plaza. Nancy embraced Betty Ford with her usual enthusiasm, and as they sat down in one corner of the lounge, Reagan handed Ford a gift. Ford was disarmed, and a little embarrassed as he fondled the present. "It'll give a different perspective to one of your enjoyments," Reagan said, obviously keen for Ford to unwrap it. Ford set it down on a coffee table and the two men sat on a sofa.

"Thank you Ron," Ford said. "But I haven't gotten you anything."

Reagan beamed. "You might think of something before the end of this convention."

The former President smiled warily and Reagan added, "You can opened it now, if you like."

"You want me to?"

"Sure."

Ford undid the wrapping and was genuinely thrilled by the gift. "Betty," he said to his wife, "come and have a look at what the Reagans have given me."

It was an ancient, authentic Indian peace-pipe.

Soon afterward Meese, Casey and Wirthlin asked Henry Kissinger to act as the go-between in complicated negotiations aimed at bringing Ford on to the ticket, and on the Tuesday afternoon of the convention the two parties met in a small boardroom in the hotel. On one side of the table sat Wirthlin, Meese and Casey. On the other side were Kissinger, Alan Greenspan, former chairman of the Council of Economic Advisers, and Jack Marsh, an old Ford White House aide. After an hour's discussion Wirthlin suggested that the points they had touched on should be typed up.

"Can we trust any secretary with this?" Kissinger asked, and when they all agreed that it was too sensitive, Bill Casey volunteered to play typist. As the author of several books he was used to typing roughly at some speed. Eventually ten 'talking points' were worked up. The Ford people left to discuss them with the former President and the two sides met again two hours later.

"We think it's now possible to influence Gerry if we get one or two points amplified," Kissinger said. "First of all, he would like a special role with Office of Management and Budget, and on the National Security Council.''

''How would you define that role?'' Wirthlin asked.

''He would want some say in running them for the President,'' Kissinger replied.

''Do you mean he would oversee them for the President?''

''That's how we see it,'' Greenspan said. ''He would have a major input on all decisions.''

There was a lull as Casey typed up a few lines. ''Would you be agreeable to that?'' Kissinger asked Wirthlin.

''I don't see any major objections there,'' the strategist said, ''but it could depend on what you mean by 'major input'.''

''We would expect that all the papers submitted in those departments would go through Ford.''

''You mean a veto?'' Meese asked.

Kissinger looked at Greenspan and then said, ''Not necessarily. But we would expect him to contribute to policy decisions.''

''Would you expect him to be able to stop something happening?'' Meese asked. ''To be able to send back a paper, control policy and strategy . . .?''

''Not necessarily,'' Kissinger repeated cautiously, ''but there would be little point in turning him into a bottleneck. He would like to be more than that.''

''What sort of staff would you want him to have?'' Wirthlin asked.

''That would depend on how we finally define the role,'' Kissinger replied, ''but I want to make it clear, gentlemen, that we are not here in search of jobs for ourselves. Our concern is in ensuring Governor Reagan is made President, and that Gerald Ford has a role more in keeping with his great experience as President.''

''On this subject of appointments,'' Wirthlin began. ''Would you envisage President Ford wanting his choices in the cabinet?''

''If he was to have a meaningful role, yes,'' Greenspan said, ''but I don't think we would make it a condition for him joining the ticket. He would just like to have a say in the kind of people he would like around him.''

The following day Ford rang Reagan from his suite saying that he wanted to see him, and was immediately invited down to Reagan's suite on the floor below. There was a far more cordial atmosphere between them now. Their differences from 1976, which had stemmed from Reagan's challenge for the Republican nomination, seemed to have been buried.

''We may be moving toward something,'' Ford said. ''If the guys can get a move on over the negotiations there may be something in it."

"Gee, I hope so, Gerry," Reagan said, handing him a beer. "I really think we would murder Carter and Mondale."

"That's what Dick Wirthlin's polls have been saying," Ford replied.

Reagan poured himself a beer and said, "One thing I didn't quite understand from the talking points was what you expected in the way of staff, if you were overseeing Budget and Security. Would you want to appoint some positions?"

"Well, I would like to have a say, I guess."

"The boys were wondering where Henry Kissinger fitted into all this . . ."

"Well, he and Greenspan are involved in the negotiations". Ford shrugged. "Bud is the kind of guy who ought to be Secretary of the Treasury, and let's face it, you couldn't do better than Henry as Secretary of State. But, Ron, it's definitely not a condition for me taking this thing."

The idea of delegating some authority had not bothered Reagan that much, for he well remembered his California days when he ran the state government like the chief executive of a corporation. There was, however, a world of difference between California and Washington DC and the situation began to worry Wirthlin and others around the candidate. They feared that Kissinger's aim would be to dominate foreign affairs as he had under Nixon and Ford. Authority would be cut not just from under Reagan, but everyone around him. No one in the immediate prospective presidential entourage would be able to match Kissinger when it came to the international political arena.

At the height of the behind-the-scenes negotiations, Walter Kronkite of CBS interviewed Ford at the convention and asked him about the idea of a 'co-Presidency'. Wirthlin was with Reagan at his suite at the Detroit Plaza during this. "Did you hear what he said about a 'co-Presidency'?" the candidate said, sitting bolt upright in his chair. "What the hell is Gerry doing? How did Walter Kronkite learn that something was going on?" He was shocked but not angry.

"It hasn't gotten that far," Wirthlin said. He realized at that moment that the dream ticket was headed for the shredder. At the next meeting between the two negotiating parties soon afterward it became clear they needed at least another day to iron out differences. Meanwhile, the 'co-Presidency' idea swept the convention floor and brought the delegates to fever pitch as they anticipated the candidate making an announcement to the convention before the close of proceedings that night. All three networks fueled the speculation, while reporters all over the convention floor checked with everybody and anybody to see if any new snippet of information could be gleaned to give credence to the rumor about the ticket. At one point CBS announced that Ford was definitely coming to join Reagan at the convention to announce their joint ticket.

"We are agreed on some points," Kissinger told Ford in his suite after his last meeting with Wirthlin, Meese and Casey, "but some areas are going to take some time to work out."

"Then it's not on, Henry," Ford said firmly, "it's just not on.' We've run out of time. I can't stall the Governor anymore. The floor's going mad over this, and I know he won't want to wait until tomorrow to announce a running-mate. It would be such an anticlimax, and it would make him look stupid. Besides, I told him I'd call him tonight."

Ford reached for the phone and rang Reagan to tell him he would not be joining the ticket. The candidate then offered the place to George Bush and went to the Convention Hall to make the announcement.

The next day Reagan was to make his acceptance speech, but before this, a smart propaganda documentary film on the candidate was shown. It had been prepared by Peter Dailey, the campaign's director of advertising. The shape of the film had come directly from Wirthlin's strategy of making Reagan better known. It showed the candidate's strong, basic Midwestern ethic, underlining that he had come out of America's heartland. It said that he had been a hardworking man at an early age and had become a union leader. Finally, his record as California Governor was made to appear particularly strong. The Reagans followed this on to the rostrum and the convention exploded into a frenzied celebration of their chosen nominee. It was Reagan's second finest hour. Only a win in November would give him greater satisfaction. He launched right into the themes of family, work, neighborhood, peace and freedom which Wirthlin had stressed should be the basic thrusts of verbal strategy. The performance was vintage Reagan, and he brought to it all his skill and experience as an actor. There was well-modulated sentimentality in his voice, which had that familiar honeyed huskiness of forty year's cultivation; it was always earnest as he made it recede to silk to project smoothness and warmth, or hover to barely whispered throatiness to demonstrate intimacy. In an effort both to appeal to the hawkish Republican faction and diffuse his image as a potential warmonger, he said, "Our strength is at its lowest ebb in a generation, and fifty Americans are still held hostage in Iran because the Carter administration lives in a world of make-believe." Later he added,

"We resort to force infrequently and with great reluctance – and only after we have determined that it is absolutely necessary . . . we are awed – and rightly so – by the forces of destruction at loose in the world in this nuclear era . . . the United States has an obligation to its citizens and to the people of the world never to let those who would destroy freedom dictate the future of human life on this planet."

Wirthlin left the convention without his ideal candidate combination as defined by PINS. In theory, the computer would have been right about the Reagan-Ford combination bringing the best possible victory. PINS was only reacting to its programming, which had been designed to show how to reach the required 270 votes in the easiest and quickest way. Yet there was no function to allow for intuitive reasoning on a scale which would have foreseen difficulties with the ticket. That would no doubt be programmable in the near future, but not yet. The result of the convention was a Reagan-Bush ticket which would be harder to sell. Nevertheless, that arrangement looked reasonably attractive and balanced. More problematic for the strategist were the issues which Reagan had so professionally tackled in his speech. Wirthlin's polls soon after the election found that not much more than 60 per cent of the nation knew what Reagan stood for, and from the strategist's experience, this was not enough for him to appear 'presidential'. Wirthlin wanted to be sure that at least 70 per cent of the nation felt they understood Reagan and his policies before he was let loose to attack the incumbent. Any less than that could cause a backlash against him if he went on the attack prematurely. The strategist took comfort from knowing that his counterpart in the Carter campaign could not do anything about this aspect of the selling of Reagan to the nation.

Caddell, however, could do something about another factor vital to Reagan's chances. DMI's post-convention polls still showed that nearly half the nation saw him as 'dangerous and uncaring' and likely to lead America into war of some kind. Wirthlin's aim in the ensuing strategic battle would be to bring that dark image of Reagan below 40 per cent. Caddell's aim would be to keep the figure as high as possible, and the first chance to maintain it at close to 50 per cent was the Democratic Convention.

COSTING KENNEDY

"My name will not be placed in nomination," Kennedy said on television in the middle of the convention. He had finally conceded defeat to Carter after nine grueling months of campaigning, and the effect of the struggle showed for the first time.

The Senator fought to remain composed, but looked as if he might break down. The picture poignantly told the story of Kennedy's own belief in himself. Until that late point he had firmly maintained a faith and hope that he would somehow hang on and win. He had proved to himself and others watching his performance closely that he had the courage of his brothers. Despite the impact of Mudd's interview, the brilliant guerrilla tactics of Caddell in thwarting him in the primaries, and the lingering legacies of his personal shortcomings and mishaps, he had battled harder than any other losing candidate most Democrats could remember. Before he bowed out completely, however, he had his speech to deliver. It was the best performance of both conventions. Like Reagan, Kennedy was brilliant with the set-piece script, which he delivered with verve and style. Both may have groped inarticulately at times during press conferences, but with the programmed delivery to rehearse and read, each was unbeatable within his own party.

Caddell and Carter had been nervous about Kennedy's months of stubbornness, but now his speech set the tone for the fall campaign. At the peak of his delivery, with the audience gripped and silent, he waded into the enemy. "That nominee is no friend of labor!" he said, and was greeted by cheers. "That nominee is no friend of the cities!" he repeated on and on, issue after issue in the same derisive and attacking style. The audience roared their approval. Despite all the attempts of Carter, Mondale and others among the Democrats, Kennedy's confidence that night brought him closer to pinning down the elusive opposition candidate. A string of less impressive speakers, including Carter, went through the same ritual with less effect. Yet Caddell was pleased. His polls after the convention showed that the event had denied Reagan the 'acceptability threshold' of 40 per cent. A high proportion of people still felt uneasy about him. Even more comforting was Carter's comeback as indicated in Caddell's 'adjusted' figures. From a low for the year of 23 per cent support on 25 July which put him more than twenty points behind Reagan, he had come to within six points of the Republicans challenger just before the start of the national battle. In pollster parlance, that 6 per cent meant it was still anybody's race.

CHAPTER 13
THE COMPUTER CRUSADE

THE SEVEN CONDITIONS OF VICTORY

"We're on a crusade," Wirthlin told Grayling Achui early in the national campaign, "and that means sacrifices."

"I still really do not want to work on Sundays," Achui replied.

"The Lord has given us this opportunity," Wirthlin said quietly, "and we must make the best of it."

"I understand that, Dr Wirthlin, but I'm used to having Sunday off. I like to go to church, and then have a break."

"All right, Grayling," Wirthlin said. "I can appreciate that."

Wirthlin had wanted a seven-day week from the Mormon contingent. In August it moved from Utah to Arlington, Virginia – the Republican campaign headquarters for the national battle. Such was his determination to win the election for Reagan that in order to make the squad respond to the disciplined conduct which would be required, Wirthlin had engendered a kind of religious fervor about the Mormon endeavor. And apart from one or two who objected to working on Sunday, they seemed happy to meet his demands. They were a tightly knit group. As well as Wirthlin, Beal and Breglio from DMI, there were survey experts Craig King, Mario Hegewald, Kemp Harshman and Gary Lawrence. Grayling Achui was in charge of a smaller unit constantly monitoring PINS, and the whole team was ably assisted by the only women in the team, secretaries Susan McKinnon and Celeste Heritage (Celeste was the only non-Mormon). Their operation was backed up by other DMI operatives, and by the 300 trained interviewers who manned the phones and stalked the polling booths to gather the vital data used to drive the PINS engine. The rest of the Republican staff at HQ largely kept themselves separate from the Mormons, who seemed a world apart in their cramped offices in the unprepossessing and undersized building on Columbia Pike South next to a Macdonald's hamburger joint. The days were long and often stretched into night shifts. PINS analysis and research became a dedicated grind with little time for relaxation, which for most of the team merely consisted of breaks to eat at nearby Japanese, Korean, German and French restaurants. Although the young Mormons were happy to be away from the staid sanctity of Brigham Young, work was intense.

In March PINS had generated twenty-one 'conditions of victory' which were closely followed by the Reagan team. By the fall these had been whittled down to just seven. Two of the conditions were as much intuitive as indicated by the system. Wirthlin and co. did not need the computer to tell them that they should have a stronger organization then the Democrats in as many states as possible. Yet this was essential if the PINS operation was to work properly. Such strength could only be achieved by raising the funds necessary to buy the people and the technology to distribute the mail, man the telephones and get out the vote. Money had become no object as the Republican campaign focused on the November election. Between 1976 and 1980, the party had been instructed by politicians, lawyers and accountants in ways of circumventing restrictions which had become law since Watergate. Republican backers had been shell-shocked by Congress's 1974 Act which had greatly limited contributions to candidates from corporations and individuals, and in the 1976 presidential election the Democrats had the financial edge over the Republicans. But all that had changed for Reagan's 1980 bid. It was literally business as usual in the exchange of money for political favors. Businessmen with the right money and connections would be promised government positions such as overseas diplomatic postings, sometimes far beyond their capacities and experience. Such was the strength of the promised pay-offs in 1980 that the money-raisers in the Republican campaign did better than they ever did in the halcyon days of the Nixon campaigns before Watergate. This success made it easier for the Republicans to set up the strong state organizations that Wirthlin desired. He wanted to be able to push the button and see things happen the way PINS indicated they should, especially if Reagan had to make sudden campaign changes and swings which would see him whisked into any city anywhere in the country at short notice.

The other intuitive factor which was part of the 'conditions of victory' was the need to construct a counter-strategy to the anticipated 'October surprise'. This was the phrase coined by DMI's Gary Lawrence which referred to the possibility of Carter winning the election by bringing home the Americans held hostage in Iran – a move certain to greatly boost the President's popularity, if he could time it precisely. Carter's press conference on the morning of the Wisconsin primary in which he had inferred that he was on the brink of bringing them home had made the Republicans wary, and Wirthlin instructed Beal to make a complete analysis of such a ploy. PINS calibrated exactly when the return of the hostages would have its biggest impact. Several surveys were done to determine the nation's reaction to a chain of events which would see the hostages brought home at various times from September through October. Would people vote for Carter as a 'thank you' for his efforts? When would they become skeptical and regard it as a cynical political ploy? Beal rang Wirthlin at his McClean offices the moment he had made the calculations on PINS.

"Dick, it looks bad," Beal said. "The reading is that if Carter brings them back between 18 and 25 October, he will get a 10 per cent boost."

Wirthlin was stunned. "That much?" he said with anguish.

"'Fraid so. But the good news is that this figure slides away after that. The people become suspicious and cynical."

"And before 18 October?"

"It moves steadily up from now at a base of between 5 and 6 per cent."

Wirthlin was silent for a moment. "Rich," he said finally, "better tell Bill Casey we should start working up a counter-strategy right away. Ten per cent could sink us. We have to come up with tactics which will whittle that down, making the worst-case assumption that Carter could do something in that week of the 18th to the 25th."

Besides the organizational strength and the 'October surprise', the other five conditions of victory were indicated, monitored, guided and even controlled by PINS. The first of these was the indication that the campaign had to solidify the Republican base and also expand it among constituencies that offered a big chance of movement toward the Reagan column. These included blue-collars, Catholics and Southerners. The second PINS objective was that most resources should be poured into a small number of states that were considered key to capturing those coveted 270 electoral college votes. Florida, Texas, the West, Virginia and Iowa gave a base of 205. Once a combination such as this was secure, Reagan would have to pick up only 65 more, and Wirthlin would be relying on PINS to highlight the best grouping of states to collect those elusive 65. But this first PINS combination was also expected to change as the campaign progressed. Unforeseen circumstances, or even a brilliantly successful execution of strategy, could see the mix change dramatically. Thirdly, PINS indicated that the campaign should concentrate on the issue of leadership; fourthly, that the decision to attack Carter's weakness-es and the man himself should wait until precisely 70 per cent of the electorate thought that they understood Reagan and what he stood for politically. The fifth, totally PINS-directed condition was the decision to refrain from big media spending until the last ten to twenty days. This took faith, for the plan was to spend nearly seven million dollars in those last days. "I feel a little like those revolutionaries on Bunker Hill when they were asked to wait 'until you see the whites of their eyes' before firing," Wirthlin told

Breglio, who was in charge of scheduling media ads. "We'll take a lot of flak over this because there will be pressure on us to spend big earlier."

THE HUMAN FACTOR

By late August Wirthlin was not satisfied with progress in building Reagan's image. The negatives about his being 'dangerous and uncaring' were still alarmingly high, and in a memo to the campaign leaders the strategist instructed them to develop themes about a Reagan 'peace' posture. Just before the commencement of the fall campaign, he asked Reagan for a meeting at the Arlington Headquarters to impress upon the candidate the importance of developing a less aggressive manner in speaking of military issues.

Wirthlin, well aware of the candidate's dislike of early engagements, wisely scheduled Reagan for an 11.30 a.m. appointment. When he arrived flanked by guards he hurried through the busy offices of the Mormon squad who had all dressed a little snappier knowing that the candidate was due for a meeting that morning with the boss. Reagan glanced at the TV computer terminals and graph-plotters as the staff made their calculations. He acknowledged one or two of them with a nod and a wave and was bustled into a more private boardroom with the strategist. Wirthlin asked his secretary, Celeste, to bring Reagan coffee (plenty of milk, no sugar). They sat at a boardroom table and Wirthlin began by telling him of the 'warmonger' image. Reagan pulled a face. His eyes bulged and he puffed out his cheeks. "The 'mad bomber' problem, eh?" he said. "Won't Carter ever give up on that one?"

Wirthlin laughed and then added more seriously, "I don't think so, Governor. It's very important to their strategy."

"Well, godammit, that makes me mad!" Reagan said, feigning anger. "Oops, not allowed to look that way, right?"

"Right," Wirthlin said, and handed Reagan the memo he had sent to other key advisers. "Governor, we've done quite a lot of analysis on this," he said, "and there are a few key phrases and words that you should try to insert in your speeches, whatever you say . . ."

Reagan slipped on his glasses. "We are not a warlike people," he read, and repeated the expression as if he was recording it. He continued: "Quite the opposite. We always seek to live in peace. We resort to force infrequently and with great reluctance – of all the objectives we seek, first and foremost is the establishment of world peace."

"Governor, phrases like that will help us a great deal . . ."

"It's a little stronger – weaker – than my convention speech . . ."

"Well, we have to hammer this theme home because Carter will be doing exactly the opposite," Wirthlin said. "We must drop your 'negatives' considerably. You have to speak in terms of promoting international stability with an aim toward world peace. I've listed a few examples there. Rather than a 'defense posture', we should use the term 'peace posture'. We should avoid references to the 'arms race', but stress the need to re-establish 'the margin of safety'."

"Margin of safety," Reagan repeated, savoring the expression. "I like that."

"All you really have to do is speak in a reasoned and non-strident way – even when you are talking about the Carter administration's likelihood of increasing the risk of war by its poor leadership."

"And you want to see all my speeches . . ."

"Well, I think we have to tighten up," Wirthlin said. "We can't afford to have the opposition or the press pounce on anything."

"You mean you want me to 'stick to the script'," Reagan said.

"Not just you, Governor," Wirthlin said, "all of us."

Wirthlin didn't quite know how to tell Reagan not to insert too many of his own little anecdotes into speeches, especially if they were out of sync with overall strategy. The strategist knew that the candidate liked to please his audiences, as he had ever since his days at General Electric when he learned to love the ringing applause he would get for his 'speech' – the address on the virtues of 'free enterprise' that he had carried through his public career. But too much ad-libbing by Reagan now, Wirthlin feared, could upset the program. He wanted the candidate to be a constant in the PINS equation, not a variable. It pleased the strategist to hear the candidate say he would 'stick to the script'. Yet he had been on nearly four campaigns with Reagan and he knew how difficult it was at times to restrain his speeches. The candidate was more reliable if he was required to act out a certain emotion. This called for a disciplined performance, and Wirthlin was confident that there had never been a politician who could deliver the appropriate pose as convincingly as Reagan. The strategist expected him to prove in the next two months that he was indeed 'the greatest media candidate' of all time. For it was those little gestures of emotion – the wrinkled grin, the rollicking laugh, the angry frown, the indignant grimace, the sly wink, the glistening eye of sadness, the hurtful shrug – that added so much to Reagan's skill as a politician. It wasn't just acting, but also knowing how to hold and subtly influence any audience, live or unseen. Over years of campaigning he had learned to perfect his skills, and now he was preparing a performance with the ambition of eventually gaining his greatest role. Yet he was not the puppet his critics and the Carter campaign were trying to paint him. Nor was he a robot. Wriggling inside the sack of campaign strictures, the real Ronald Reagan wanted to get out. He had a file full of half-fictional stories with which to make his political points. Wirthlin and others had so far failed to make him see that there was a sophisticated press waiting and hungry for his sometimes mindless, often meaningless homilies. No matter how much they liked Reagan, the media covering a Presidential campaign were not going to let him get away with half-truths and unverifiable distortions of fact.

There was, however, a rapport between the media people and the candidate, although he was often uncomfortable with them. He was too polite not to answer a question, and not afraid to hold an impromptu press conference, and this helped maintain his popularity with journalists who tended not to like Carter. Many thought the President cold and aloof or even unctious at times. He was not a natural back-slapper or teller of jokes. At heart, he wasn't 'one of the boys'. There was an intellectuality about him that did not endear him to some members of the press who despised such traits. But Reagan's relative popularity did not spare him some biting criticism in August. The high-rating CBS evening national news program anchored by Walter Kronkite ran a short but damaging documentary on Reagan's 'inaccuracies'. Using a split-screen technique, they showed the candidate making a questionable point. The shot would be frozen and shifted to the left. The commentator would say 'wrong' and the facts would appear on the right. After several examples had appeared, Reagan was interviewed about the errors, and he squirmed his way through answers in a less convincing way than he had when answering the question about the Polish joke in the first TV debate in the New Hampshire primary. Back at Arlington, Wirthlin, Meese and Casey sweated.

"We've got to do something about this," the usually benign Meese said agitatedly.

"You've seen the memo," Wirthlin said with an exasperated gesture as he flicked off the TV set, "and I have spoken to the Governor."

"That sort of thing," Casey mumbled in his bullfrog manner, "could wreck the whole campaign."

"We need someone on board the plane with him all the time," Wirthlin said, "someone he'll listen to."

Casey started cleaning his glasses, and grunted, which was usually the signal for another comment. "Why can't we have a roster of senators and congressmen rotate on the plane?" he asked. The others silently ignored this suggestion.

"It's got to be someone like Stu Spencer," Wirthlin said.

Meese shook his fleshy jowls vigorously. "Don't think Nancy would like that," he said, "not after Stu's performance in '76 with Ford against the Governor."

Soon after the CBS mini-fiasco, Reagan told a live audience that some noxious materials in the air "might be beneficial to tubercular patients. The breezes that blew off an oil slick on the Santa Barbara coast around the turn of the century, purified the air and prevented the spread of infectious diseases." In another speech, the concerned-looking candidate suggested that "growing and decaying vegetation is responsible for 93 per cent of the oxides of nitrogen abroad in the environment." Reagan had confused nitrous oxide, the natural product of plant respiration, with nitrogen dioxide, a government-regulated pollutant. It invited ridicule, and he was greeted in some states with placards pinned to trees that said: "Chop me down before I kill again".

The candidate was against regulation of industry, and not much concerned about environmental pollution. He would look for every tiny 'factoid' in the obscure right-wing magazines that he read which backed up his views. He felt that added vivid 'weight' to his anti-big government themes wrapped in the basic line, "get Government off the backs of people and industry . . ." which he used repeatedly in the campaign. Reagan's dubious statements had always been coupled with his great skill as a story-teller. He could conjure powerful images of incidents, some of which had never occurred, but which were useful in his role as a performer-communicator-persuader-salesman.

Yet it wasn't just this propensity to slip a doubtful line into one of his speeches that troubled the strategists. He was also straying from the agreed policy lines that Wirthlin and the rest of the team had tested against PINS to see if they should be played up or down, or avoided. One major issue was China. Reagan had always been ambivalent about Communist China, and he told newsmen in August that he still recognized Taiwan. "I want to re-establish official relations between the US Government and Taiwan," he told reporters at Dulles airport. This not only contradicted recent changes in public opinion, but was said at a time when vice-presidential candidate George Bush was being dispatched to Peking to give the appearance that a new Reagan administration would strengthen US ties with China. Reagan could have avoided the issue, but his impetuosity over a gut hatred of Communism per se, and a sense of loyalty to Taiwan – an old American ally – got the better of him.

'Bloopers', as the pouncing press called the candidate's misplaced, off-the-cuff remarks, were becoming a daily event in the last weeks of August, and the lull period before the campaign began in earnest in September was proving damaging. Wirthlin moved quickly and arranged for Reagan's speeches to be written in time for clearance by himself and others who knew the exact script as prescribed by the PINS programming. Scheduling and advance work were revised accordingly and Wirthlin hired Ron Walker, who had been Nixon's chief advance man, for just that purpose with the Reagan drive. But the problems increased on 22 August when Reagan flew to Dallas to speak to a national meeting of evangelists. When his address was over he was surrounded by a gaggle of newspeople, and while aides struggled to push him away, several reporters started asking questions. It quickly became an impromptu press conference.

"How do you feel about the theory of evolution?" one woman from a local TV station asked.

"Ah, there are great flaws in the theory of evolution," Reagan said carefully, not wanting to upset his hosts, who could help with the right-wing fundamentalists and Born-Again Christian vote. He then added, "Perhaps the schools should teach the creationist theory as well." The candidate had tried to have it both ways, something he had done when necessary ever since those awkward Hollywood days in the late 1940s when he had astutely walked the tightrope between left-wingers on one side and witch-hunters on the other. On this occasion the media and his opposition jumped on his statement and, citing the evidence of the daily bloopers, implied that he might not be intelligent enough to hold down the nation's toughest job.

A few days after the creationist comment, Reagan was speaking at the Michigan State Fair. He was reading diligently from the script when he noticed a female Carter supporter near the front of a big crowd. She began heckling him. Reagan looked away from the script.

"Now I'm happy to be here," he said with obvious irritation, "while Carter is opening his campaign down there in the city that gave birth to, and is the parent body of, the Ku Klux Klan."

When his speech was over, he hurried to a waiting car to avoid the press. As it sped away, his press secretary Lyn Nofziger said, "You know that remark . . ."

"I know, I know," Reagan said, waving his hand and sighing heavily. "I should never said it."

"It was wrong, Governor," Nofziger said, lighting a cigar in quiet exasperation. "First of all Tuscumbia, Alabama, is not the home of the Klan. It didn't give birth to it. Second, Carter was heckled by the Klan yesterday, and he attacked them."

"It was just a dumb thing to say," Reagan said, shaking his head. "I'll have to apologize to the Governor of Alabama."

"And the Mayor of Tuscumbia," Nofziger said. "Boy, are the press gonna give us shit for this!"

Reagan and his entourage flew on to Wexford, Virginia, where he had rented an estate for the campaign's duration, and that night Nancy Reagan spoke to her husband about all the mistakes that had occurred. They agreed that a professional political operative should join the campaign plane to make sure Reagan did not stray from the set script. They both knew that no one could do this better than Stu Spencer, so they decided to bury the hatchet and enlist him.

Wirthlin rang the veteran Californian consultant, who had been acting on a part-time basis for the Reagan campaign since July, and he agreed immediately to join the candidate on all his scheduled trips. Spencer arrived at Republican HQ a few days before commencement of the fall battle, and stopped in at the offices of the Mormon team to be briefed by Wirthlin. Achui was sitting in front of a terminal TV screen watching a graph trace itself out when Spencer leaned over his shoulder. "Hey, what's this?" he inquired.

Achui was pleased at the opportunity to explain it to him, for he knew of Spencer's reputation as one of the nation's most respected political operatives.

"This is a simulation of the Governor's vote in New York right now," Achui said and then began explaining what he meant.

But Spencer didn't seem to be listening. "We used computers in the sixties," he said interjecting wistfully. "We could analyze the way districts voted or intended to vote. When we knew that, we hit the fuckers with the right message. My company was the first to do it."

"Yes," Achui said slowly, "but this is far more . . ."

Spencer had turned on his way to Wirthlin's office. "Hi, Rich," he said, acknowledging Beal. "Who's your computer say is going to win? Anderson?"

Beal laughed, and watched Spencer disappear into Wirthlin's office.

Achui turned to Beal. "So that was Spencer," he said, in surprise. "You know, he only picked up on one little aspect of PINS. He didn't understand it."

"Well, that doesn't matter," Beal said with a shrug.

"He doesn't have to know. He has a very important job on the plane. He'll be able to control the Governor and make sure he stays close to the script. Stu's also popular with the press and knows how to use them."

"Got a little job for you," Casey said, as he greeted Robert Garrick, a high-powered Californian public relations man, into his second floor office in the Arlington HQ. "Dick Wirthlin says that bringing the hostages back from Iran could mean a 10 per cent swing to Carter. We want you to monitor every damn thing Carter is doing about Iran. It's a 'hostage watch'."

"You mean stay in touch with the families of the hostages?. . ."

"Yeah. You can check them for advance word of their release," Casey mumbled rapidly. Only an acquaintance like Garrick could understand all he said, so smothered in grunts were his utterances. "You can, you know, use all your military contacts to keep an eye on movements of aircraft, such as big C-5A transporters on the East coast."

"Anything that could make a fast trip to Iran."

"Right. Planes, that could, for instance, transport impounded shipments of fighter plane spare parts which could be used in a trade for the hostages. You can use some of our staff here to check the tail numbers of planes."

"Who do we have for that?"

"Some first-rate people with CIA training. They came across with Baker and Bush when they joined our campaign."

CHAPTER 14
PINS AND NEEDLES

THE MEANNESS FACTOR

"The election will help decide whether we have peace or war,"
Jimmy Carter said, in the opening remarks on his first campaign
stop in California early in October. The President had been forced
out of the Oval Office to campaign, and these remarks caused the
press in a packed high school gymnasium in Los Angeles to snap
out of their collective reverie. There was a scribble of shorthand, a
playing of tape recorders, a sudden increase in the whirr of
cameras, and then a chaotic rush to find phones. Jimmy 'nice guy'
had turned tough. He was actually saying that choosing Reagan for
the Presidency would mean war.

To be absolutely certain no one missed the point, Carter
repeated the statement at another stop two hours later, and so
began a series of concerted broadsides aimed at upturning
Reagan's election bid. The tactic had its seeds in Caddell's findings
in May and June, which said nearly half the nation thought Reagan
was a dangerous 'hip-shooter'. But there was one significant
deviation. The President himself was going after the challenger.
Normally such a burden would be borne by surrogates – the
Vice-President, cabinet members and other party functionaries.
Richard Nixon, for instance, had done this with great success in
1972 by using administration officials to rebuke challenger George
McGovern, for whom Caddell was working at the time. Officials
acted as hatchet men, usually in response to a McGovern attack or
claim, and so kept Nixon above the sordid battlefield of the
campaign. Nixon simply sat back in the Rose Garden and acted
presidential.

Unfortunately for Carter, many of his key administrators felt
the 1980 fall campaign should be fought on the Government's
record. This would have meant spending much time on explaining
accomplishments to the nation, which had an in-built skepticism to
the administration's efforts. The economy was not helping their
feelings. Caddell had won the battle against those backing the
record, and had convinced Carter that it was impossible to mount
an effective support for it in such a short time. Instead he put
forward the 'attack Reagan' strategy. Carter liked it more as he
became increasingly frustrated watching Reagan, however falter-
ingly, build his claim to being capable of taking over the Oval
Office. Although Reagan's lead in the polls had sunk gradually
through September, he still led going into October. This irked the

President, who had little regard for Reagan's intellect and policies and was annoyed to think it possible that the Republican could beat him. At a meeting in Carter's small hideaway study in which he preferred to work rather than the larger, more accessible, Oval Office, Caddell went through his latest poll findings on the perception of the two candidate's characters.

"Half of California think Reagan's a 'hip-shooter'!" Carter said as he ran his finger down a column which showed each state's attitudes. "It's his own state!"

"That's encouraging," Caddell agreed. "We can afford to hit really hard."

Carter nodded. "I've got to get into this," he said. The strategist could see what he called the 'Bantam rooster quality' rising in the President as he added, "I think I'll enjoy it."

"You can afford to tarnish your image a little," Caddell told him. "It's so strong at the moment."

"Anyway, it won't matter if I can do the job on Reagan," Carter said with quiet aggression. "We can knock him right out of it." Caddell noticed a glint in Carter's eye as he smiled coldly.

"If you push his warmonger image through 50 per cent," Caddell said enthusiastically, "the damage to Reagan could be irreparable . . ."

Despite the desire for battle, however, there was one major drawback – the President's method. Somewhere between the tactical idea and the execution of the attacks, the message was not as incisive as the Carter team would have liked. It may have had something to do with the President's slightly maudlin twang and the sing-song cadence of his words. Or perhaps it was his uninspiring manner. Delivery and style, in fact, were problems that had dogged Carter perpetually. Although he was a disciplined, successful campaigner in general, he was not capable of really firing either a live or a TV audience. Carter regarded himself as a man far better suited to matters of substance, and he enjoyed tackling the big problems of Government. He had the intellect to grapple with large conceptual problems like the Middle East crisis, and to work hard toward solutions. He may not have brought to the Presidency the vision of a Richard Nixon on foreign policy, or the worldly education of a John Kennedy, or the political skills of an LBJ, or the punch of a Harry Truman. Yet he did have an excellent cerebral capacity and the precision-like mind of an engineer, which by training he was. But following through on a fine-tuned strategy with real finesse and showmanship was beyond him. No matter how much he jumped up and down, or banged his fist, he could not bring a crowd to fever pitch. Campaigning at its best was too much like acting, and while he could carry much in his head and repeat it all, often the impact simply was not there. Even if he believed what he was saying about Reagan, his words were not forceful, and therefore appeared less credible. As he attacked, the media began analyzing Carter's character rather than examining the possibility of the message's veracity.

As Carter stepped up the attacks, Caddell tracked their effect with his polls. Should the President be held back, stopped, or told to kick harder?

"We see it as dead even," Paul Maslin, his assistant told him in his Pennsylvania office. He was in his mid-twenties, another of the short-in-the-tooth pollsters. "Jimmy's doing well. He has lost a couple of points in terms of his positive image, but Reagan is still way up there on negatives."

Caddell frowned. "The thing is," he said, stroking his beard, "how do we play it now? I have a feeling he is going to go too far. I told him to frame it all carefully."

"That's the way of all candidates, isn't it," Maslin said. "Once they get into it, they overrun."

"Yeah," Caddell nodded, staring ahead, "they do have minds of their own."

At a Chicago fundraiser reception in the backyard of a Democratic supporter's mansion the next day, Carter was speaking to the assembled politicians; there was a group of press people roped off in one corner. To the candidate's embarrassment, after a minute of his address, many people resumed their conversations and small talk.

"Your votes will decide . . ." Carter said more stridently than was necessary for this audience which was exclusively Democrat, ". . . whether Americans might be separated black from white, Jew from Christian, North from South, rural from urban."

There was a hushed silence.

"Jesus," said one press man, "does he mean it?"

"Who the hell cares?" another replied. "He said it, and it's white hot!"

SCENE ONE: ACT HURT

At Arlington HQ Wirthlin was delighted. Carter and Caddell had fallen into a trap the Republican strategist had set for them as long ago as June. For several weeks now the media had been warned by Republican party operatives including Wirthlin, Lazalt, Nofziger, Spencer, Deaver, Casey and Meese that Carter would exhibit 'the meanness factor', a phrase coined to depict the attacks by the President on Reagan. Wirthlin and his team had calculated that

Caddell would be left with very few options in the fall campaign, and one of them would almost certainly be an all-out effort to 'demonize' the Republican candidate. The surprise for Wirthlin was the intensity of the Democrats' efforts and also the fact that Carter himself was vociferously spearheading the strategy. Surrogates had been expected to carry the main attack. But they were not receiving the media attention required to make the strategy work. Even Vice-President Mondale, who was saying tougher things than the President, was not getting big coverage. So Carter had entered the fray, and this certainly did galvanize the media. Until October of his fourth year in office Carter had managed to maintain his image as a nice, religious, honest, sincere and fair man. Even when he criticized Kennedy, it appeared to be just sniping. But now Carter was machine-gunning Reagan, and that was big news.

Wirthlin's task was to make sure Reagan responded accordingly. He rang Spencer, who was with the candidate campaigning in Ohio.

"Ron is mad," Spencer said. "He is really riled up about Carter."

"You've got to restrain him," Wirthlin said. "Tell him I've already picked up some cracks in Carter's image. If the Governor attacks back at this stage it will be premature and give credence to some of Carter's claims."

"Don't worry, Dick," Spencer said, "he's ready to 'aw shucks' it. He's geared for it. Ron will stick to the script. He'll play the sad, wounded bear at a press conference this morning."

Wirthlin had also found that Carter's attacks were influencing Reagan's image. He was still seen as dangerous, and Wirthlin felt that if Reagan could be seen as uncombative under pressure from Carter, then it would be the beginning of the drop in the Republican's darker image. The press conference in Ohio would be an important test.

Reagan did not let his strategist down. When a reporter asked him what he thought of Carter's remarks in Chicago, the candidate responded in a manner worthy of the Oscar he never received in Hollywood. While inwardly seething over the attacks he said: "I can't be angry. I'm saddened that anyone, particularly someone who had held that position, could intimate such a thing." With head tilted and face creased in a frown of despondency, he added, "I'm not asking for an apology from him. I know who I have to account to for my actions. But I think he owes the country an apology." There was much pity and sorrow in his voice, but no bitterness. It was a tactical masterstroke, and a definite turning point for the fortunes of the campaign. Reagan for the first time had looked more worthy of the Presidency than the incumbent, and the timing was nearly perfect for Wirthlin's strategy. Within weeks he wanted to build Reagan's credibility to a point where he could begin the counter-attack against Carter.

At the end of the first week in October, Wirthlin began evaluating the unusually concentrated battle of the negatives. He was not surprised to find Reagan still struggling with his image. The strategist expected this to soften as the full impact of the PINS strategy worked its way into the psyche of the nation through media messages, the press, media and speeches. The number of people who found the Republican candidate 'dangerous and uncaring' had dropped only marginally, to 44 per cent. However, the strategist was now reading the start of an erosion of Carter's 'nice guy' image with such statements as: "Carter will tell the truth even if it hurts him politically to do so." Several months ago PINS had indicated that this decrease would be important to a Reagan victory, and by end of the first week in October, with a little more than three weeks until the election, the system was showing signs of being accurate. Yet PINS calculations were a silent, slow business which required much patience, and even more faith, in the operation. Not everyone shared the Mormons' belief in PINS as Carter drew even with Reagan in the polls. At the end of one high-level meeting, a key Reagan aide traveling with the candidate on the plane took Breglio to a quiet room in the Arlington HQ building. Locking the door behind him, he turned to the strategist and said, "You don't really expect us to believe you and Dick, do you? You're the only people saying that Carter's catch-up is only temporary. Many polls outside are telling us Carter is already ahead. What gives, Vince?"

Breglio had just updated the candidate and all the main advisers on how well the strategy was doing, assuring them that it would soon pay dividends. He had sensed some shifty-eyed reaction from several skeptics. "We know what we are doing," Breglio said.

"Well, I'm bloody pleased for you, because some of us don't," the aide replied.

"Be patient," Breglio said coolly. "Our strategy is based on a whole range of things dovetailing in the last weeks and days. If you want to join the panic merchants, then do."

"I'm not panicking," the aide said.

"Well, if you're not, it's a very good impression!" Breglio said goodnaturedly.

The aide was still dissatisfied. "Another thing," he said. "Some of the guys are worried about our advertising."

"We know it's bland," Breglio said, "but that's deliberate. We want Reagan straight-to-camera."

"I'd say dull rather than bland."

"You're comparing it too much with the Democrats' ads. We know they look more professional. We know they are more slickly phrased. But this isn't a competition to see who can deliver the best smart-ass line about the opposition. When you have a strategy like ours those things are trivial. Our ads fit our overall plan."

"In 1976 we used some of the best advertising ever," the aide persisted. He had worked for Ford in the last presidential election.

"And you lost," Breglio said softly. "We are going to win."

The aide stared back. "We would like to see some evidence of it," he said coldly.

"You may not for some time," Breglio replied. "Strategies like ours take time to work through. We have not designed it to win on day one, because day one doesn't count. Everything we are doing is designed to weave together in the last days."

"Vince, a lot of people just don't believe in Dick and his magical computer system."

"There's nothing magical about it. It just imposes discipline on our methods. The computer makes us more systematic, and allows us to integrate all the thousands of variables going on out there that no single mind can keep track of."

"But what if the computer is wrong, Vince? What are you going to tell us the day after Reagan is beaten? 'Oh, gee, sorry folks, the computer didn't work right.' Is that it?"

"It won't be the computer's fault," Breglio said. "It will be ours."

The aide nodded almost imperceptibly, and then unlocked the door. "I just hope you guys are on the right track," he said with a sigh. "There's a lot riding on a Reagan victory."

Breglio immediately reported the criticism to Wirthlin and found him in a foul mood, which was out of character. Even he was beginning to feel the pressure, Breglio thought.

"Have you seen the godammed papers this morning?" Wirthlin demanded angrily. "Not only are we getting flak for our polls and strategy, some bastard in the building is leaking very confidential stuff."

He handed Breglio a copy of the *Washington Post* and a clipping from the *New York Times*. Breglio read them, and shook his head in anguish. "Well, I can tell you it wasn't me."

"It must've been someone!" Wirthlin said. He marched out of his office and into where the Mormon squad was working.

"Which one of you miserable assholes leaked this stuff to the *Post*?" Wirthlin raged. His outburst startled all of them. They had respected the boss for being a perfectionist, but they had never seen him lose his temper or swear. "Come on!" he persisted, "which damned traitor has been spilling stuff to reporters?"

When several of them protested their innocence, Wirthlin stormed out, slamming the door behind him. Achui turned to Beal who just shook his head in surprise. "What was that all about?" Achui half-whispered.

"God, I don't know," Beal said. "Everything seems to be cracking up. The *Post* reported not only a secret DMI poll, but some pretty knowledgeable insider interpretation."

"We gotta mole?"

Beal took a deep breath and began tapping an instruction into the computer terminal. "Must be," he said, "and I don't want to be there when Dick gets his hands on the guy's throat."

Two hours later, Wirthlin returned looking decidedly sheepish. He apologized humbly to all of them. "I had lunch with the reporter yesterday – not realizing that everything I told him would be used," he said humbly. "I'm afraid I was the leak!"

With pressure mounting from both inside and outside the Reagan campaign, Wirthlin thought it best to go public to back his claims that Carter was not leading in the race. He was concerned that confidence in the Reagan camp could diminish as criticism of the campaign mounted, and there was also the credibility of his own position. The strategist was secure enough about his planning and the kind of strategy he was trying to direct. But because PINS was unobtrusive, and less colorful than past methods, the press demanded action and accountability for Reagan's slippage as reported by the continual daily 'horse race' polls, which were nowhere as accurate or probing as DMI's. Gone were the days when consultants and party functionaries met daily to discuss tactics and decide where they might send the candidate in the afternoon. The computer-driven strategy had programmed the candidate's plans weeks in advance, while still reserving the flexibility to change them within hours.

At a packed press conference in a New York hotel, Wirthlin began by explaining the precarious position for Reagan across the nation. Out of the seven big states of California, Pennsylvania, Illinois, Texas, Ohio, New York and Michigan, Reagan was behind in the last three. California, his home state, was a worry. He only had a three point lead there. Ohio was also of particular concern because PINS originally had indicated it as a 'must win' state for Reagan. While Wirthlin was explaining this, some of the journalists had been examining the press releases which showed the breakdown of the state voting support for each candidate, and the suggested electoral college voter tallies, which showed Reagan just ahead. One journalist interrupted Wirthlin.

"These figures don't seem to add up," he said. The strategist stepped down from the podium to put the matter right, but he too became confused. There did seem to be something wrong with the additions of state groupings. Beal, who had set up the conference, grabbed a press release and slipped out a door to a small adjoining room. The problem set the reporters off and the questioning became intense.

"Why is it that your poll findings are so much at variance with everyone else's?" one reporter asked.

"Hasn't it always been the case that your role is to put a rosier perspective on the figures for your candidate?" another questioned.

Wirthlin quietly defended his position. "There would be no point in me giving the candidate the wrong impression," he said. "I have to give him accurate information."

Beal read and reread the press release, trying desperately to find the error, but he could not. Another member of the Mormon squad joined him. "Heck," he said despondently, "they're beating Dick up royally in there." At last Beal found the simple error made by a typist copying the data coming out of PINS. But he was too late. The conference had been a disaster and the reporters left unconvinced, and if anything confused at a higher level.

"He'll never forgive me for this," Beal mumbled to Breglio as he prepared to explain the error.

BREAK IN THE SOUTH

Morale in the Mormon squad had reached its low point in the campaign by 7 October and it was not helped by the initial readings of PINS for each state's predicted voting. It was 4.24 p.m. and Beal and Achui were running simulations of fresh data coming in. New York made them wince in despair. Reagan was still a yawning 12 per cent behind Carter there. That major block of electorate college votes was all but a write-off. Ohio still looked bad for Reagan, so did Missouri. The researchers were both looking at small TV terminals which traced out on the screen the way the votes for Reagan, Carter and Anderson were moving. The graph's vertical axis marked the percentage vote for each candidate, while the horizontal axis indicated the date. Simultaneously, an electronic graph plotter linked to the terminals traced out the jagged lines on paper.

"Hey!" Beal suddenly exclaimed as he looked over at the 'arm' on Achui's plotter. It was tracing out the vote for Mississippi. "Reagan's level there! He's got him!"

"I was about to check it," Achui said, less enthusiastically, for Mississippi was a small state with few electoral college votes.

"But I've just done Tennessee," Beal said excitedly, as he typed in an instruction to trace out Louisiana. "Reagan has edged closer there too."

Both men glanced at each other, aware of the implications of a possible trend if other Southern states showed a similar increase for their candidate. They watched intently as the arm moved laboriously and wrote LOUISIANA in the right-hand corner of the graph paper. The arm then swept down to the left axis and began its trace. First, yellow, for Anderson. It chattered its way slowly, almost touching the bottom line horizontal axis. Anderson, who would finally secure 5-10 per cent of the national vote, was predictably nowhere in this state. The red line for Carter followed. The trace began high and arrogantly, for this was not too far from the President's home territory and was part of Caddell's brilliant strategy of 1976. Then it dipped, recovered and dipped again. Back the arm went to the left for the Reagan trace in blue. It started about half way down the vertical axis, well below Carter and took a nose dive heading for the yellow Anderson line. Then it climbed like a sluggish World War Two bomber toward the red. It dipped, dived, picked up suddenly and finally edged up. Beal gave a yell of anticipation, for his experienced eye told him that there was a definite and consistent increase in that last gradient. Eventually the blue line peaked and stopped just above the red. "Hot dog!" Achui cried while Beal looked closely at the graph and then requested a hard copy of the straight figures on the vote since the beginning of the campaign a month ago. It was quite clear. Not only was Reagan 2 per cent ahead of Carter in Louisiana, the graph told the picture of the steady trend toward the challenger. They then ran the simulations on Alabama, Kentucky, Arkansas, South Carolina and several other Southern states. The break to Reagan was statistically small but widespread and definitive.

Beal scurried to a phone to alert Wirthlin who had joined the campaign plane for a brief time. The strategist decided they had to move fast. This certainly looked as if the PINS strategy was beginning to show itself up for the first time in an area vital to both candidates. The Southern bloc had been solid Carter country since 1976. Now, suddenly, definite cracks had formed in an edifice which was in Carter's own backyard. Wirthlin's tactic here was to consolidate the break, because it would be a psychological blow to Carter. After explaining his move to those on the plane who feared that Reagan's drive had lost momentum, Wirthlin ordered a campaign blitz. The plane was to make new stops in the South, and Breglio started buying peak time in the media in specific cities. Half a dozen states were going to be hit with Ronald Reagan's 'talking ahead'. He would speak straight-to-camera in spots of thirty seconds, six seconds, five minutes and even half an hour. Wirthlin was after the wavering 'undecideds' in the Southern states who may have voted Democrat and for Carter in the past. The trickle of support for Reagan could fast become a flood. Bill Timmons was asked to mobilize the different state organizations ready for the campaign thrust and a Reagan visit.

This sudden Southern assault perplexed some of the aides on board the campaign plane. Why was the candidate being sent to these states at this critical time when his whole effort seemed to have lost thrust? Why hit relatively small towns when a much bigger effort could be made in Chicago or even Manhattan? When confronted with these grumbles, Wirthlin tried to explain his moves by saying the election strategy was a game of probabilities. Given the risk, you put the campaign resources where the pay-off gave the largest number of electoral votes. He liked to use a gambling analogy, and would say it was as if a gambler had to put so many chips on so many squares. When he saw the vote moving Reagan's way in the Southern states, he planned to take some of his chips away from the big Midwest states and Pennsylvania, and put them right into Carter's backyard – Louisiana, Alabama, Kentucky, Arkansas and others. The hope and risk was that eventually the bet would pay off on both numbers – more immediately in the South, and when success of the PINS strategy began to show itself, in the Midwest and Pennsylvania as well. Timing was critical. If there was panic and no method, money could be thrown at important states before the other effects of PINS – media reports, advertising, surrogates' speeches and the general thrust of the strategy – came through. It would be much more effective, for instance, to attempt to take New York very late in the campaign. That state had rejected the challenger so far and it was going to take time for the character perceptions of the candidates to form more fully. If Carter was seen as 'mean', and Reagan as less of a warmonger and more of a leader, then Reagan could perhaps make a late stop in New York and attack his opponent, backed by a hugh media blitz. But in early October, according to Wirthlin, that would have been a big waste of time and resources. Reagan's candidacy just did not have credibility there and in other states, yet.

The Arlington HQ strategists found this philosophy difficult to explain to those on the plane who were experiencing the hectic rush of take-offs and landings. The press on board didn't help because they easily became disgruntled and bored. Numbed by having to listen to the basic Reagan speech up to seven times a day, they were hungry for 'excitement' in the form of a head-on debate between the two combatants.

CHAPTER 15

BATTLE OF THE BOX

DEBATE DEBATE

With his bearded face a map of constant harassment, an overweight Caddell hurried past the White House security guards at the southeast gate, his permanent pass flopping in the breeze. A battered briefcase dangled from one hand, and under his arm were several folders which carried evidence about his attitude to a debate which he was about to put with characteristic cogency and logic to the President. It was 11 October, and media pressure was mounting for a nationally televised confrontation between Carter and Reagan. Caddell was against it. He gave Carter only a 25 per cent chance of winning, and was about to tell him he thought it dangerous. It would give Reagan a platform in front of a huge audience, and this could shatter Caddell's own carefully constructed plan for victory.

Caddell had been aiming at keeping Reagan below the 'threshold of acceptability' but a special TV debate forum would enable him to pose as presidential. The cameras could dispel the spookiness about his 'bomb-thrower' image, which the Democratic strategist had worked so hard to maintain. No matter how Reagan gaffed, Caddell knew that he would be able to act benign. And he could well come across looking better than the President, especially in delivery. Carter had really only been effective as a speaker when he gave a sermon in his local Plains church. There he inspired the smaller audience, and the locals hung on, and understood, his every word. Outside that setting, however, he often sounded elliptical. It was something he could not avoid, and it would sound most glaring when contrasted directly to Reagan's smoother style. The Republican had made a career out of plain speaking as opposed to speaking in Plains.

Caddell claimed that to win this debate – in other words, have a long-term impact – Carter had to win most decisively, and the strategist thought that was impossible against Reagan. Caddell had explained this to Carter and the other advisers, but the President had left himself without options by not debating Kennedy in the primaries and by saying earlier, when challenged by the press, that he would debate Reagan. There was no way of avoiding a contest. The only slim hope was that Reagan would shy away too, which would have suited Caddell perfectly.

Meanwhile, the Democrats hammered away at the challenger's image. Rafshoon had been running TV ads showing man-in-the-street interviews saying that if Reagan had been President for the past four years "he would have gotten us into a war by now". Others called him 'scary'. Still more ads had clips of Reagan making statements about the arms race, followed by Carter commenting that the business of running the Presidency was never a matter of "dealing with another shoot-out at the OK Corral". This ad was run often in California, Reagan's home state, where the election was very close and Caddell was reading that his strategy of keeping up the doubts about Reagan were working. By mid-October the strategist had Carter consistently ahead. According to Caddell's calculations there was no need to debate. Carter was going to win.

Wirthlin's PINS reading was that Carter only slipped into the lead briefly on 14 October when he went two points ahead. The Republican strategist was firmly convinced that this was only a temporary bump in the national picture. Far more important was that Reagan had never been behind in electoral college votes, and Wirthlin predicted the candidate would soon begin to make real impact across the nation. The strategist too was reading that *his* candidate was the front-runner, and front-runners had no need to debate. He thought it was futile, short-term thinking to go into the 'underdog' or 'defense mode' and risk all in front of eighty million viewers. The PINS analysis in fact was indicating to Wirthlin that his strategy was working itself through mostly on target. Two days after Carter had the lead in the national vote, Reagan had it back again, and the margin was six points which meant a jump of eight points in Reagan's favor in just two days. The sceptics and gut politicians in the Reagan camp wanted to know how Wirthlin explained such a change of fortunes. He told them it was because voters had not liked Carter's Christian-against-Jews, North-versus-South outburst in Chicago, and that the impact of this had taken several days to pervade the electorate. "It takes a week to get secondary coverage in the press and media," he claimed, "and this, coupled with the growing impact of the PINS strategy, worked strongly in the Governor's favor."

However, the fact that Carter had been reported in the lead for a brief period (14 October) did the damage, along with the continued problems of the big industrial states – Ohio, Illinois and Pennsylvania. A great sense of urgency developed on the plane and the candidate's advisers, including Nofziger and Spencer, worried about it openly with Reagan and some members of the press. Reporters realized that they might be on to some thrills at last and some began baying louder for a TV contest – a toe-to-toe slug out. A drama was being built out of no crisis at all, according to the cooler heads at Arlington. When Wirthlin learned of the pressure building up for the debate, he told all the advisers: "You are putting a lot of political capital on the table for an hour and a half of TV." They wanted to know if the six point lead would be enough of a cushion to ensure victory if Carter managed to bring the hostages home. The strategist could not say that it would be, but he explained patiently to all of them that a debate 'win' for Reagan would not necessarily increase his lead by more than 1 or 2 per cent at the most, going on past and recent history of such events. This would not be enough to ensure victory with a predicted 10 per cent swing to Carter, if the hostages were returned in the week 18-25 October. Other tactics would have to be used to tackle this, such as Bill Casey's 'hostage watch' operation, and the planned counter-strategy blitz on TV. Given the delicacy of the vote if the hostages were returned, there would be even more risk involved if Reagan were to lose a point or two because of the debate.

Bill Timmons, in charge of mobilizing the Republican Party across the nation, backed Wirthlin. Timmons told Reagan how a great force of direct mail, media money, radio and TV tapes and people organized to drive the voters out in force, was ready for the last two days of the campaign which would help deliver a knock-out to Carter. Yet while the two people with the strongest overview of the election battle among the Republicans did not think it necessary to debate, most of the rest of the key advisers favored it.

Finally, Reagan made his decision and told Wirthlin: "If I am going to wear Carter's shoes, I'm going to have to debate him."

THE BRIEFING BOOK

The debate – a televised event to rival anything in US sport – was set for 28 October in Cleveland, and both candidates began preparations for the biggest test of their political lives. Carter spent many evenings after work at the Oval Office studying his Briefing Book, which was the complete strategy for the debate. This 100-page looseleaf folder had been devised by Caddell. He had worked out the framework in a 30-page memo. The detail – such as the exact answers by Carter to likely questions by the panel of journalists, the likely responses by Reagan, and how Carter should rebut them – had been filled in by Martin Franks, a researcher for the Carter-Mondale Committee, and David Rubenstein, deputy director of the domestic policy staff. They had been assisted by Sam Popkin, an associate of Caddell's who was a professor at the University of California at San Diego. Popkin had advised the Carter campaign on debate strategy in 1976.

The Briefing Book gave Carter much comfort because it seemed to cover the contest from every possible angle. Caddell had pinpointed the exact groups at whom Carter should aim his responses. The strategist had analyzed in clinical detail the public perceptions of both candidates which guided Carter on how he should present himself, and how he should try to portray his opponent. The Briefing Book became his bible. He took notes and expanded or contracted answers to suit himself, while never straying far from the original text, which he practiced, in some cases, word for word. The President had been apprehensive about debating Reagan because of the ex-actor's camera skills, but with the Caddell strategy firmly in mind, he felt more secure and self-assured. Carter was confident that what he lacked in speaking ability and camera presence would be easily compensated for by this comprehensive, if not brilliant battle plan.

BAKER'S HALF-DOZEN

James Baker stared at the stack of documents on his desk at Arlington HQ. The latest addition to the pile was a folder containing one hundred photocopied sheets. Like most of the pilfered documents from the White House, it had been passed on to Baker by one of the tight band of about six ex-CIA men working for the Reagan campaign. Several of them had come with Baker from the campaign of ex-CIA Director George Bush, and they were employed to use their dubious talents of 'intelligence gathering'. Baker, a former Houston lawyer who had had considerable political experience, including the management of Bush's bid for the 1980 Republican nomination, was more than a little nervous of all the material pouring in from the zealous activities of the intelligence people. He was a quiet political operative concerned about propriety, and had never given orders that anything should be stolen. But in the hectic days of the the last weeks of the campaign, the pressures mounted. Everything that came in from the opposition camp was considered without questions being asked as the countdown to the debate began and the time when the hostages could be returned drew nearer.

As a lawyer and a Republican politico, Baker was alert to the possible Watergate connotations. Pilfering opposition debate documents was nothing like the widespread allegation of criminality that was associated with the Watergate episode of the 1972 Republican campaign. However, what worried Baker was the possible link to the original mid-1972 'third-rate burglary' in the Watergate building beside the Potomac river in Washington DC. Then, the White House 'plumbers' group of ex-CIA men had broken into the Democratic campaign HQ to place listening devices in it, and obtain the Democrats' campaign plan for George McGovern (to which Caddell had also contributed heavily). The question which entered Baker's mind was whether the 1980 CIA people at Arlington had done any of their own 'plumbing' to obtain documents. After contemplating the valuable Briefing Book, Baker decided to turn a blind eye to any possible dirty trick perpetrated on Carter. He did not know the mechanics of how the Book reached him, so it was not his responsibility, he told himself. Baker had already pleased the candidate in the way he had negotiated the event so that it would be close to the election in the hope that this would help offset the impact of Carter's possible 'October surprise'. Now the Briefing Book was a further chance to impress Reagan. It would be of considerable help in the debate preparations.

CARTER'S COACHING

A tape of Reagan giving a stock response to an economics question was frozen on a frame of the candidate. "That's the kind of answer he should never get away with", Caddell told Carter as they prepared for the debate in the Aspen Lodge at Camp David. Caddell, Jordan, Powell, Rafshoon and Eizenstat were participating in coaching Carter through tapes of Reagan's TV debate performances over the years. The two most significant were one with Robert Kennedy in 1967, and a recent encounter (on 21 September 1980) with independent presidential candidate, John Anderson. Carter was surprised and impressed. "He's real slick," he commented about Reagan at one point. "A good speaker too, I guess." Even in the ebullient atmosphere engendered by his closest aides and his wife, Carter was becoming more aware of Caddell's warning that he would have only a small chance of 'winning' the debate, where a victory as such would be measured by nothing less than a complete humiliation of the challenger.

This awareness spurred the President on to greater effort in his rehearsals, and instead of eschewing·simulated debate sessions, he encouraged them. Caddell's associate, Sam Popkin, was chosen to play Reagan because he had helped prepare Carter's Briefing Book, and was most knowledgeable on the Republican, whom he had researched and studied for many years in California. Although Popkin, a bulky forty year old, did not look like Reagan, he had learned by heart Reagan's responses to certain questions, which had varied little from 1967 to 1980. The Georgia 'mafia' and Caddell fired questions at them both and encouraged Carter to humiliate his opponent with as much presidential demeanor as possible by giving succinct answers and rebuttals which were intended to expose Reagan as unfit for the job he sought. All agreed that Carter looked most impressive in rehearsals. And few had doubts that he was far better prepared than he had been for his debate against Ford in 1976, thanks to the thoroughly researched Briefing Book.

REAGAN'S REHEARSALS

In the backyard of Reagan's estate at Wexford, Virginia, the candidate, wearing a short-sleeved open-neck shirt and casual slacks, sat in the sun listening intently to briefings from Wirthlin and economist William Simon. Wirthlin, jacket off and looking relaxed, was taking full advantage of the opportunity that the debate had given him to drive home PINS strategy. He advised Reagan to use the themes which had been extracted from years of research, rather than make his message diffuse by reaching out for specific groups in the expected huge audience. This was in keeping with Wirthlin's scheme to give Reagan a more presidential mien. He was to appear a man of vision and verve, rather than one of detail and diligence. He had to be perceived as a decisive leader instead of a dithering loser. DMI's incisive probing into the nation's feelings about the economy had uncovered simple thoughts which Reagan planned to commit to memory and regurgitate in his answers, and especially in his final statement. Some of the lines such as "Are you better off now than you were four years ago?", "Is it easier for you to go and buy things in the stores than it was four years ago?", "Is America as respected throughout the world as it was?", and "Do you feel that our security is safe, that we are as strong as we were four years ago?", had come almost word for word from the questions DMI had put to tens of thousands of telephone respondents across the nation in 1978, 1979 and 1980. To each of these queries the interviewers had been given a resounding "NO" from a large majority of the nation. At this, the most critical moment of the whole campaign, Wirthlin had a chance to put his PINS strategy into operation with the biggest one-time audience. The candidate's responses would be subtly yet directly matched with the feelings, aspirations, thoughts, fears and hopes of the nation. It was another opportunity, too, for Reagan to appear a prospective statesman of peace.

With Baker preparing Reagan for the Carter strategy, Wirthlin further planned to remove any chance that the Republican would be seen as 'losing' the debate. He knew that his opposite number in the Democratic camp would advise the Carter team to persuade the press and media after the debate that the President was the winner because of his more substantial answers. So Wirthlin devised an operation to influence more strongly the media's post-debate election analysis. Both Caddell and Wirthlin had seen how Ford had been depicted as the debate loser in 1976 because the media made much of his gaffe on Soviet domination in Eastern Europe. The first public reaction had declared Ford the winner. The second reaction, influenced by the media, perceived him as the loser. With this in mind, Wirthlin designed an 'instant' polling operation which would be run during the actual debate. DMI's offices would be hooked up to two hundred TV sets in private homes in Portland, Oregon. The sets would have rheostats, which would allow viewers to register responses to answers as they were given by the two candidates. The responses – either negative or positive – would be automatically registered at DMI's operation in McClean, and then phoned through to Wirthlin in a booth at the back of the debate theater. He, in turn, would phone Ed Meese who would be sitting off-stage near the candidate. As soon as the debate was over they would brief the press if Reagan did better.

While the preparation for the debate went on, Wirthlin directed that the ads for the full Reagan counter-attack be made ready, for he expected that by the end of the third week of October the Republican and his policies would be understood by at least 70 per cent of the electorate – enough to allow him to shift to the offensive against the President. Wirthlin was still nagged by Reagan's 'dangerous and uncaring' image which hovered above the acceptable 40 per cent level. Yet he took some comfort from this figure, for some of it was made up of those who actually *approved* of the candidate's aggressive tendencies in military matters. The strategist was beginning to pick up in his polls that 'dangerous' equated to 'strong' in some corners of the country, especially the South. When this was taken from the disturbingly high 40 plus per cent, it was found to be within an acceptable range. This meant that Reagan could be more himself when he campaigned in the South, as long as he appeared as the peace candidate in, say, the East and Northeast. To consolidate the peaceful image, Wirthlin asked Henry Kissinger and several other well-known and nationally respected Republicans to join the campaign plane. There were responsible types like Elliot Richardson, the former Government jack-of-all-trades cabinet member, Anne Armstrong, former Ambassador to Great Britain, and Howard Baker, the Republican Senate Minority Leader. All carried the message that Reagan would not wantonly involve the nation in war, and the candidate himself weighed in on 19 October with a half-hour TV address on foreign policy and defense. In it he mentioned the word 'peace' no less than 47 times. Five days later, another strong indicator that PINS was coming through on target and heading Reagan for an upset win, was registered at Arlington.

Grayling Achui had been running through routine simulations

when he suddenly gave a yell and ran out into the corridor to find Beal. PINS had Reagan ahead by a massive 11 per cent. Both researchers had been recording leads of from 5 to 8 per cent daily, but such a large divergence amazed them. Smallish leads of up to 6 per cent could be wiped out by one or two incidents in a day. But anything over 10 per cent was different. Beal checked through to see if the result was unreliable because of poor sampling. Everything pointed to an accurate reading. Two other surveys that day indicated that the lead was more like 8 per cent, so this became the official figure in the records. Yet both noted the substantial drift in the upward direction, which prompted Beal to comment: "Reagan is going to win, and win big."

Reagan rehearsed the debate in the garage of the Wexford estate, with David Stockman standing in as Carter. Stockman, a Republican representative from Michigan, looked quite like the President. He had gray hair and was about the same build. But even more remarkable was his command of the issues and his mock tactics with Reagan, which would prove to be almost exactly the same as Carter's in the actual debate. So comprehensive were Stockman's attempts to pin Reagan down that the candidate became exasperated as the panel of Jeane Kirkpatrick, journalist George Will, and others, fired questions.

In the post-mortem Reagan was not satisfied with his performance, especially his defensive responses to Stockman's accusations, so he decided to say, "There you go again," if Carter cornered him. He practiced this as much as he did the simple, "Are you better off now than you were four years ago?" line, which he thought would impress the audience more than Carter's double-layered convoluted replies. But it wasn't just committing lines to memory, as Carter was also busy doing. Delivery would count far more. With the whole show now based on a script – the Carter Briefing Book – the professional actor held the edge over the amateur performer, long before they walked on to center stage.

THE ENCOUNTER

A smiling Reagan loped across the podium and shook hands with the President. This gesture set the pattern for the next ninety minutes of the debate, which was notable for its lack of spontaneity. Carter, on advice from Caddell, opened up on the first question – on the military – and leapt straight into his presidential routine: "I've had to make thousands of decisions since I've been President, serving in the Oval Office," he said, and added that he had "learned in the process". But although this had come straight from the Briefing Book, it did not seem to work.

Carter sounded more like a learner than a leader.

Reagan answered by slamming home the peace theme with: "I believe in all my heart that our first priority must be world peace." He than proceeded to use 'peace' as if mentioning it a certain number of times would cast the right spell on the audience. He told them: "America has never gotten into a war because we are too strong," which, like many of Reagan's lines, had a superficial appeal. On analysis it meant precisely nothing. But this did not matter, for very few of the audience, estimated at eighty million, would be bothering to dissect each phrase. Reagan also added that he was "the father of sons; I have a grandson" – which was all part of the plan to alleviate his image as a potential 'mad-bomber' with a large percentage of the nation.

Question after question, Carter followed his brief, with even more apparent diligence than the professional actor. But the President reached out perhaps too much for the constituencies he had been instructed to mention. Reagan, in contrast, used his one-liners, as he had all his life, and stayed within the broad fundamental themes: "We don't have inflation because the people are living too well; we have inflation because the Government is living too well . . . the budget for the Department of Energy is in excess of ten billion dollars, and it hasn't produced a quart of oil . . ."

Caddell tried hard to follow Caddell's instruction of cornering Reagan, rather than attacking him directly. The President used the words 'dangerous' and 'disturbing' many times to describe Reagan's positions: "This attitude is extremely dangerous and belligerent in its tone," he said, "although it's said with a quiet voice." With this, the camera caught Reagan's reaction – a slight tilt of the head, and a look of irritation which seemed to say, "Aw, c'mon, you're not still trying that one on!"

As the debate progressed, Wirthlin's TV polling hook-up was operating and he was telling Meese of the reactions of the people who were twisting their rheostats in Oregon. "Not much happening here, Ed, either positive or negative . . .", he said, and "very strong, very positive here, now it's a turn off . . . good positive response to that one . . ." Wirthlin and Meese scribbled notes and prepared themselves for the public relations exercise which would follow later with a bevy of reporters all demanding reactions to the debate.

At one point, Carter remarked: "Governor Reagan, as a matter of fact, began his political career campaign around this nation against Medicare." The President then spiritedly defended the concept of national health insurance, and said that Reagan opposed this proposal. Wirthlin did not pick up a positive or negative response to this comment, but then Reagan replied: "There you go again," and the rheostats became hot and positive in the strongest public reaction thus far in the debate. Carter's accusations had been accurate enough, but Reagan's avuncular indignation had dramatized Carter as a naughty little boy telling tales he shouldn't, and it worked. In one stroke, Reagan had pulled Carter down from his Presidential loftiness, and had made him look mean and uncharitable – which had been the Wirthlin-directed ploy since June.

Soon after this, Carter made the one gaffe of the contest. "I had a discussion with my daughter Amy the other day, before I came here, to ask her what the most important issue was," he said. "She said she thought it was the nuclear weaponry and the control of nuclear arms." Wirthlin found that the public response to this was strongly negative, and it was clear that the remark was seen as contrived. Carter did not finish the thought but went on to describe the terrible destructive force of nuclear weapons, and his closest aides, watching the debate on TV, groaned in horror. The idea behind Carter's reference to his little girl had been right, but pathetically executed. Caddell and other advisers had wanted the President to invoke fear concerning the bomb – the implication being that it was safe in his hands and not in Reagan's. Carter had taken his cue from a TV ad made by Tony Schwartz for the 1964 Johnson campaign against Goldwater. However, the impact of this ad – called the Daisy Girl Spot – was created by brilliant use of visual and sound impact. An innocent child was seen dissecting a daisy and counting petals as she went. Then came a countdown by a disembodied voice and finally a hideous dissolve into an atomic explosion. Carter had tried to verbalize that devastating film concept, but had merely made himself look foolish in the process. The only person in politics who could have done this successfully, and with emotion, was standing next to him on the debating platform. Yet Reagan was not about to do it, for he rather liked the idea of America increasing its number of nuclear weapons, and he was there to reduce fears about the bomb, not increase them.

The closing remarks clearly demonstrated the quintessential difference between the two candidates. Carter closed first, and reached out indirectly and directly to the South, women, Anderson voters, college students, independents and suburbanites. He thanked the people of Cleveland and Ohio for being "such hospitable hosts during the last few hours of my life," which again sounded odd and contrived. Carter struggled to appear convincing in his more upbeat final remarks, but seemed to spoil them by repeating how much he had learned as President. His determination to follow the Briefing Book had at various times in the debate made him appear the solemn, patronizing teacher, and at others, the keen student. He looked edgy, and like Nixon two decades earlier in debates against John Kennedy, had seemed shiftily conscious of his more telegenic opponent. Where the President had seemed humorless and cold, Reagan was able to smile. Whether as man or actor, or both, the challenger had won the emotional battle, and also the contest of perceptions. Reagan had not seemed a bomb-thrower and he had not come across as uncaring. And despite the simplicity of his closing remarks, which were direct and memorable ("Are you better off now . . .?"), he certainly was not seen to be the simpleton politician Carter had tried to portray him as. The combined sound and sight impression caused the less complicated messages to linger. Reagan had opted for hackneyed, straightforward, but carefully selected themes in his final statement as if he was doing a commercial. And he was. His message left a deeper imprint on the bulk of the audience.

When the debate was over, reporters swarmed all over the stage and theater as members of the Carter and Reagan campaigns quickly made their points about why each candidate had 'won'. All the President's people insisted that Carter had been more substantive in his responses, and Reagan's people claimed he had been more impressive and direct. The latter had instant poll data to back up their claim.

Wirthin ran a poll after the debate. He was able to measure some vital improvements in the major responses from the electorate that the PINS strategy was programmed to influence. The surveys indicated that the fear of Reagan getting the US into an unnecessary war had at last dropped from 44 per cent to 40 per cent, and Wirthlin felt he had won the strategic battle with Caddell over the 'dangerous and uncaring' factor. Now he felt safe – in the South – to push two 'peace through military strength' ads which had been made in the last few days. Furthermore, Reagan had consolidated his appearance of being a sound potential president, and he had seemed competent enough to handle the job, which Carter had made out, rightly, to be the toughest in the world. Reagan also came across as a strong figure by a 2 to 1 ratio. The vital 'undecideds' votes, which could swing the election either way in the tense final days, had begun to break for Reagan. They were ignoring Anderson, and opting less for Carter.

Wirthlin now judged that his packaging of the candidate, and his camouflaging of some of Reagan's more extreme positions by the use of semantics, particularly euphemisms, was beginning to work well. The nation was set to buy him on election day. Now the strategist decided the time was perfect for letting Reagan loose to attack Carter.

CHAPTER 16

VICTORY BY COMPUTER

THURSDAY 30 OCTOBER

It was not yet light when Wirthlin arrived at an apartment in the Washington suburb of Falls Church, Virginia. He was there for a usual 6 a.m. meeting with Meese, Casey, Garrick, who was in charge of Casey's 'hostage watch', and Peter Dailey, Reagan's ad man. The daily rendezvous reviewed and previewed strategy, and the main topic, as it had been for several weeks, was the 'October surprise'. The previous night's debate had given Reagan a 2 per cent lift, and his lead over Carter had consolidated at around 7 per cent with clear indications that this would firm even further for Reagan in the last days. Yet Wirthlin was far from complacent. "Carter could still win," he briefed the others, "but he has to create a special new strategy to give him the sort of boost needed."

"Well, it won't be the hostages," Casey said gruffly.

Wirthlin nodded his agreement. "Either they won't be released, or if they are, there will be too much skepticism to make it effective. We are already days past the date of the maximum effect."

"Then how could Carter still win?" Meese asked.

"If he uses his time to build up leads in Texas, Michigan, Ohio and California, and our momentum drops, he could still do it," Wirthlin warned. "We have to keep our two Southern flanks – Texas and Florida – intact. We must add Arkansas and Louisiana to the Governor's schedule, and drop Kentucky and Tennessee. Then we must focus on the industrial states and keep our California base together."

Despite their confidence over the hostage situation, Wirthlin was still concerned enough about it to make sure that a counter-strategy was ready. There was always the chance that if Carter brought home the hostages he could receive a vote of emotional thanks from enough extra people – mostly among the undecideds – to challenge Reagan's lead. It might not be even half the maximum 10 per cent he could have obtained, yet it was conceivable that it could drag enough votes back to the Carter column to give him hope. Apart from the powerful TV and radio ads that had been prepared and Garrick's intelligence operation, Wirthlin had briefed key surrogates on the counter-strategy. People such as Bush, Ford and Kissinger were primed ready to go on TV if Carter created hostage news.

Just before midnight on the same day, the lights were still burning in Caddell's offices. They were a hive of activity. The strategist was hunched over his desk digesting the lastest survey figures which had just been brought to him by his assistant, Paul Maslin. Caddell was particularly interested in the data concerning the President's handling of the hostage crisis. Despite Carter's approval rating – 51 per cent thought he was handling the issue well, and 38 did not – the strategist now felt that the Carter Presidency hinged almost entirely on this issue. If Carter could not maintain credibility with it, Caddell feared that the electorate's attention would move to the administration's overall record. The tactic of making the major issue one of a choice between the two candidates had not worked, mainly because Reagan had come out of the debate looking a credible alternative for the Presidency.

The TV nightly news, one of the important rough barometers for the strategists, was still dominated by the crisis in Iran, and the President was figuring prominently. As yet the electorate's attitudes had not hardened toward Carter, and it seemed important for him to prolong the drama without too much theater, which could make the media, and the nation, cynical about the timing. The uncertainty crept in because the Iranians were unpredictable, although they seemed to be playing it right for Carter by indicating certain demands for the safe return of the hostages. Could it be an opportunity for a media event which would give Carter his second term in office?

FRIDAY 31 OCTOBER

At mid-morning, Wirthlin headed the last campaign strategy meeting at Arlington HQ and made a prediction about the Tuesday result based on a PINS analysis carried out at 7 a.m. The straight vote – the Polaroid snapshot of the election from the previous night – had Reagan at 44 per cent, Carter at 37 per cent, Anderson, 10 per cent and undecided, 9 per cent. This still gave Reagan his 7 per cent lead, but the PINS 'movie', in which all the elements representing the political environment were computer-simulated, told a more significant story. Also computerized in this PINS run-through were: adjustments for turn-out as predicted by Timmons' calculations state by state; the voting intentions of undecideds; the continuing decline of the Anderson vote; trends detected from more incisive questioning than simply, "who do you intend to vote for?"; historical voting patterns; and subjective judgements by the selected experts. The adjusted result gave Reagan 50.0 per cent, Carter 40.5 per cent, and Anderson 9.3 per cent. Unlike every other poll in the nation (most of which were describing the race as a toss-up), the PINS program suggested a

Reagan victory of 9.5 per cent, which was approaching landslide proportions. The PINS prediction for electoral college votes was even more certain of a big Reagan victory. The 'worst-case' scenario gave Reagan 290 votes, which was clear of the required number of 270. A 'reasonable-case' scenario had him at 386 votes. The PINS strategy had indicated the campaign should spend six million dollars in the last week, which was the biggest such one-week blitz in politics. Concurrently, Reagan and the whole Republician organization was to focus its attention on siphoning off the extra votes in key states of the industral Northeast and the Great Lakes.

Less guardedly optimistic now, Wirthlin told the last meeting about Reagan's consolidated base among Republicans, the Western vote, Catholics, union members, disaffected Democrats and political moderates. They were staying with the challenger, DMI's surveys indicated, no matter what Carter did with the hostages.

The type of campaign the President was now running had begun to etch itself into his face. A strain, even a desperation dominated his expression as he embarked on the most grueling day of his campaign so far. Air Force One took him to five states – Mississippi, South Carolina, Tennessee, Florida and Texas. It was a last-minute dash to the South which reflected his troubles. Even worse, from Caddell's point of view, were the measures of skepticism in reporters' questions to Carter concerning Iran. The strategist feared this was the first sign of a possible hardening of the nation's attitude. He knew Wirthlin had been planting a cynical view of the 'October surprise' for months, and that his efforts had hemmed the President in as the days dwindled to a precious few before the election. News items on TV that night again featured Iran as the lead item. American officials were waiting for the Iranian Parliament to meet on Sunday. More waiting. More apparent impotence on America's part, and more frustration. Was it another false start, similar to the one on the morning of the Wisconsin primary? Carter's one slim hope of retaining his Presidency now seemed dependent on him doing something dramatic to rivet the nation's attention.

At the end of the day, Reagan looked confident and buoyant after his trip to Pennsylvania, Illinois, Wisconsin and Michigan. It too, had been a tough tour, but it had been made as a safety measure rather than in desperation. These were important states with big electoral college votes that had favored Reagan for weeks, and Wirthlin expected him to take them all.

Armed with the latest PINS figures, the strategist flew to Grand Rapids, Michigan, and waited for the candidate at the airport. Jack Germond and Jules Witcover, two journalists from the *Washington Star*, spotted him. "Can Reagan win the Midwest?" Germond asked.

Wirthlin grinned broadly, "Yes," he said with a conviction that expressed a lot more than his simple reply.

"Do you think he can win the election?" Witcover asked.

Wirthlin's smile turned mysterious. "I really can't say anymore at the moment," he said. "I have to brief the Governor first."

Despite his reserved demeanor, Wirthlin had become popular with the press because he was a source of plenty of facts, figures and some useful comments. But none of the press had bothered to interrogate him fully to find out the true depth of his influence on the campaign. Neither had any of them tried to understand how PINS operated, although several had visited Arlington HQ and had noticed the computer hardware. Most of them shied away from the technology, and the few, such as Theodore H. White, who asked questions, seemed intimidated by the atmosphere, and left without attempting to probe too deeply. The media and press had not yet adjusted to the new realities of political technicians and computer technology. They preferred to feed off the more colorful 'gut' political operatives around the candidate such as Stu Spencer. His robustness and profanity had most of the media on board the campaign plane bluffed, and he was the most accessible operative who spoke their language and gave them one-line quotes and titbits about the candidate. The media and press tried to create an atmosphere of excitement by exaggerating the role of certain operatives and advisers on board the plane. Spencer, for instance, did play an important role in disciplining the candidate to 'stick to the script' – which had come from the planners at Arlington – and in on-the-spot tactics at which he excelled. But he had not been involved in the major overall strategy which guided, directed and controlled the whole campaign from February to November.

The media attention given to him and other operatives on the plane suited Wirthlin and the Mormon team, who wanted to keep secret the way they arrived at strategy and decisions. Only one reporter, David Broder of the *Washington Post*, took time to ask questions on PINS during the election, and he was given a superficial view of the system, on the understanding that he did not publish anything until after the election. Now, at a critical time in the election, Wirthlin was not hounded by a horde of reporters. He had almost complete freedom of maneuver to mastermind the vital last days of the campaign in secrecy, and to direct and inform the candidate.

Late on Friday night, Wirthlin met with the Reagans in their hotel suite. "You're going to win," he told them ebulliently. "We have a 'worst-case' scenario saying you'll take at least 290 electoral votes, and that you will win the national vote by 9½ per cent."

"What about Iran?" Reagan asked.

Wirthlin allayed his fears. "Well, Governor, our prediction is that it will not have any major impact, even if he brings them home."

"Oh, Dick," Nancy said, "I hope you're right!"

SATURDAY 1 NOVEMBER

While Wirthlin was all but gift-wrapping the Presidency for Reagan, Caddell was reading a completely different scenario to the Democrats. He had Reagan only 4 per cent ahead on Friday and claimed that by Saturday this had closed to 1 per cent, or too close to call. Caddell had the hard information at his fingertips and emerged as Carter's most powerful adviser in the last few days. No one else in the dispirited Carter camp had any fact-based bright ideas, and the stategist's strongly articulated if convoluted theories outweighed everything else. He reveled in his moment of glory.

Caddell knew that since 1948 there had always been an incumbent party resurgence at the end of the campaign, if it was close. He had the race close, so to fit the historical data he was now predicting a surge of support from 'weak' Democrats who were expected to 'come home' to the party and support Carter. This would be helped, he suggested, if the President was to act as the underdog. He and his team were to hint strongly, or plead, that things looked bad in an effort to frighten Democrats out to vote. This had happened to Carter, Caddell believed, in the 1980 primaries against Kennedy, and in the 1976 presidential fight against Ford. That it should happen again was a logical deduction, if indeed Carter was that close to Reagan. But it would be futile if he was nearly ten points behind – as Wirthlin had Carter by Saturday night.

Then there was Iran. Responses to several questions in surveys until Saturday made Caddell feel that the crisis was still serving Carter well. On the broad but related question, of how Americans viewed the US in the world, the positive response had not diminished from a position of several months ago. More pertinently, attitudes about the conditions for the release of the hostages had not slipped either. The number suggesting that conditions were right was steady, and the number saying that they were bad had not increased. Based on this data, Caddell felt Carter was holding the line on Iran, and that the nation's view of his handling of the crisis had not yet soured. This, and the expected last-minute surge from Democrats, gave the hope that the President still had a strong chance of winning. Caddell had always put great store by the effect of events in Iran, and his strategy was largely based on that big event. Wirthlin was also very concerned with its effect, but in contrast his PINS-based strategy was that a great variety of factors of varying influence, including Iran, combined to affect national voting patterns.

Wirthlin awoke in Grand Rapids on Saturday to a phone call from the PINS nerve center in Arlington. It was good news for Reagan. The vital chunk of undecideds across the nation, who could swing the election either way, were breaking three to two in his favor and holding well. Translated into electoral college votes this was another factor, Wirthlin believed, that was strengthening Reagan's grip on the election.

The strategist joined the campaign plane, where his presence was overshadowed by that of former President Ford, who was there to help Reagan win Ford's home state of Michigan. However, some of those on the plane, including one or two of the more astute members of the press, took the arrival of Wirthlin as an indication that they might be with the winning team. But whenever they asked him if he thought Reagan would win, he would smile enigmatically like Mephistopheles and say, "I think so."

Still the press was more interested in Iran than anything else. As they pumped the advisers for information, Wirthlin's counter-strategy had already been set in motion in anticipation of Carter trying something over the weekend. Reagan had been directed to say nothing. He would adopt a studied pose of speechless caution while Republicans such as Kissinger, Ford and Bush would use the media to go on the attack over the issue.

SUNDAY 2 NOVEMBER

The sound of the Marine Corps helicopter split the silence of the early morning as its rotors disturbed the tranquility of the trees around the White House front lawn. Once it had landed, the lonely figure of the President emerged and walked toward the building in the half light. In full view of TV cameras, he was greeted somberly by Vice-President Walter Mondale, and then by national security adviser Zbigniew Brzezinski, who overdid it by putting his arm around Carter's shoulder and handing him papers. The well-staged 'October surprise' had arrived on the second day of November. But was it too little and too late? Carter had learned in the middle of the night that Iran had put up several conditions to be met before the hostages could be returned. Again, with all the drama of a long-running 'soap', the nation's focus was squarely on Carter and the crisis, which was exactly where his stategist wanted it to be.

Less than two hours later, Wirthlin directed poll-taking across the nation to measure the electorate's response to the 'new' developments in Iran, and found that Reagan's support was still climbing toward 11 per cent. Another afternoon poll registered no change. Wirthlin reported the situation to Reagan, who was besieged by the media as he left a church in Columbus, Ohio. He had no comment, except to say that it was all "very sensitive".

At mid-day, Bush went on 'Face the Nation'. He, like Reagan, said it was all "very sensitive", then he threw a cautious, wordy counter-punch at Ayatollah Khomeini, who he said was "trying to manipulate the election". Next into the ring was Kissinger on ABC TV. He jabbed hard and accused the Iranians of "trying to tell the Americans how to vote". Finally, Ford went on 'Meet the Press'. Although not as quick on his feet, what he said carried weight, and he surprised everyone by delivering a vicious verbal uppercut. He was skeptical about Carter's timing concerning the crisis, which implied that it was all staged, presumably with the Ayatollah's connivance. The combined attacks were designed to take the sting out of anything Carter said, unless he could tell the nation the hostages were coming home on a specific date.

When he did appear on national TV, on Sunday at 6.22 p.m., there was still an atmosphere of hope and expectation. In an effort to make the most political capital out of the situation, Carter began by saying that the Iranian proposal was a "significant development". It was the first sign that it wasn't what he hoped for. He went on to imply that the Iranian demands were concrete, but too high, and that they would be difficult to negotiate. There was no release date. Now the question was, had expectations been built up too much? As far as the election was concerned, did it even matter anymore?

MONDAY 3 NOVEMBER

Twenty-four hours before people went to the polls to cast their vote, Beal and Breglio had settled in with a computer terminal at the Century Plaza hotel suite where Reagan would be staying later that night. The terminal was linked to DMI's computers in Los Angeles and Washington. An early morning simulation run of the PINS program had the two men whooping and yelling at the top of their voices. Reagan was going to win, PINS predicted, by 10.6 per cent. (This was, in fact, the actual winning margin.) Two Spanish maids cleaning the suite were astonished at their behavior.

"Come over here!" Beal said. The two maids looked quizzicaly at each other and joined the two men at the terminal. "Reagan's going to win!" Beal said excitedly. "He is going to be President!" He pointed at the graph on the TV screen which showed the Reagan blue line national vote significantly higher than the Carter red line. But the two women did not speak English.

"No understand," one of the maids said, and then broke into giggles as she watched Beal's dance of anguish at not being able to communicate with them.

On the plane later in the day, Wirthlin had a different communications problem as he joined the celebration to end the campaign. He sipped mineral water as the others took champagne. Nancy Reagan, with whom he had built a strong trust and friendship, approached him. "Dick, are we REALLY going to win?" she asked, weary after a hard day's final campaigning.

"Nancy, we are really going to win," Wirthlin replied with a huge grin, but he still did not think the Reagans had fully grasped the fact that the White House was theirs.

By contrast, the tension in the Carter camp was almost unbearable for the key advisers. Caddell had begun to read on Sunday night that Carter was in trouble. The strategist's polls then were indicating that Carter was behind by five points, although things seemed extremely unsettled. Caddell was beginning to get less favorable answers to questions about Iran. A higher percentage thought it would be a long time before the hostages would be returned. Suddenly a higher percentage thought the Iranian's terms were unreasonable. Also Caddell noticed some worrying figures about the decline of America's position in the world. More seemed to see a decline. The strategist's interpretation was that the President's campaign had finally been unable to prevent the nation's frustration and anger from entering electoral calculations enough to destroy Carter. His position had slipped by Monday, and Caddell was suddenly having to explain how it could deteriorate so quickly. In two days, Carter had seemed to fall away somewhere approaching ten points. Whereas Wirthlin's PINS calculations saw a gradual improvement for Reagan since before the debate, Caddell's poll results, at his own admission, were 'jumping all over the place' on Sunday, after having had the two candidates just about even on Saturday. Late on Monday night when Caddell went to his Pennsylvania office he received confirmation of a pending landslide against the President. All his staff were waiting for him. The atmosphere was depressed.

"How bad is it?" he asked Maslin.

"Ten," Maslin replied. Caddell mouthed something under his breath and sat down at his desk to examine the figures. All except Maslin drifted silently into the waiting room and began making coffee.

"The data's consistent, Pat," Maslin said quietly, "right across the board. The most critical groups are all gone." Even the 'weak' Democrats that Carter hoped would come home had fallen from 9 per cent for the President to just 3 per cent. They had gone to Reagan in their droves, as had Catholics, independents, women and even upper-income white voters who had been suspicious of the Republican. The trends were so definitive and uniform across the nation that Carter would be lucky to win even 50 electoral votes out of a possible 538.

"It's a disaster," Caddell said, and then quickly picked up the phone to warn Carter's closest advisers.

The President was flying somewhere over Kansas when Caddell finally reached him at 4 a.m. Carter had seemed confident, and had been positive in his remarks to the press. He had been told that the election was very close over the weekend and he felt that the Iranian crisis had been handled well under the circumstances. Now he was optimistic.

"Hi, Pat," Carter said happily, when he picked up the phone on Air Force One, "What's happening?"

"Well, Mr President," Caddell said, steeling himself. "It's gone."

Carter said nothing. Gone. All those years of toil and battle, and power and decision. He was going to be defeated and the Presidency would not be his anymore. Blown away. Carter could hear Caddell giving him details about a margin of 7 to 10 per cent, and saying that they needed to decide what he should say when he arrived in Plains. But the President wasn't concentrating. "You all work that out with Jody," he said. "I'm going to take a nap."

Moments later, when he had rung off, Caddell buried his face in his hands.

TUESDAY 4 NOVEMBER

At 11 a.m. at the Century Plaza Wirthlin gave Reagan his final briefing of the campaign and warned him of the impending landslide victory. "You are going to win 489 electoral votes, by our projections, Governor," Wirthlin said cheerfully. "Even Kentucky fell to us this morning."

Reagan laughed. He was practically speechless.

"You had better get your acceptance speech ready," Wirthlin added. "Today you're the President-elect."

A few minutes later Reagan drove to Pacific Palisades to vote.

"Who are you voting for?" one reporter asked as the press and media swarmed around the candidate.

Reagan turned to his wife. "Nancy," he said.

"Do you think you have won?" another press man asked.

"Now, you know me," Reagan smiled. "I'm too superstitious to answer that."

"George Bush says you're in like a burglar."

Reagan laughed. "I think he was just using a figure of speech," he said.

At 7 p.m. that night the NBC network reported that Indiana, Florida and Mississippi were Reagan's, which meant that the bottom had fallen out of Carter's Southern base, which PINS had indicated on 7 October would happen. A half hour later, the network gave Reagan Alabama, Virginia and Ohio. Carter had only scored in one state, Georgia, his own. At 8.15 p.m. NBC projected Reagan the winner. Carter, gracious in defeat and wanting to get it over with, rang Reagan. It was only 5.15 p.m. Pacific time and Reagan was in the shower. His surprised aide, Mike Deaver, said, "It's Carter on the line." Reagan put a towel around himself and waddled to the phone.

"Congratulations, Governor," Carter said. "You've had a good victory. I'm conceding the election to you."

"Well, thank you, uh, Mr President," Reagan said, "that's very nice . . . so early."

"We want to have the best transition in history," Carter said. "Goodbye and God bless you."

Reagan put the phone down slowly. "He has conceded . . . already," he said incredulously. "I just don't believe it." But he did. As his key strategist had been telling him for some time, Reagan was going to be the 40th President of the United States of America.

Wirthlin's experiment to control the political environment by computer and program the run of a candidate into the most powerful office in the West had succeeded.

PART THREE
1981–1984

PROGRAM FOR A PRESIDENT

CHAPTER 17

THE ENDLESS CAMPAIGN

AFTER PINS, PACS

Ronald Reagan's historic programmed victory was the beginning of an even more ambitious experiment, again masterminded by Richard Wirthlin. His aim was to contruct another larger Political Information System, but not merely to win an election. Now the strategist had a grand secret concept for a computer program to guide and help drive the Presidency.

But first, Wirthlin had to establish the path of the new Government, for Reagan had put him in charge of the transition team from the winning 1980 campaign. The strategist set out his ideas in his Initial Actions Plan for the Reagan Presidency which the political tacticians and 'technicians' inside the White House were to follow. The plan became known as the 'First Ninety Day Project'. Basically its directive was that the Presidency itself should establish a set direction, and not be distracted by simply reacting to the myriad events which could impinge on the Oval Office. Wirthlin's plan was not a directive for the whole adminstration, but simply for the office of Presidency. The project pinpointed the most important goals of the new Presidency for the first few months, and beyond. Wirthlin's aim for the Presidency was to set a tone and objectives. It was the job of the rest of the administration to make sure Reagan's wishes were carried out. The President was to act like the chief executive of a big corporation who delegated greatly, and who kept the office of the Presidency as a precious resource to be used sparingly for the dictating and overseeing of his main aims in both domestic and foreign affairs.

Despite Wirthlin's control over the transition and his personal involvement with Reagan, he did not want a job inside the White House. He was not concerned with joining the power scramble that always ensued around a new national leader. Secure in his own considerable business achievements, his deeply religious private life and role as adviser to his good friend, Wirthlin preferred a detached view of the Presidency from the comfort of his Washington DC suite a quarter mile from the White House. He felt he could better serve Reagan this way, and at the same time continue to work for the Republican Party from which his company, DMI, now received a one million dollar a year contract. Just like Caddell with Carter, Wirthlin could rely on 'power by association' with the President, which would help all his interests.

However, Wirthlin was aware of the shortcomings of Caddell's efforts to influence the Presidency from the aloof position he was about to take himself. The Republican strategist saw the need for a vehicle on the inside, especially if his new grand scheme was to have any chance of long-term success. So at Wirthlin's request, Reagan agreed to set up a totally new White House office – the Department of Planning and Evaluation, also known as P & E – which would be run by Wirthlin's partner, Richard Beal.

Once this was in place, Wirthlin sent Reagan a memo which in essence said: "To provide leadership you must engage in a perennial campaign". This sagacious move was a primer, a hint, for Reagan and his staff of what Wirthlin had in mind eventually for the Presidency. The concept of a perennial campaign was something to which they all could relate, because they had just seen – even if some had not fully grasped – how the strategist had directed Reagan toward victory by selling him and his policies to the American people. Now Wirthlin was subtly advising the White House that running the Presidency smoothly was very much like running for office. Where the aim in the election was to win, the object now was to 'win' major goals the Presidency set itself, in everything from bringing down inflation to expanding the military. In both an election and a Presidency, Reagan needed a mandate – popular support and acceptance of his aims and the way he should achieve them. This was the guiding principle by which the White House staff would go about achieving Reagan's goals. Again, as in the 1980 campaign, a continual loop of manipulation or persuasion would be set in motion. First, a policy would be developed (for example, to expand the military). Second, the polls would indicate the policy's acceptability by the public (more than 55 per cent of the nation think that the US should have a stronger military). Third, more polls would indicate how the policy should be packaged and sold to the nation (by having the President make a prime-time TV address expounding on the 'peace through strength' theme used successfully in the 1980 campaign). Fourth, polling would be carried out to measure the effectiveness of the selling.

In the initial burst of the Reagan Presidency this method was used mainly with domestic affairs. With the White House thinking strategically, Wirthlin was able to turn his mind to his grand scheme for guiding the Presidency, which had been inspired by the great success of PINS. Just as PINS was fueled by data – demographic, historical and up-to-the-minute surveys – any new system inside the White House would need information too. But in order to drive the Presidency on the same principle a lot more data would be needed. DMI's great experience in extracting the right facts and figures about the nation over twelve years was more than useful here. Wirthlin knew that all the extra data he wanted was to be found in the Government agencies, most of which kept vast statistical records. He told Reagan that the new P & E Department was meant to "view the whole statistical community from the President's perspective". In other words, the Department had to have the authority to order in all the data it required. Such a move was sure to give new meaning to the old cliché that 'information was power'. P & E would run a Big Brother to PINS called PACS, Political Agenda Control System, an innocuous sounding name for something which had enormous potential power for Reagan, especially if it eventually worked to Wirthlin's satisfaction.

"We want the Presidency to have a strategic thrust," Wirthlin told Beal when the Department was first set up. "It must have a focus. The idea is that you think strategically and have access to the Presidency. We'll initiate a set of ideas consistent and coherent with all the President's aims." Like PINS, PACS, when fully operational, would be a computer-based system which could integrate and monitor thousands of measurable 'variables' ranging across every possible group or subcategory of the population. As in the campaign to elect Reagan, the 'What if' questions put to the system could give guidance to every step the Reagan Presidency was considering. "What should the President do to make sure he maintains support – from all groups in the 'coalition' that voted him into office – for his increased military spending? Should he rattle the saber against the Libyans in the Mediterranean to send the Soviets a message, and also boost support at home? What if he used gunboat diplomacy in Latin America? Would that hurt his re-election chances? How should the President handle the falling support from women who still find him 'dangerous and un-caring'? . . ."

The system would always be used to guide the Presidency and maintain Reagan's popularity no matter how dangerous, unpalatable, narrow or delicate his goals. Wirthlin was well aware that it would take some time for his plan to be effective. An initial drawback to P & E was the fact that it did not have the institutionalized force of, say, the National Security Council. It would take time for the new office to gain the respect of all in the White House. The question was whether Beal would cope. There was no doubt about his brilliance or technical skills, which had been used to great effect with PINS, and he had shown an ability to cooperate with others in the 1980 campaign. But Beal was primarily an academic who had taught at Brigham Young University in the specialist area of International Relations.

Whether he had the ruthlessness necessary to fend off the bruising elbows of politicians in big government was another matter. How, too, would he handle being so close to the President, with whom he did not have a close personal relationship?

At the beginning of the Reagan Presidency none of this mattered too much, and Beal became caught up in White House activities in the bewildering rush to cash in on the new President's election success and push through as many items on the agenda of goals as possible. Initially one of PACS' main functions of helping the President stay on top of the agenda – the schedule and basic strategic plan for reaching Reagan's main objectives – worked well. Beal's role was to inform the 'guards at the door' to the Oval Office, Meese, Deaver and Baker, about what Reagan had to do to reach his main aims. For example, the Pentagon and the Defense Department might be lobbying for a new weapons system in a few months' time. Assuming the President was in favor of it, he would need to know what to say, and when and where to influence Congress and the public to accept the weapon's manufacture and later deployment. Beal's job was to create a strategy to cover every contingency to achieve objectives.

In the early months of the administration the 'perennial campaign' concept worked powerfully and suited Reagan himself perfectly. He was happy to ride along on the momentum built by his thumping landslide victory and the push of the strategists. His role in the manipulation-persuasion loop was the same as it had been in the campaign. Reagan was the key salesman and his best medium was TV. No one could handle it better. His ideas would be given flesh by the communications experts, and then the master communicator would deliver them with great professional skill and style. This was Hollywood, TV hosting, campaigning and big politics all in one, and Reagan loved it. No more was it just a matter of repeating the campaign slogans, such as 'Get government off the backs of the American people'. Reagan was actually doing it – his way – with the budget and tax cuts he had promised. A key to the strategy was receiving a positive response and support from the big TV audience. Reagan came across well whenever he sold, and there was subsequent pressure on Congressional representatives to support the President's proposed legislation. Tough, back-up lobbying from a specific group, such as businessmen, would make sure that local Congressmen were bombarded with calls demanding that they support the particular Reagan initiative. Nothing, it seemed, could stop the new President in those early days.

SHOOTING UP THE RATINGS

Reagan stood frozen for a split second as the sound of six bullets split the air. A secret service agent shoved him from behind and Reagan bashed his head on the door of the limousine as he was bundled onto the floor.

"Take off," veteran agent Jerry Parr yelled to the driver, "just take off!"

Reagan groaned in agony. "You sonofabitch," he said. "You broke my ribs." The limousine sped off toward the White House. Reagan began coughing up blood, and Parr had the driver change direction and head for George Washington Hospital. The swift action by the agent saved Reagan's life, for a bullet had lodged an inch from his heart and he needed immediate surgery.

The President's courage endeared him to the nation. Despite his natural fears, he still managed the one-liners at the most critical moment of his life. To his wife, who had rushed to his bedside, he said, "Honey, I forgot to duck." To the doctors who were preparing for an emergency operation, he quipped, "Please tell me you're Republicans." It was the stuff of which legends are made, and the White House made sure that the nation was given as many bulletins on his jokes as his condition.

A week after the assassination attempt on 30 March 1981, Beal met with other members of the White House staff including Meese and Baker in the West Wing. He had with him some data on DMI's latest surveys of public reaction to Reagan. His popularity had rocketed.

"The public impression of Reagan is not misty any more," Beal told them. "The shooting had turned out to be important to his image. The President is seen as human, warm and courageous." The very attributes that Wirthlin had been packaging as part of Reagan's image during the campaign to combat the picture of him as 'dangerous and uncaring' had now been highlighted dramatically. It had taken a shooting to do it, and it became important to the continuing campaign to sell the President's policies to Congress and the nation. The White House communications staff and strategists saw their opportunity of exploiting the enormous sympathy in the nation for the brave and fortunate leader. When he had recovered they capitalized fully by asking him to make a televised speech on his radical economic program in front of a joint session of Congress. Reagan gave an emotional, overwhelming performance to which the nation responded fully, and the atmosphere this created helped greatly in the implementation of his policies.

BRIDGING THE GENDER GAP

Wirthlin's polls in the early months of the new Presidency isolated a glaring problem which had nagged Reagan in his two major campaigns for the Presidency: the 'Gender Gap'. This was pollster shorthand for the fact that there was a large gap between male and female support for the President. Women were more suspicious of Reagan, and genuinely feared he would lead America into unnecessary war. Their worries were accentuated by events in El Salvador. From the outset of the new administration it became clear that the White House was determined to flex America's military muscle in the Western Hemisphere, where it claimed that the Soviet Union had intervened through arms supplies to leftist guerrillas. The administration moved quickly to portray El Salvador as the key 'domino' in Latin America. If that country was to fall under the control of a left-wing regime, they claimed, this might cause a domino effect in America's backyard right through to adjoining Mexico. However, the administration found that action, even covert, was difficult, for the Vietnam experience was still fresh in the minds of the US media and the public. Yet the Government persisted in gearing up for increased activity in Central America to stop Marxist rebels in El Salvador. American women became concerned. From the White House's point of view, the El Salvador issue had not been handled well. Some intelligent survey work would have warned that public attitude was mixed about American involvement. If there was to be any, the issue would have to be better packaged and presented to the nation.

Wirthlin had monitored Reagan's image for twelve years and had subcategorized it into hundreds of perceptions which were continuously filed on computer. The strategist was always looking for ways to reconcile image problems. He could not do much about the packaging of the El Salvador issue, which was in the control of the White House tacticians who began to play down America's involvement. Wirthlin was however able to offer advice on the Gender Gap, which was a direct result of El Salvador.

DMI's surveys had probed the electorate to ascertain how Reagan's actions and policies could narrow the Gender Gap and make women less suspicious of the President and more favorable toward him. The strategist's computer analysis indicated that one way was to appoint a woman to the Supreme Court Bench. Even before a vacancy occurred Wirthlin had a profile of what sort of woman would be acceptable to the President, Congress and the nation. It added up to Sandra Day O'Connor. She joined the Bench early in the new adminstration when Associate Justice Potter Stewart stepped down, and the appointment paid more than one dividend. At the height of the furore over US intervention in El Salvador early in the year, the Gender Gap had been 12 per cent. After O'Connor joined the Bench, and Latin

America was temporarily less of an issue with the media, it had narrowed to just 5 per cent. Also Reagan was seen to deliver on promises because he had said during the campaign that he would appoint women to key posts. Surveys had found that Carter had not been perceived as delivering on promises, so the contrast was useful for Republican propaganda. Furthermore, it broke Reagan's image as a 'tradition-bound conservative'. It did not matter that O'Connor was not going to behave any less conservatively than anyone else on the Bench. More important was the fact that Reagan, a right-wing Republican, had given a woman a key job on the judiciary.

This strategy was a classic example of how Wirthlin would have liked P & E to work on scores of other issues in a finely-honed overall plan for the Presidency. But by the late summer of 1981, he realized that not everything was going according to plan. P & E was, in fact, running into trouble. Beal had begun to operate the department over a much wider territory than Wirthlin had in mind. The key difference was that where Wirthlin wanted P & E to lay a smooth path for Reagan to implement his goals, Beal was getting involved in the internecine power struggles which decided political tactics and policy. With the assistance of Grayling Achui, who had worked closely with him in the 1980 campaign, Beal was preparing a computer-programmed set of tactics which went far beyond the brief of campaigning by persuading public opinion. P & E was entangling itself in the competition among key advisers to run the Presidency. Soon the knives were out for Beal and the fledgling department.

THE OVAL OFFICE – ON AUTOMATIC PILOT

The Libyan SU 22 jet twisted and banked steeply in an effort to evade the F14 Sidewinder missile. It failed and was blasted into a thousand pieces which showered the calm Bay of Sirte waters on the Libyan coast. It was early on the morning of 19 August 1981 that two jets from the US Navy's aircraft carrier *Nimitz* were involved in a dogfight in which two Libyan jets were shot down. The next day President Reagan, wearing a peak cap captioned 'Commander-in-Chief', and his counselor Edwin Meese appeared on board the aircraft carrier *Constellation* off the Californian coast to watch a show of US Navy air power. According to Hugh Sidey in *Time* magazine of 3 August 1981, "Reagan knew the confrontation was coming and so did his men, right to the fighters in the F14s." Soon after the incident, Beal confirmed in a filmed interview for a British documentary that the conflict and Reagan's special appearance had been prepared as two sequences in a 'pre-scripted event'. The reason was primarily to boost the

President's popularity, and to help support a big build-up of military forces. It was also meant to send the Soviet Union and its supporters like the Libyans a message: "This was a far tougher and more belligerent American administration than the previous one."

"After four years of Jimmy Carter's bad timing and timidity in foreign affairs," Sidey commented, "the world has had to make quite an adjustment. The Soviets, while continuing to denounce Reagan on the surface, have grown oddly silent beneath the waves."

The Bay of Sirte action came soon after Reagan had fired 12,000 air controllers who were striking illegally. Wirthlin found that these carefully considered hard-hitting decisions had worked. His surveys showed that support for Reagan had deepened across the country. A big percentage of those questioned felt both initiatives had been "clearly in the national interest". The Libyan incident particularly was the culmination of the efforts of a team of technicians – political tacticians, pollsters, marketing and advertising people – who dominated the early period of the Reagan Presidency. They included advisers Meese, James Baker and Michael Deaver, pollster-strategists Wirthlin, Beal and Robert Teeter, and a team of 'communications' people led by David Gergen who handled the media.

Until the Libyan incident most of the press and media had given Reagan an extended honeymoon because of the assassination attempt and his stunning victories with Congress, particularly with intricate budget and tax proposals which reversed the policies of two generations. He had also had a reasonable meeting with European leaders in Ottawa, and had appeared to take firm action with both the air traffic controllers and the Libyans. Very few regular White House correspondents were questioning the President's actual role in all these 'successful' initiatives, apart from applauding his TV performances. However, there was plenty of guessing about how the Presidency actually operated. With Meese feeding Reagan strategies and policy initiatives to be ratified, the Oval Office seemed to be on automatic pilot, and for a short while the Presidency was programmed in much the same way that Reagan's campaign had been. Meese reveled in his sudden rise to prominence and the press began referring to him as Prime Minister, or even President Meese. As well as P & E, Policy Development and the National Security Council reported directly to him. Because of his support from Beal and others Meese was able to translate the President's ideas into substance, and he was seen as Reagan's conceptualizer and the main policy funnel to the President. In those early stages his closeness to Reagan (he had been chief of staff with his Californian administration in the 1960s and 1970s) and his command over the flow of ideas made him the White House's prime mover. The press became fully alert to his power when the two Libyan jets were shot down in the Bay of Sirte. Meese waited until six hours after the incident before waking the President at 4.30 a.m. to give him the news. The media wanted to know why he had delayed, and Reagan obliged by saying, "If our planes were shot down they would wake me right away. If the other fellow's were shot down, why wake me up?"

Soon afterward, like a lawyer counseling a client, Meese broke in when reporters tried, during a photo session, to question the President about the MX missile. "Mr President, you're not obliged to answer any questions," Meese said.

When another reporter asked Reagan why the administration's decision on how to base MX missiles was slipping behind schedule, Meese interrupted and said that it was right on schedule, with a decision due in a few weeks. He continued to shield and protect Reagan from the media, who were beginning to suspect the President's ignorance of key issues. Matters were not helped by Reagan's embarrassingly weak displays at press conferences in which he showed a lack of briefing and knowledge. Apologists for the President referred to his habit of delegating authority just like a chief executive of a corporation, and compared him to Jimmy Carter who immersed himself in detail even to the point of scheduling who could play on the White House tennis courts. However, the longest honeymoon for any President since Roosevelt was over, and observers in Washington turned their attention to working out who really had the power in the White House.

Late in 1981, the battle for influence in the Oval Office shifted. With P & E not showing its early effectiveness, and bigger battles with Congress in play, James Baker, the White House chief of staff, moved up next to Meese in the power hierarchy. The tacticians had begun to take charge.

REAGAN'S DIRTY LINEN

The President had been diligently working his way through a six-inch pile of folders on his Oval Office desk when he came across a press item which angered him. It was a detailed internal analysis of his Gender Gap problem which had been written by Beal. Reagan immediately rang Wirthlin to complain that he did not like his dirty linen being washed in public. It was an embarrassing moment for the strategist who had placed Beal very close to the President. Beal had been writing many reports without consulting Wirthlin, and one of them concerned Beal's own appraisal of the Gender Gap and how the problem should be tackled. The report had been widely circulated in the White House, and finally leaked to the press. The problem was further aggravated by Beal not returning Wirthlin's calls.

Beal's over-zealous activity was in part attributable to his faith, for as a devout Mormon he took his role in Government very seriously and adhered strictly to the church's Doctrine of the Covenants, which dictated that "All men should uphold their Governments . . . Governments were instituted of God for the benefit of men." Inextricably bound to this was a total, almost blind dedication to the nation's leader, who in this case happened to be well disposed to the church's views on most issues. It was no coincidence that Mormons poured into the new administration, especially the CIA, the FBI and military intelligence where loyalty to the US Government is an important requirement. In theory, at least, Mormon spies and others dealing with sensitive intelligence work were less likely to be 'turned' by the KGB. Beal's dedication caused him to become precipitately involved in trying to see that some of Reagan's more extreme aims were achieved, and this brought him into conflict with some of the more moderate people in the White House, such as James Baker, the powerful chief of staff. One of these aims was the slashing of social security, which Beal and others felt should be pushed through with other legislation in the initial months while Reagan's popularity was still high, especially after the assassination attempt. Baker was annoyed that a social security package should be rushed through. He complained that the political arm of the White House, which worked with members of Congress to ease the passage of proposed legislation, had not had enough time to consider it properly. Baker made sure that some of the proposed cuts were eventually dropped. After that incident, he and his deputy, Richard Darman, were on the lookout for any more plans from Beal that did not meet with their methods and moderate politics, which were often a long way from Reagan's more right-wing views. This, plus the Gender Gap incident and some less than brilliant plans emanating from P & E, did not help the new department's reputation. Beal seemed to feel that proximity to the Oval Office was power alone, not realizing that his power was Wirthlin's power. P & E had been set up as his vehicle. When it stayed within its brief it worked well for the President in those early months following Wirthlin's Initial Action Plan.

P & E's failure to provide a strategic overview was a disappointment rather than a blow to Wirthlin, for he knew that only someone as close as he was to the President could have developed the department the way he intended. But Wirthlin had made the decision to stay out of the White House, which meant that a fully operational P & E department – tapping into all sources of Government information to guide the Presidency – would have to wait for a more propitious moment. In the meantime, Wirthlin continued to take a key advisory role for the President by 'laying out the numbers' on the nation's mood. He remained Reagan's seeing-eye dog through the maze of public perceptions on every major move the President made. The strategist could not avoid flak from all White House factions, for his job was to read the public mind for the President rather than push for a particular line. Yet because he remained outside the White House, and because of the impotency of P & E, he was not seen as a rival to anyone's power pretensions. Wirthlin could not set policy, but he could counsel, and because of his connection with the President, he could have influence.

The strategist's eyes were set firmly on the future. He had to consider such questions as, how would this action or that gesture affect the President's public standing, and in turn, his chances for re-election? Even as early as 1981 Wirthlin was preparing for his expected role as strategist for the 1984 Presidential campaign – if Reagan decided to run – which would use an even more sophisticated PINS simulation system. Wirthlin had, in fact, never stopped fine-tuning it.

CHAPTER 18
BLOODY BUT UNBOWED

THE CADDELL INTERVIEW

Pat Caddell, head bowed and hands in pockets, was strolling along K Street in Washington DC when he heard his name called. He turned and could see people in a taxi waving at him. He stopped as members of a British film crew jumped out and ran toward him. Caddell was aware that they were in town making a documentary on Reagan's Presidency and his election victory in November 1980, nearly a year ago. The strategist had not been keen to be part of an inquest into 1980, and had not bothered to answer the crew's pleas for an interview. However, its researchers had been persistent, and when they finally spoke to him in person, he agreed to be interviewed.

Three days later the crew were set up in the strategist's office waiting to catch him, *cinema vérité*, as he came to work. Caddell lumbered in to be greeted by a cameraman and sound technician. He was not amused and mumbled an expletive as he examined the appointments book on the desk of his secretary, Harriet. Without another word he marched into his office and slammed down a folder on his desk, swearing vehemently. He had just had a disagreement with a client and was in no mood to be interrogated on camera about last year's election. Although TV was central to his own operations as a pollster-strategist, he often detested the medium and despite his reputation as being one of the most open, candid and informative of all political operatives in the country, he was sometimes suspicious of journalists' motives.

The director – leading British film-maker Jack Grossman – the interviewer and the crew hovered outside until beckoned in by the secretary. Without saying a word, Caddell gave them the distinct impression that they were encroaching on his precious time. There were no introductions, no small talk, in fact, no talk at all as the crew readied itself. There was no rehearsal, and the interview began amid much tension. Caddell was defensive when questioned about the 1980 campaign, but loosened up when the interviewer, Edwin Graham, switched to more general areas, and to his thoughts on the Reagan Presidency. "Have modern election techniques driven some of the better people out of politics?" Graham asked.

"Oh sure," Caddell replied candidly. "We [political consultants, strategists, pollsters] have pre-empted the political system. We decide who are the best and more likely people to be successful, and so we have contributed to the decline of political parties. I'm not sure it's healthy at all, and it's a question that bothers me greatly."

"What sort of people do you look for?"

"We look for people who give quick and often facile answers. People who look good on TV and who can project the kinds of messages we want to project. Whether or not they understand them is a different question. Because of TV, we don't look for people who have deep, thoughtful, complex and complicated approaches to life, because we wouldn't be able to put them on TV."

Caddell refused to name any examples, but he did say this new breed had formed into a professional class of politician who were among the most 'gutless' people he had ever met.

The interviewer switched to questions about the style of the Reagan administration. "If anything," the Democratic strategist said adamantly, "they are the most ideological administration we've ever had. They do most things because they believe in them, and they use politics well to back up their goals." He was asked to expand on that and be more specific. Did he mean their approach to Latin America? "Well, yes," Caddell said. "There are a number of issues in which this administration seems to be willing to say – 'I believe this is right and we will try to do this, come hell or high water.' Then they use techniques [the manipulation loops] to steamroll public opinion – the public consensus – and they seem to have less interest in the public process than they ought to."

"You were recently quoted in the *New York Times* as saying you 'could kiss Wirthlin and Beal' for using 'themes' to help run the Reagan Presidency," Graham said. "What did you mean?"

"I spent a lot of the last four years in enormous frustration trying to make the Carter administration understand the importance of sending larger signals – of having themes with which to lead public policy. By that I mean I wanted the administration to spend a lot more time and effort in explaining where it was going and what it was doing so that it could attract support. This is an essential part of the process of governing."

"And are you saying that Wirthlin and Beal do this well?"

Caddell nodded. "These Reagan people clearly understand the importance of thematic approaches in their explanation of their policies," he said. "By contrast, I ended up with an administration that was proficient at getting elected and then kicked politics out the door. They thought government in a vacuum was efficient government. That usually ends up in disaster – at least in terms of public support."

The crew had filmed Richard Beal on camera the previous day

in the White House's Old Executive Office Building. Beal had implied that US action against Libya in the Bay of Sirte in August had been a 'pre-scripted' event and part of a theme. In other words, the White House had planned to provoke the Libyans into attacking their naval force in the Bay so that it could teach the Libyans a lesson, which would also be a signal to Libya's friends in the Kremlin. This was supposed to be part of a larger theme to demonstrate that the Reagan administration was much tougher than its predecessor, and that it would not stand any nonsense from Soviet surrogates like Libya or Cuba. In the subsequent action, two Libyan jets were shot down. The interviewer wanted the Democrat's reaction to this.

"That's technicians getting carried away!" Caddell said vehemently, "I can understand their argument for focusing attention – early in the administration – on economic issues, for in fact, they have been trying to redirect the Government. They use themes to that end. I also understand that they use their economic reasons [themes such as 'getting Government off the backs of industry and the people'] as a shroud for a lot of ideological moves. OK, that's acceptable." Caddell leaned forward on his desk. "But the idea of scripting events – of shooting down other people's jets – is godammed – pardon me – is a very, very dangerous thing to do. That's technicians getting way out of hand in their responsibility as public officials." The strategist thumped the desk. "And if that's in fact what they are doing, then the American media has missed its obligation to expose it. As a technician, I will tell you that's dangerous! Dangerous! DANGEROUS!"

Graham and the director, Grossman, were pleased with this response, for Caddell had appeared very aggressive. Instead of mumbling into his beard as he had with other replies, he had made his points forcefully. Now the interviewer tried to draw him on his views about 1984. Whom did he think the Democratic candidate for the Presidency would be? Caddell thought it was too early to say because the conditions were not similar to those in 1973 and 1974 when Carter had emerged as a contender for the 1976 presidential battle as a reaction to Watergate and the end of the Vietnam war. "We are in a very exciting period," he said, "where Reagan's initiatives are attempting to supplant the consensus in America with an ideological rigidity."

"Do you hope to be the pollster for whomever emerges as the Democratic nominee in 1984?" Graham asked.

"Given the direction of the country [under Reagan] I would like to take a position larger than that of a pollster," Caddell began. "I am desperately concerned with the direction this country is going. I don't think that technicians like me can any longer say 'I am only responsible for getting a candidate elected.' We have a greater responsibility for the people we have had elected."

"Then you want some sort of role in Government?"

"No. I want to shape political strategy. I think my ideas will pan out to have some viability."

"Between now and 1984?" the interviewer asked finally, and Caddell nodded emphatically.

When the filming was over Graham expressed his fascination with the final Caddell answers. What ideas, he wondered, did the strategist have in mind? The interviewer and the director resolved to watch Caddell's moves closely to see how his concepts would develop and influence the 1984 presidential election.

RISE OF THE TACTICIANS

Republican Senator Jepsen from Iowa started crying. He had been sitting at his desk in his Washington DC office speaking softly and hesitantly about competing claims on his loyalties, when he slumped forward and broke down. The Senator had been one of the most outspoken leaders of the opposition to the US sale to Saudi Arabia of military communications planes and equipment (AWACS) worth a record eight billion dollars. It was late 1981, and the US House of Representatives had rejected the deal. The White House needed a majority victory in the Senate for the deal to go through. James Baker had directed a highpowered lobby which entailed a combination of personal cajoling, patriotic pleading, some old-fashioned horse trading and tough political pressure. In Jepsen's case, for instance, the President was on the phone personally reminding him how he had supported the Senator's underdog candidacy in 1978. His party and country needed him, Reagan said. Eventually people such as Jepsen cracked, and the sale became one of the biggest foreign policy coups of the Reagan Presidency.

It was a most important victory. If Congress had turned down, the sale, Reagan's ability to conduct any effective foreign policy would have been called into question. If he could not deliver on this promise, how could foreign leaders trust any other commitment he might make? In Europe as well as Middle East capitals, US allies had awaited the vote as a test of Reagan's credibility in defining American policy. Two days before the Senate vote, there appeared to be 55 Senators committed to or leaning toward rejection, which was a few too many. Baker and his aides directed the President to the wavering Senators and briefed him on the best way to persuade them to change their minds. In the end it was a selling job, and Reagan became fully aware of the effectiveness of Baker and his staff.

The President appreciated the marketing end of the political business better than anything else, and the success meant that the stocks of the former Houston lawyer were high for the rest of Reagan's first term in office. Until the AWACS deal, Baker had been handicapped by not being a Californian insider, and by the fact that he had fought against Reagan, first for Gerald Ford in 1976, and then as director for George Bush's presidential bid in 1980. But his managerial and decision-making skills soon gained him respect among the more laid-back Californians. Added to this was Baker's personal security. He was as rich as Reagan and from one of Houston's oldest familes. He was also used to the hurly-burly of big business in Texas, so it was perhaps inevitable that he would emerge powerful in the struggle for control of the White House, which to him was just another big corporation. Some insiders even referred jokingly to him as 'JB', a jibe related to his love of the TV series *Dallas*, starring 'JR'. Key to Baker's power in the White House was his control of the staff. He and his people were responsible for turning Reagan's broad goals into legislative reality. In so doing, the Baker group, which was the acceptable face of moderation in the conservative White House, took the far-right-wing sting out of Reaganism on most policy positions, particularly in the case of economic and domestic issues.

The Baker team was called the Legislative Strategy Group (LSG) and its core included coordinator Richard Darman, Congressional liaison Kenneth Duberstein, cabinet secretary Craig Fuller, Baker and Meese. Since there were few issues which did not have legislative implications, the LSG became visibly involved in a wide range of issues. Its tight, powerful organization took power away from the stategists, policy developers and all areas of the administration from State to Commerce. In the battle for influence in the most important political center in the world, such control caused tensions. The issue focused as a fight between the moderates led by Baker and Darman, and the Reaganites led by Meese, who while a member of LSG, was concerned that the President's more right-wing ideology was being ignored. So were many other groups in and outside the administration, such as the Heritage Foundation, who saw Reagan's more radical goals as being thwarted by the moderates. A main factor in the struggle was the mastery of the paper flow to the President, which fell into the hands of Richard Darman – described by one neutral inside observer as having "intellectually the sharpest mind in the White House, with elbows to match". Viewed as more moderate than Baker, he had risen to fame in 1973 for being a self-imposed victim of Richard Nixon's 'Saturday night massacre' when Elliot Richardson resigned as the US Attorney-General. (Darman served under

Richardson in five cabinet departments – State; Health; Education and Welfare; Defense; Justice and Commerce – in the Republican administrations of Nixon and Ford.) Richardson had refused to obey Nixon's order to fire Watergate special prosecutor Archibald Cox, and Darman, who had been working for Richardson, walked out with him.

Almost anything that went to or came from the President passed through Darman. It was a tedious, demanding role involving fourteen-hour days, not compatible with the more relaxed attitude of the Californians. Yet Darman was not simply in control of the 'in-out' basket. Like a young Stalin in Lenin's Russia, he learned fast that guarding the information flow meant power. Administrators liked to call it 'quality control'. Darman became a setter of standards, rejecting material from advisers that he considered "not of proper intellectual quality to go to the President." The White House thus had its best political editor since Bob Haldeman of the Nixon years. Darman often asked for more information and was always involved in condensing it in something digestible for Reagan. "I read slightly more than the President," Darman said in a sardonic understatement to the *Los Angeles Times* in 1981. He was also able to be selective. Anything that did not quite suit the moderates' ideology could be thrown out, or modified – a situation which bestowed subtle power on the ambitious forty year old. Big names like Secretary of State Al Haig as well as lesser known operatives like Richard Beal ran into difficulties with him and lost, as did those wanting the Reagan Presidency to be far more conservative. This, naturally, created enemies. However, what kept Darman and Baker in full flight was their continuing successes. LSG scraped together enough votes in the Congress in many major legislative battles by being well managed and efficient, and by making an excellent choice of tactics for each occasion. With each issue, once the objective was known, Darman began by asking a set of questions. "What was our target coalition? Did we avoid the Democratic leadership or go the bipartisan route? Who were the key people to rely on as leaders or mediators? Did we stage a massive grass-roots campaign [for instance, by using Reagan in a major TV selling address of a policy goal]? Or did we take a behind-the-scenes negotiating tack? What leverage did we have? What were the fallback positions? What did we have in reverse and when should we have used it?"

In the brilliant first year of his Presidency Reagan had been able to follow through vigorously on his economic package as set down by Wirthlin in the Initial Actions Plan. Reagan was very popular, while Democrats were still shell-shocked by Carter's crushing defeat in 1980, and by the Senate having a Republican majority.

During 1981 the White House was able to bulldoze its way into the House of Representatives (still with a majority of Democrats) and divide and conquer the various factions in the Democratic Party while relying on the almost completely party-whipped Republicans to support Reagan. The White House used him via the media to reach the grass-roots supporters, and the President was hailed as the smartest Congressional operator since LBJ or even Franklin D. Roosevelt. However, after the euphoric first year things became tougher, and Reagan had to learn to compromise just as he had in the course of his first term as Californian Governor.

Achieving the right conciliation on issues was the job of the LSG, and it took over. It was nothing for the group to alter decisions made by the cabinet or coming from the Oval Office in order to accommodate political pressures from Congress and elsewhere. Sometimes it was simply a matter of semantics which made the Reagan Presidency appear more flexible. When, for example, a resolution calling for a freeze on the production of nuclear weapons seemed likely to pass in the House, the LSG convinced Reagan that, contrary to policy pressed by the State Department, he must embrace an alternative resolution that included the word 'freeze'. The group used its power to neglect certain issues that didn't suit its more middle-of-the-road stance. Onto the shelf went the program to dismantle the Department of Education, and the attempt to pass a constitutional amendment to ban abortion. Legislative issues that did not go well for the Reagan administration were handled so adroitly by the LSG that they were not seen as central to the Reagan program. Contentious voting rights amendments, for instance, and the much heralded New Federalism (increased power and finance to the States) were put on the back-burner. The controversial Social Security package was watered down.

Semantics, too, played their part in reversing Reagan's position on taxes, about which he had been most adamant in his election campaign. He was only going to cut them, he said, not increase them. However, as President, he had to make a big U-turn in the summer of 1982. Reagan accepted, and even lobbied hard for a $98.6 billion three-year tax increase that had been fashioned by Republican Senator Robert Dole. The LSG convinced Reagan that without the extra funds his economic program would be dead, and that his political popularity would fall dramatically. It excluded anyone from its meetings that opposed the Dole tax bill, and referred to it as a 'tax reform' package when consulting with the President. Reagan got the message and when selling it to the nation, used the same term. He followed this up soon afterward by endorsing a Congressional proposal to raise the Federal gasoline tax five cents per gallon. The idea was to use the money to repair the nation's highways, bridges and mass-transit systems, although he had previously said that only a 'palace coup' could get him to raise taxes to do so. 'Editor' Darman had put a red line through 'tax' and scribbled above it 'user fee'. As long as the dreaded word 'tax' was omitted, the boss was happy.

Whether or not Reagan was fully aware of it, a part-palace coup had taken place from the end of 1981. Reaganism had been replaced by Bakerism, at least on many economic and domestic issues.

Nevertheless on at least one issue the President was adamant. He, would not countenance any slow-down in military spending. According to *Time* magazine of 13 December 1982, "Baker so nettled Reagan at one meeting by pressing for excise taxes and defense cuts, that the President took off his glasses, glared at his aide, and asked, 'If that's what you believe, then what in the hell are you doing here?' " Prudence stopped the mild-mannered chief of staff from telling him.

CLARK AND FOREIGN POLICY BY SPASM

'Reagan Chooses Nitwit as Minister', read the headline in an Amsterdam newspaper. The London *Daily Mirror* commented: "America's allies in Europe will hope he is never in charge at a time of crisis." These were some of the harsher judgements made on William P. Clark in February 1981 after he had testified before the US Senate Foreign Relations Committee on his qualifications to serve as US Deputy Secretary of State. He was unable to identify the Prime Ministers of South Africa and Zimbabwe. He was ignorant of the state of nuclear weapons in Europe or the upheavels in the British Labour Party. Clark had proved to be an appointee who rocketed to new heights of ignorance for such an important foreign policy post. Perhaps only in the US could such glaring old-boy-network patronage have been tried, let alone accepted. Clark was a good and trusted friend of Reagan's. He had been chief of staff in 1967 when the then Governor Reagan wanted his Sacramento California office reorganized. Clark was the insider's insider. He had hired Meese and Deaver to the Reagan governorship, and it was Meese that made a personal plea to him to join the Reagan presidential administration as Deputy Secretary of State, primarily to act as a watchdog over the unpredictable Secretary, Al Haig.

Clark was not all that keen to join at first, and candidly admitted, "I didn't know any more about the subject [of foreign affairs] than any casual reader of *Time* or *Newsweek*." However, he relented for the sake of his old friend Reagan. When the undistinguished National Security Adviser, Richard V. Allen, was forced to resign early in 1982, Clark moved into the position which needed even more expertise than anything he had done at State. This job had been held down recently by such heavyweights as Henry Kissinger and Zbigniew Brzezinski who had been the closest advisers to Presidents Nixon, Ford and Carter. It demanded a deep knowledge of defense, foreign affairs and even economics to be run to its full potential. In practice, the role was that of sieve and synthesizer of all national security matters filtering through to the Oval Office. With Clark indelicately placed there, the hope that he would never be in charge in a time of crisis must have turned to an eel of fear in the bowels of European allies. After his inauspicious debut in front of the Foreign Relations Committee, few observers were convinced by White House public relations claims that Clark had learned "a lot" as Deputy Secretary of State. His new role was hyped up as 'managerial'. He would be a 'mediator' between the Haig *v.* Baker-Darman factions. For all that, it left Reagan with just two people who had any real expertise in foreign affairs – Jeane Kirkpatrick, Ambassador to the UN, and Haig – and by early 1982 the latter was on the way out. Nevertheless, Clark was assured of far greater access to Reagan than anyone else. Soon he had taken from Meese control of the NSC's information flow and was seeing the President daily on matters of foreign policy. This upset Baker and Darman, for so long as Meese was the funnel for NSC paper flow, they virtually controlled what the President read on foreign affairs. Furthermore, Clark was a noted right-wing hardliner, who indulged Reagan's prejudices.

When Haig quit in the middle of 1982 the vacuum of foreign affairs expertise in the Reagan administration was all but complete. Haig's successor, George Shultz, had gained international respect as an economist and as a member of the giant Bechtel Corporation, a construction company which had extensive dealings with Middle East countries, particularly Saudi Arabia. Initially, however, he preferred to take a low-key stance and stay out of the news as much as possible. Shultz was far more inclined to try to solve problems, rather than just taking ideological sides, like Clark. "Clark only had to look at CIA reports coming in to him every day to bolster his own thin knowledge and attitudes, on the Soviets, for instance," one White House aide noted. Shultz, on the other hand, was held in such high regard that he could begin to maneuver for more moderate positions on world issues without upsetting the right wing of the White House and Congress. His influence, while held from public view, was powerful during the summer of 1982, when he turned the White House away from its policies of applying sanctions to the European allies for their participation in the Soviet natural gas pipeline project. He thus lessened the strains in relations with Europe, where he was the most respected person in the Reagan administration.

By late 1982, as the President battled with Congress on major issues of foreign policy and national security, Clark and Baker emerged as rival architects trying to accomplish Reagan's goals, which included his efforts to continue military build-up, win Congressional approval for deployment of the MX missile, and bolster anti-communist forces in Central America. Clark advised Reagan that he could risk being more hard-line and militant. Baker wanted the President to be more flexible and compromising – as he had been on domestic and economic issues, mainly as a result of his chief of staff's subtle directives. It became a battle between two hard-working and soft-spoken lawyers. Clark's style acted like a sedative on the White House and his demeanor, which appeared benign, polite and thoughtful, was mistaken by many for sagacity. Yet his much-vaunted managerial skills made him a formidable force. Both he and Baker shared a conservative outlook, but where Clark reinforced Reagan's gut political instincts, Baker appealed to the President's political antennae by making him more aware of Congress and public opinion. The differences were highlighted when Reagan was pulled in two different directions regarding military spending. Clark wanted Reagan to ignore Congress and push maximum increases, whereas Baker wanted compromise because he was more in touch with realities on Capitol Hill.

Clark's basic hard line was backed by Meese and Casper Weinberger, the tough Defense Secretary, another of the front-line members of the administration with meager knowledge of foreign affairs and defense matters before taking office. Weinberger was an easy captive of the Pentagon on account of his right-wing views. He had been Director of Finance during Reagan's governorship before serving Nixon, first as chairman of the Federal Trades Commission, then as director of the Office of Management and Budget, and finally as Secretary of Health, Education and Welfare. In the Reagan administration his political skills were stretched one hundredfold as he took charge of demanding 30 per cent of the entire US budget for the military. He naturally sided with anyone, particularly Clark, who would push, squeeze and cajole every extra dollar for the biggest military machine in history. Against this hawkish combination were set Baker, Darman and to a lesser extent George Shultz, who was gradually having a greater influence on Reagan's foreign policy.

COMPUTER FOR CONFLICT

In October 1982, William Clark, Reagan's security adviser, asked Richard Beal to join the National Security Council. The invitation was music to Beal's ears, for he had considered quitting the administration and going back to teaching. Since the Department of Planning and Evaluation had run into political opposition a year earlier, Beal had been in a frustrating period of limbo. His spirits had been lifted in the middle of 1982 when Reagan sent him to India to arrange for Prime Minister Gandhi's visit to the US – a move that went some way to improving US-Indian relations which had been strained for some time. Beal had spent much of 1979 at Jawaharlah Nehru University in New Delhi on a visiting Fulbright-Hays scholarship, which added to his broad knowledge of international relations. Back at P & E after his diplomatic mission to India, however, his fortunes dipped again when the *Washington Post* obtained a simulated projection from P & E of the President's chances in the 1984 presidential election. This indicated that Reagan would lose to John Glenn and just beat Walter Mondale. The President was naturally unhappy about the report, although Beal was not reprimanded by him directly. It was then that Beal thought seriously about leaving, but Clark came to the beleaguered strategist's rescue. Clark knew of Beal's expertise in the study of crisis in international politics, and asked him to join the NSC to create a computer system which could be relied on to give Reagan answers and options in times of international, and even internal, strife. Clark, conscious of his own lack of knowledge of foreign affairs, was happy to introduce an all-powerful computer rather than call on assistance from others who might weaken his influence with the President. As Beal reported directly to Clark, the system would be under his control and would thus increase his power, especially if access was limited to just a few key NSC staff, such as Beal and Robert 'Bud' McFarlane, the deputy director of the NSC.

When Beal joined the NSC late in 1982, he immediately began designing the new network which promised to transform a vital part of the Presidency. Nothing tested the mettle of a President and those around him more than a crisis like the Iranian hostage incident, or the 1962 attempt by Russia to place missiles in Cuba. The former academic and devout young Mormon suddenly had the responsibility of taking crisis management into the computer age, with all the consequences that this implied. The world had become Beal's laboratory, and he now had the opportunity to develop fully a network with which he had experimented over a decade. But instead of wargaming on university computers he was now dealing with actual events.

Richard Beal had learned the basis for the development at NSC at the University of Southern California between 1972 and 1974 under Charles A. McClelland. Beal had come from the relatively isolated world of Brigham Young University with an MA and a burning interest in international relations – how nations related and reacted to each other, especially in times of political tension. Those who worked with him, such as fellow students Nancy Wilshausen and Frederick Rothe, found him very ambitious and "incredibly bright". "He was easy to get along with and always patient and helpful," Wilshausen said, "but he worked so hard and put on so much weight that I worried about his health."

Beal quickly taught himself to program computers at USC because he became aware early of the advantages of technology in his field. He went on to make a science of political study, which hitherto had been considered an art. Tantalized by the possibility of being able to predict international crises, Beal became a master of the technology and applied it to studying WEIS – World Event/Interaction Survey. Its aim was to link a variety of different intelligence data into a dynamic graphical pattern which could highlight peaks and troughs of activity between nations. In turn, this could indicate if a war was brewing somewhere in the world. This 'intelligence' data was restricted at USC to collecting clippings from the *New York Times* and London *Times* newspapers and filing them under different headings. These showed, for instance, whether nations were talking, fighting or cooperating with each other. While on face value the basic data seemed flimsy, the two newspapers concerned had a history of covering events sometimes with greater depth and accuracy than government intelligence agencies, for reporters could often go where CIA people, for example, could not. More impressive were the scores of categories collected from the papers which could be programmed to show trends. By linking all the categories such as 'force', 'request', 'deny', 'demand', 'warn', 'threaten', which showed the relationship between certain nations over twenty years, it was possible to consider the peaks and troughs on a graph. When the bumps were spotted, the theory went, potential areas of trouble could be isolated. This was about as far as it could go in the university computer room. However, some useful indications emerged from those basic patterns. For example, WEIS discovered that crises occurred whenever the system appeared overloaded: an increased level of threats and warnings was an obvious indication of coming conflict. On the other hand, if communications, even aggressive dialog, fell away this could also indicate a conspiracy. A military attack might be imminent. In other words, 'underload' meant potential crisis too. In a study of the period

1966 to 1976, WEIS uncovered 'critical stress points in the flow' in events from the June war (Israel-Egypt) of May-June 1967, right through to the Lebanese civil war and Syrian intervention in the period September 1975 to May 1976. Beal and the other students were excited by the fact that if the US Government had been using such a system, it may well have been able to predict, for example, the surprise attack on Israel by Egypt in the Yom Kippur War of October 1973. Some saw the possibility of taking the concept to a highly sophisticated level so that coming wars could be accurately predicted and acted on, and Beal decided to make the development of WEIS his academic speciality.

Not surprisingly, Clark's offer was beyond Beal's wildest dreams, and within weeks of his unpublicized switch from P & E to the NSC, boxes of equipment were obstructing the corridor of the Old Executive Office Building's second floor outside his office in Room 200. He had asked for and received the latest and best technology. There were six powerful Digital computers, scores of terminals, and General Electric scanners and processors. The scanners could 'read' and electronically edit all the intelligence coming, in standard form, from all the sources the US Government could reach worldwide. The CIA, the NSA, the military and State Department officials would be sending input to the proposed system via satellites and other means of communication. WEIS had come a long way since the primitive days of newspaper cuttings, although reliable information from journalists would still be used in the new advanced system. When the huge amounts of data arrived daily the processors and scanners would strip away excess words to the bare essentials and store the information on computer. A message would appear on TV terminal screens telling the users that filing had taken place. The detail could be flashed up if requested.

Beal aimed to link and synthesize information so he could monitor trouble spots anywhere in the world, whether they be the China-Vietnam border, the Iran-Iraq war, or Beirut. The strategist hoped that by the second half of 1983 or early 1984 the President would not just be relying on data taken individually from the military, or the CIA or the NSA. The National Security Council would have the capability to integrate and sift all the data coming in to the White House – in keeping with the NSC's true role – so that the Commander-in-Chief could press a button and see the options at his disposal in a crisis, with summary reports. Beal, in fact, did not want the system to produce just summaries. He was determined to introduce computerized maps of the trouble spots which would allow the President to make an instant decision on, for instance, where an invasion force might be landed. This visual data of an area would be supplemented by satellite photos and other information which could make or break a mission. Beal, for example, was particularly concerned with the failure of the US military to free hostages in Iran. In his opinion, if some of the top-level decision makers had had a better understanding of the distances, the soil topography and conditions in general, the rescue mission might have been successful. Yet the strategist's ambitious project was not merely aimed at presenting military options to the President. He wanted the Commander-in-Chief to push one button and see the problem, and then be able to push another and see all the economic, cultural and political conditions connected with the trouble spot.

Suppose, for example, the President was considering invading a country near US borders because he believed it posed a threat to America's national interest. The computer system would be able to present the President with instant details of actions which could put economic pressures on the country rather than invading it. He could also see the political ramifications of a decision to invade, such as the effect diplomatically on allies and enemies. Beal's aim was to avoid the President being backed into a corner and left thinking he had just one military option open to him in the event of a crisis requiring immediate decisions. The strategist's idea was to provide in addition quick diplomatic and trade options which could possibly avoid confrontation and military risks.

The same principles were to apply to internal US crises, and Beal had been asked to monitor the potential trouble spot of the 1984 summer Olympics in Los Angeles. In late 1982, those in charge of security were preparing for it as if they were certain of a terrorist attack. The Olympic Law Enforcement Coordinating Council began cooperating with Beal and the President. Twenty-seven subcommittees in charge of everything from intelligence to communications were set up. If the worst were to happen, as it did in Munich in 1972 when Israeli athletes were taken hostage, Reagan would be better prepared than any previous leader of a nation hosting an Olympics.

Although Beal had failed at the Department of Planning and Evaluation to set up a system to guide the Presidency by computer, he found himself directing an effort to control and computerize international and internal crises – the most important aspect of the Presidency in the nuclear age.

FACING REALITIES

At the time Richard Beal was being resurrected at the White House, key members of Kennedy's staff were preparing something similar for the Senator. Dr Larry Horowitz and Robert Shrum had written a 'Black Book' which was to be Kennedy's strategist path to the Presidency in 1984. They wanted to put pressure on their boss to make a decision to run by the end of 1982 for they feared if he left it any longer it would be too late. The other leading Democrats, Walter Mondale and John Glenn, had already clocked up nearly two years' campaigning.

The Horowitz–Shrum document showed that they had learned many of the lessons of failure in 1980. They planned to ask Caddell, the person who had done most to ruin Kennedy's 1980 bid, to be the 1984 strategist. In addition, Kennedy now had his own PAC – Political Action Committee – which used computerized direct mail for raising funds and attacking opponents, which had been the method used against him in 1980. Furthermore, there would be more emphasis on controlling the candidate through staged media events to ensure regular publicity, and deft slogans and themes would be developed to carry the campaign. Kennedy would not be hidden from the press, but he wouldn't be handed to them on a platter either. His on-the-trail campaigning would be used judiciously, and his forceful oratory would be continually scripted to hammer the main themes.

A practice run took place in November 1982 when the partially 'new look' Kennedy fought for and won his Massachusetts Senate seat comfortably. Michael Kaye from Los Angeles, who had been California Governor Gerry Brown's ad man, handled the TV ads. He took note of Caddell's methods of shattering Kennedy's image and decided to use the same tactics, but in reverse. The Senator was portrayed emotionally as the good family man – the caring father. As family head responsible for his own children and those of his slain brothers, there was plenty of genuine heart-warming material to use. Caddell was commissioned to poll the effectiveness of the advertising. Yet the concern was not how well it was received in Massachusetts, but in nearby New Hampshire, the location of the first 1984 primary and the graveyard for countless past presidential hopefuls. Caddell's secret findings had some influence on Kennedy. On the one hand, the ads had some positive effects. On the other, they had not totally dispelled the basic character problem.

The Senator also had to consider the decision that he and his wife Joan had taken to divorce. That would not be finalized until late 1983, which did not leave much time for Kennedy to build a strong new family image. He did not need telling that it would be better to run for the Presidency with a wife at his side. If he decided that a new marriage was imperative for running, he would have to marry again soon after his divorce. The rush to the altar, Kennedy realized, might look too contrived.

After consultation with his family, Kennedy began to see a bid for the Presidency in 1988 as more compelling. The Chappaquiddick incident would be almost two decades behind him by then. A whole generation of voters born after the incident would come on to the electoral rolls. Also, given another five or six years from now, he would have a decent chance to find a suitable new wife and even start another family. Moreover, he would be able to avoid running against Reagan, a formidable opponent at any time. If Reagan was to win office for two terms, the Republicans in 1988 would be forced to field a new candidate, which would improve Kennedy's chances. By then the Senator would be gambling on the electorate's swinging to a more liberal Democrat in reaction to eight years of right-wing administration. In the end, it added up to a decision not to run in 1984.

In a successful 'media event' he held a press conference and used his children, who were placed in front of the cameras, as the reason for his decision. They did not want him to run again because they feared the strain of another campaign, and the dangers it would pose. Kennedy's critics were cynical about his using the family this way, although his children, especially Patrick, did have some influence over his decision. Whichever way it was viewed, the Senator made his point dramatically and forcefully. In essence he had been beaten again – this time before he even started – by the strategists and their technology. But if he was to run again, he planned to use *them* to give himself a greater chance of victory.

CHAPTER 19
TUNING UP FOR 1984

THE SOOTHSAYER

In a tongue-in-cheek ceremony at the *Washington Post* early in November 1982, Richard Wirthlin was given the 'Crystal Ball' award for being the most accurate of the nation's political forecasters in hundreds of congressional and gubernatorial races in the mid-term elections. He had called only three wrong. Despite the gimmickry, Wirthlin, with his usual grin, readily accepted the award. In the home of political symbolism, you took what 'winning' accolades were on offer. Celebration of 'victories' in the election game were becoming annual events for the Republican strategist. The year before, at a much-publicized advertising function, Wirthlin had been made Adman Of The Year for 'selling' Ronald Reagan to the American people. None other than the President's daughter Maureen Reagan had handed him the plaque.

Meanwhile, less publicly, the strategist carried on with his continual polling and tracking for Reagan and the Republican Party in the inexorable build-up to 1984. Day in, day out, evening calls were made randomly to 150 or more homes scattered from coast to coast. With a 1500 sample collected each week to ten days, DMI took the nation's pulse and learned what it was thinking about today's and tomorrow's major concerns and issues. In conjunction with this, Wirthlin never stopped refining his PINS system which distilled meaning from the plethora of survey data choking his computer banks. He could, for instance, examine the 'fairness issue' – the question of whether Reagan's policies benefited the rich more than the poor – to see if it affected the Gender Gap issue. If so, how? Because lower income bracketed women were disproportionately affected by the recession? Did it mean that long-term economic improvements which benefited lower income persons were important for Reagan's election chances? Added to this were another thousand factors which had to be monitored as the next presidential election drew nearer.

THE HOUSEWIFE PROBLEM

Early in 1983, Wirthlin visited the offices of the Republican National Committee in Washington DC to meet with its fast-talking director of communications, William Greener. Greener had a problem: how could he explain to the nation, particularly housewives, that the Reagan administration had inflation under control? He wanted to know how to pitch the RNC's latest multi-million dollar TV campaign. He knew from Wirthlin's advice that it was wise to use a woman in the ads, not the least reason being the President's persistently nagging Gender Gap problem. But what would she say?

Greener reached for a thick black folder of DMI's surveys which completely filled a bookshelf covering a wall of his office. "Dick, we have licked inflation," he said in a frustrated tone, as he leafed through some of DMI's figures on the economy, "but no one is giving us credit for it!"

Wirthlin took a folder from his briefcase. "Why don't you view inflation like a thermometer which measures the rate of increase," he suggested, "rather than like a pregnancy – which is the general view."

Greener blinked. "C'mon Dick," he protested, "this is serious."

"I am serious," Wirthlin said. "Little old ladies are still going into stores and finding that the price of soap is going up. So you can craft an ad which says, 'Well, things are finally looking up, although prices are still way too high. But they are not going to go up the way they used to before we elected President Reagan.' "

Greener suddenly understood as Wirthlin added, "The message should be that people's paychecks can now handle the rate of increase in inflation."

"That's it!" Greener said. "We've been trying to work it out for weeks! Dick, you're as important to the Republican Party as Einstein is to physics!"

Wirthlin's insights had come more from hard work and experience than genius. He had been examining every cog in the PINS system, including advertising which he had been testing on audiences for three years in order to find the right style for 1984. In 1980 he had selected two test sites in Texas and California and had measured the effects after they had been run on TV, which proved a costly business. Operatives had to keep ringing until they found a suitable sample of respondents. Since then, however, DMI had tested a series of ads in a better way. Operatives would ring a random sample of people and ask them to watch a particular program – for example, CBS's '60 Minutes' on Sunday evening – without telling them why. Then they would be asked a series of standard questions after the show. "Did they remember the ad? What in particular did they remember about it? Did they have any objections to it?" The answers eventually allowed DMI to tell the difference between a good and a bad political ad.

These refinements led to the most effective Republican ad campaign in the history of the party. While the creative ad people still had a part to play, by 1983 they were being guided more than ever by the strategists who knew *exactly* what they wanted to say to lift support for their candidate.

THE BEAUTY OF KATIE

"What do you consider the most important problem facing America today?" the operator at DMI's McClean office asked.

The woman on the other end of the line in Lubbit, Texas, replied "Environment," without hesitation. The operator quickly keyed in a request from the TV terminal screen in front of him. A second later fifteen questions on the environment appeared. When the replies came through, the operator had learned what would be important in terms of the respondent's vote. This way the thoughts of thousands of voters who considered the environment to be the number one problem were collated over two years and DMI learned how Reagan should tackle this issue and many others, whether in a speech, which broadly agreed with the special voter group's perceptions, or by composing a suitable advertisement. An important improvement in the PINS technology of 1980 was the introduction of Computer Assisted Telephone Interview (CATI, as in 'Katie'), which greatly increased the speed and efficiency of analysis for the 1984 campaign. The interviewers didn't have to sit juggling scraps of paper: operating now was simply a matter of calling up questions from the computer via the terminal in front of them. CATI also allowed operators to manipulate the data inside the computer.

"Who do you think is the best Democratic candidate for the 1984 Presidency?" the operator asked, and the respondent in Texas answered, "John Glenn." The operator looked at the screen for the next question and said, "What do you like most about John Glenn?" The woman in Texas replied, "I think he's a decisive, strong person. He'll make a good leader." When the 37 minute interview was over, the operator wanted to review the past week of interviews which he and DMI's large team of operators had made. Calculations by the computer recorded instantly how many times the words 'decisive' and 'strong' had been used to describe Glenn, Mondale and Reagan. Then other questions, such as "Tell me the kinds of people who are using these descriptions?" were asked of the system. In this way, DMI was gradually calibrating a mosaic of opinion on the way every group in the community viewed the possible presidential candidates which Wirthlin planned to have established long before the beginning of the election year. Allied with greater efficiency was the capacity to interview many more people, so that by the end of 1982, DMI had made in-depth surveys of more than 125,000 citizens, which was far more than it had done for the 1980 election. The nation's fears, feelings, aspirations and thoughts which again would determine voting patterns in 1984, had been measured and would be tracked continuously.

The most critically important factor concerning CATI, however, would not be seen until the heat of the election battle, from September through October 1984. Wirthlin planned to carry a 14 lb piece of equipment in his briefcase which he could use with a phone anywhere while he was away from the Republican Campaign HQ. He would only have to plug it in to have full access to all PINS data and simulations. Within a minute the strategist would have results of the last survey calculations – a saving of 24 hours compared to the 1980 campaign. Information on what the nation was thinking about an issue, or how they intended to vote, would be literally up-to-the-minute. Wirthlin was excited by the prospect of the increased power and efficiency this would provide in the hectic last weeks and days of the campaign, especially if it was to be a close election. He savored the thought of starting each day with instant data on how the campaign strategy was working, or not working, and where the problems would be. Tactics could be adjusted and changed by the hour to the Republican candidate's advantage. This, in turn, would make the candidate look particularly sharp, for he would be able to address a problem very quickly and appear on top of his election bid. It also meant that should the Republican candidate look like a hopeless outsider with only weeks to go, he still could not be written off as the loser. The pace of the strategist's analysis and directives could swing votes radically in a state or county or across the nation. By early 1983, Wirthlin was already well prepared for the 1984 campaign. The only question now was whether the 'greatest electronic media candidate of all time' planned to run again.

MR WASHINGTON COMES TO TOWN

"A racist appeal," Caddell called Republican candidate Bernard Epton's media advertising. The outburst to the press came at the height of the historic mayoral battle in March and April of 1983, for the right to run Chicago. Caddell, who had devised the strategy for the Democrat's black candidate, Harold Washington, appeared indignant and irate. He was reacting to a typical TV commercial which described Epton as a distinguished legislator, lawyer and businessman . . . honored repeatedly for his services to his country and his community". Washington, the ad noted, was found "guilty of converting clients' money to his own use . . . barred from practicing law for five years . . . convicted and jailed for repeated tax violations . . . he didn't even file his tax returns for five years . . ." The ad ended by urging Chicagoans to vote for

Epton "before it's too late". This final phrase inflamed the situation because it implied that having a mayor with such a record would be disastrous for the city.

Among the hired-guns – the consultants behind the candidates – Caddell's words and actions stirred things up even more. David Sawyer, the consultant for incumbent Mayor Jane Byrne, who had been defeated by Washington for the Democratic nomination, accused Caddell of injecting racism into the vitriolic Chicago battle. "Caddell made sure Washington only appealed to a narrow black constituency," he said just before the Epton-Washington contest, "and he used race to make white voters guilty about not voting black."

Whatever the claim or counter-claim, Caddell's enthusiasm for the big political area had returned. As 1980 faded into a bitter memory, he had consoled himself in 1981 and 1982 by seeking new business. He still had a $250,000 annual contract with the Democratic National Committee, and Hollywood, always of interest to him, had proved an attractive diversion. He had applied his marketing and survey techniques to the film industry, and in particular the handling of the film *Reds* made by his old friend from McGovern days, Warren Beatty. Caddell had helped pinpoint the markets to which the film should be sold, and it had been a satisfying catharsis for him. The theme of *Reds* – the Russian revolution and the evolution of socialism in the US in the 1920s – was allied to his obsession about the 'alienated' electorate. It was this that had drawn him back to political reality and Chicago to help Washington. In a classic divide-and-conquer maneuver, the strategist first split the Democrat vote to give Washington the primary, and then indicated how to muster enough support for him to defeat Chicago's traditionally weak Republican candidate. Washington's win added to the growing list of major cities – Los Angeles, Detroit, Atlanta, Washington, New Orleans and Newark – with black chief executives. It was achieved by Caddell engineering record black voter registration and turnout, with just a smattering of white support.

Caddell had probed the national electorate with his polls and by early 1983 had found that the time might be right for the emergence of a serious black candidate who would represent the 'alienated', otherwise known as the 'coalition of the rejected', whom Caddell reckoned had been ignored by the Reagan administration. The strategist saw an opportunity for wooing the 'disaffected working class', and also the 75 million Americans who were eligible to vote in 1980 but who did not do so because none of the candidates appealed to them, or sought their support. This huge group – 46 per cent of the adult population – Caddell believed was the source of a possible new power in the Oval Office and Congress.

A candidate to fit this scenario was the Reverend Jesse L. Jackson, a vocal, radical, black activist from the 1960s era of protest. Jackson was instinctively addressing problems and issues which Caddell had been finding and searching for in his polls, and as the Democrat's official pollster Caddell was giving his advice to the potential candidate, although he was not part of any proposed Jackson campaign. He had shown Jackson the numbers and pointed out the science of the possible, just as he had when Jimmy Carter emerged to address the concerns of a large proportion of the electorate almost a decade earlier. The strategist and Jackson both spoke of America's eighteen million black voters as being the "cornerstone of the real silent majority that can create new political options in 1984". Jackson saw a chance also to galvanize "six million Hispanics, six million young people graduating from high school, women, more than half a million native Americans [Indians], 40 million poor whites, and 'moderates' who would respond to an appeal for moral decency and enlightened economic self-interest." The figures of such rhetoric were beyond Jackson's wildest hopes, but Caddell had demonstrated in Chicago how to isolate some sectors of the, so far, mythical national coalition and target them for considerable support. The technology, tactics and desire were strong enough to have an impact in the 1984 Democratic primaries and significantly change the options. Caddell had also shown in Chicago that money was not the most vital factor. In the primary election Jane Byrne had raised $11 million for her campaign. Richard Daley had $4 million. Yet they both lost to Washington who had less than $1 million. Further incentive for Jackson was the fact that blacks such as Tom Bradley as Mayor of Los Angeles, and Alan Wheat and Ron Dellums as Congressmen from Missouri and California, had proved that they could run and win in areas that did not have majority black populations.

As the strategist watched Jackson prepare for his candidacy, he mused that his coveted theories could now have wide application in the 1984 presidential election. Apart from Jackson who would at least appeal to 'rejected' Southern black voters, there was liberal Senator Gary Hart of Colorado who planned to be the candidate of 'change' in 1984. He also wanted to appeal to disaffected voters, and Caddell hoped to be his strategist in the primaries. In 1972, Hart had been Senator McGovern's campaign manager when Caddell had been the strategist. Hart fully appreciated the value of guerrilla tactics in primary elections, especially when opponents had much more money.

CHAPTER 20
THE BRITISH CONNECTION

MAGGIE'S MARKETING

"How do I look, Denis?" Margaret Thatcher nervously asked her husband backstage as she stroked her expensively coiffeured hair.

"Smashing, darling," Mr Thatcher replied, "absolutely smashing!" They could hear the end of party chairman Cecil Parkinson's laudatory introduction. The band began playing her theme song: 'Who do we want, who do we need? It is a leader who is bound to succeed: Maggie Thatcher – Just Maggie for me . . .' The British Prime Minister cleared her throat and strode out on the stage to be greeted by the carefully orchestrated 'wild' cheers of five thousand Young Conservatives. Balloons went up and streamers were thrown at the party political rally in the national election campaign of May-June 1983. Thatcher gave her distinctive stiff-armed waves of acknowledgement and after five minutes stepped up to the lectern. Her eyes flicked down to the two TV sets lying on their backs in front of her and concealed by two open-topped boxes. Offstage a camera transmitted word images off a rolling script to the sets and the picture was reflected up to two clear plastic screens in front and to the side of her. Thatcher, reading her rally speech off the screens which were invisible to her audience and the wider electorate beyond the TV cameras, was able to convey the impression of word-perfect self-confidence and sincerity.

Every aspect of the rally, right down to the aptly named 'Sincerity Machine' for reading, had been copied directly from American presidential elections. Yet this was only the superficial public façade of a campaign which employed many techniques used in Ronald Reagan's 1980 presidential campaign. Technology, polling research, advertising and the use of broad strategy along with sharp tactics played a part as never before outside America.

Two men, Gordon Reece, who changed Thatcher's image, and Christopher Lawson, in charge of 'marketing', were responsible for the packaging and selling of Margaret Thatcher. And although the Conservatives had nothing like the PINS system, the planning principle was similar. Reece, an eminently suitable former TV producer of everything from religion to light entertainment, took leave from the services of Armand Hammer, the great American industrialist and art collector, in order to market the Prime Minister. In the 1979 election Reece began the modification of Thatcher's unappealing image when he changed her hairstyle, which had hovered somewhere between 1950 and 1959, threw away her hats, and made her dress with more femininity. He trained her lordly voice to be less so, making it more sympathetic and less hectoring, so that her utterances developed a huskiness at times reminiscent of her friend Reagan. When he was satisfied, Thatcher was made to work in front of a video machine to relax her strident manner, and again major improvement was made. The lady would never come across as warm, yet she might be thought less patronizing.

When Reece returned for the 1983 election, it was all too easy. He just stood back and advised quietly. But he was still needed on occasion. Just at the odd moment the bossy old Maggie emerged and was met with meek reproval from the media, especially at her first press conference of the election when she played stern headmistress and was almost seen to give two ministers a verbal spanking. Reece wanted more of the Mother Hen, and he got it when Ministers James Prior and Francis Pym spoke at cross-purposes to her on a later occasion. This time she showed greater restraint: they were just straying chicks, not naughty boys.

The Conservatives had also learned to use the media American-style for well-timed 'photo opportunities'. Typical of this was a media event in the sanitary surroundings of a Cadbury's chocolate factory in Bournemouth. "Would you eat a chocolate, Prime Minister?" one photographer asked.

"Of course," Thatcher replied, "I thought you would never ask." She munched away. "Oh, that was a nutty one," she said. "Let me have a soft one. I do like the soft centers more." Cameras clicked and whirred as the Iron Lady and nemesis of the Soviet Empire proceeded to devour several more of Cadbury's latest production-line offerings. A few hours later the event was broadcast to the nation on seven consecutive TV news programs. Nothing remotely connected with any issue in the campaign went with the items, yet it was effective, simply because the PM was seen as campaigning 'among the people'. In reality she had broken from the past completely, for her campaign was only nominally about meeting people on the trail. Instead she was striving, with new heights of professionally staged media banality, to win votes.

More important than the image-making and the staged events for TV, was the work done on the hidden election by sixty-one year old Christopher Lawson. He had been hired by Cecil Parkinson late in 1981 to be the Conservatives' first-ever Director of Marketing after spending a decade in the US as president of Mars Snackmaster, Inc. There he learned all there was to know about marketing products, and also made a study of US election techniques. Lawson realized that the basic principle of selling a politician and selling a product was the same. The best communications methods had to be used to get the message across to consumers and voters, who, in the age of mass marketing, TV and computers, were one and the same. While Thatcher was not an actor like Reagan, she was nevertheless a quick and eager student. She was not a great communicator, but she could project the right image for the British electorate, and as Prime Minister was willing to work hard at delivering a script in her own haughty, determined style.

When the man from Mars began his job at Tory Party HQ there was no need to start putting new wrappings on Thatcher. That had already been done successfully by Lawson's friend Reece. Lawson had to concentrate on marketing the party and its leader to the nation. First, he took charge of party broadcasts and worked at coordinating the Tories' publicity machinery more effectively. Then, as if he were about to introduce a new candy aimed at a wide market, Lawson hired a team of pollsters headed by John Hanvey of Opinion Research Centre (ORC) which was part of the US Louis Harris group of companies. (Harris had originally polled for John Kennedy in the 1960 campaign for the Presidency.) Their brief was to find out what flavor Tory Party the wider public wanted, or would find acceptable. First, however, came the bad news. The initial secret polls found the Conservatives running third behind both Labour and the newly formed Liberal–SDP Alliance. Lawson asked his pollsters to find out what the electorate was thinking in much the same way Wirthlin did in the late seventies in preparation for 1980, and was doing in the early eighties for 1984. Lawson's options were limited in early 1982, with Tory support soft in many places throughout the nation, apart from the southeast of England. He told Cecil Parkinson: "We have to concentrate everything on the marginals." The marketing man was convinced from his research that a strong selling campaign in areas and seats that could swing either way would encourage voters to vote for Government policies. Neither of the opposition parties was equipped for such an operation, so Lawson felt from his product marketing experience that he could fill a vacuum. The polls indicated that support for Labour and the Alliance was also soft, and people were rejecting the Tories rather than positively supporting the opposition.

A few months after Lawson's appointment, Argentina invaded the Falklands. Thatcher's handling of the confrontation and the subsequent quick and fortunate victory boosted the party image and the stature of the leader. Suddenly 45 per cent of the nation was suporting the Conservatives – the same percentage that had voted Thatcher into power – and Lawson's job was made that much less difficult. The war had proved a godsend for the party-planner, and the trick now was to capitalize on the break and maintain the Tories high popularity above the opposition parties. Lawson felt confident that if his market surveys extracted the right themes through the rest of 1982, Thatcher would be re-elected whenever she held an election. The hard evidence showed that there were really no burning issues in the land that were highly dangerous to the Conservative Government. The survey polls had uncovered, for example, important distinctions in the way unemployment was perceived. Most people saw it as a 'problem' but did not blame it on the Government. Unemployment was seen as troubling every country in the industrialized world. While it was definitely viewed as Britain's major problem, surprisingly few people thought that any party could do better than Thatcher's. This in turn allowed the Tories to sail through four years and into an election without being forced to worry about the mounting numbers of unemployed. As long as the problem was advertised and accepted as insoluble it could be ignored. Labour concentrated its attack for the greater part of the first two weeks of the short four week battle of May-June 1983 on the Government's unemployment record. Thatcher and her team simply claimed it was not their fault, and in every Tory election broadcast it was stressed that no Labour Government had ever reduced unemployment. Lawson used his marketing experience here by directing Thatcher and her ministers to reinforce the advertising by repeatedly making this point. He believed that on the same principle as an advertising slogan for a product, if it was catchy enough and repeated often enough, people would understand, retain and repeat it themselves. Just as Reagan had been directed to say 'peace' in all his speeches in 1980 as much as possible in order to allay fears that he might lead America into war, the Conservatives defused unemployment as an issue by claiming that nothing could be done about it.

When its thrust on unemployment failed, Labour moved into the attack with the nuclear weapons issue. But the Tories felt comforted here too by surveys which had discovered that only 7 per cent of the nation saw it as a problem facing Britain. However, when the same people were asked what they thought the major issues in the campaign would be, they counted nuclear weapons among them. In other words, while a small minority were concerned about it, a majority felt that only the politicians themselves would make it a big issue in the campaign. This, plus the knowledge that few people understood the intricacies of the nuclear argument, allowed the Government to continue with its policies of increased deployment of nuclear weapons. All it had to do was to appear firm and united on the issue because few people were found in the polls to understand where Labor stood on the issue. And that was not surprising, for Labour didn't seem to know either. The differences within the party surfaced in the pressure of the short campaign. Former Labour Prime Minister James Callaghan did not want to get rid of Polaris nuclear submarines. The Deputy Leader Denis Healey wanted to use them as bargaining chips in talks with the Russians, and Party Leader Michael Foot wanted to dispose of them in the life of the next Parliament. Healey and Foot reconciled their differences in the second week of the election, but the media highlighted the fact that Labour had gone into the election without a watertight clear policy on the issue. This gave the Minister of Defense, Michael Heseltine, the chance to put Labour on the defensive. Lawson directed him and other ministers to trot out the line that nuclear weapons had "kept the peace for nearly forty years in Europe". Again, the sheer weight of repetition, especially when Labour could find no unified argument against it, defused the issue.

Nuclear weapons, in fact, became the issue that never was, thanks to Heseltine. He had long been used by Thatcher to counter, not the Russians over nuclear weapons, nor the opposition parties, but CND, the Campaign for Nuclear Disarmament. This group had harassed the Government for some time over its weapons policy and had threatened to explain the argument against the escalation of nuclear arms to an ill-informed public. If CND had succeeded they might have lifted nuclear weapons from a politicians' issue to a real public issue. Consequently, the group was subject to coordinated attacks from linked anti-CND fronts which included a Ministry of Defence unit known as DS 19 under the direction of Heseltine, which used computerized direct mail to discredit the nuclear protesters, in peacetime Britain's most concentrated Government propaganda campaign.

Leadership, too, played a major part in the contest, and Lawson decided to play indirectly on Thatcher's reputation of being a strong leader after the Falklands war. The morning the Conservatives launched their campaign to muzak strains of 'Land of Hope and Glory' and 'The Dambusters', Thatcher called her party manifesto a "robust work containing proposals which are both sound and adventurous . . . it will ensure Britain remains a steadfast ally." The words 'robust', 'adventurous', 'steadfast', along with 'responsible' and 'resolute', had been the most commonly found descriptions of Thatcher in surveys, and so they formed the campaign theme. Lawson's pollsters had also found that although the vast majority approved of Thatcher's handling of the Falklands war, they did not consider it prudent to trumpet on belligerently about the victory. Consequently, it was implied, though rarely ever said, that the 'resolute' leader had fought for and won 'freedom' in the Falklands. In the year prior to the election, the victory had been played out as a propaganda tool by the Government to extend the memory of the 'win'. This helped keep Thatcher's popularity inflated until the campaign, when the Tories changed gear and looked ahead. Labour itself eventually introduced the Falklands issue into the campaign in anger and frustration rather than as a sensible tactic. Ill-prepared vitriolic attacks on Thatcher by Denis Healey and Neil Kinnock only worked in the Tories' favor, and the press and media focus was placed on the nature of the attacks themselves rather than the issue. Knowing that the polls had given the Falklands factor as Thatcher's main electoral asset, the Tories, led publicly by Parkinson, reacted with righteous indignation and were in fact able to benefit indirectly from it in much the same way as Reagan had gained from Carter's attacks on him in 1980.

FOOT'S FOLLY

"Michael, pretend there's a pretty girl behind the camera," Foot's film-producer wife, Jill Craigie, said, trying to entice a smile from him during the making of a Labour Party broadcast at his constituency, Ebbw Vale, in Wales. Yet not even she could draw more than a flicker from this intense, serious politician. Foot was a print media man who hated having to act. He preferred the old-style address in packed halls where he could cling doggedly to a rambling method of oratory. In Scotland, after one such speech, he was exhilarated by his own rousing performance. "Forget the polls," he said to his aides. "I'm feeling something different among the people. This is a different election from the one the media is covering." And he was right. His address had not been recorded by the TV cameras, and even if they had been there, they would have found it impossible to capture anything. His lengthy peroration was too discursive for extracts on TV or radio. Instead, the items that night were dominated by the Prime Minister inspecting lobsters in a City market.

Ironically Foot was one of the first to debate politics on British TV in the forties and fifties. But unlike Reagan or Thatcher, he never bothered to adapt it to his advantage. Foot followed the advice for first-time TV performances of "Don't worry about the camera, let it find you". He took this to extremes during the 1983 election and, unlike his rival, never contemplated stopping for an hour's photo opportunity to fondle a calf in a Yorkshire farmer's paddock. When the camera did catch up with him, he was seen early in the campaign to be wearing strange glasses and wielding a walking stick. This vision contrasted starkly with that of Thatcher, who always looked trim in her matronly prime. Even when Jill Craigie changed her husband's glasses and took away his walking stick, he still appeared out of touch, like a lost academic. The predominantly Tory-supporting media, which had long realized that the election was a one-horse race, were merciless in their characterization of the hapless Labour leader, for they had never quite forgiven him for not stepping down in favor of Denis Healey. (They had seen Bill Hayden do this in Australia a few months earlier to make way for Bob Hawke to lead the Labour Party. Hawke's skills in front of the cameras helped him win against Australia's conservative Liberal Party.) Healey would have been a tougher leader and such a move would have given the election some semblance of a contest, although Labour was outpointed in so many ways that the vote margin probably would not have been narrowed significantly.

Advertising was one area which made the battle look as if someone with a time machine had brought together two opposing parties from different centuries. The Tories considered some of the very top agencies in the world for their work before again settling on Saatchi & Saatchi, who ranked in the top ten, and who were certainly the slickest and biggest of the British companies. The agency diligently followed Lawson's themes under strict supervision. Not to be outdone in a small way in the promotional stakes, Labour gingerly and begrudgingly took on an agency for the first time ever, called Wright & Partners, a small group which had started in 1980. It adopted an underwhelming, 'Think Positive, Think Labour' line which was certain not to offend many people in the advertising-shy and wary ranks of the party. While Wright aimed at the fringe press with its ads, Saatchi ran concentrated multi-page ads in the main dailies with a strong negative approach. One of these compared eleven points of the Communist Party's manifesto with Labour's which were seen to be the same. Another listed fifteen points under the heading, "Putting a cross in the Labour box is the same as signing this piece of paper". Each point had been drawn directly from polling analysis. One said: "I agree that Britain should now abandon the nuclear deterrent which has preserved the peace in Europe for forty years. I fully understand that the Russians are not likely to follow suit." Another, based on Labour's policy to leave the European Economic Community, proclaimed: "I empower the Labour Party to take Britain out of Europe, even though my job may be one of the 2½ million which depend on Britain's trade with Europe." Every point could have been turned on its head by Labour and argued in defense of its policies, but they were not prepared for it. Saatchi ran these negative ads through TV and radio in an attempt to leave the voter with the thought that there was 'no alternative' to supporting the Conservatives, which was another overriding theme derived directly from polls. The advertising was successful in keeping the focus off the depressed state of the economy and on the fitness of Labour to govern, something that Carter failed to do with Reagan. (In 1980, although the Iranian hostage crisis was at its height, Wirthlin kept the focus on the economy enough to upset Carter's plans.) Despite all the Tory propaganda about being "on the right track", and economic recovery being "on the way", Lawson realized that the Thatcher Government could not run on its record so he directed a negative campaign against Labour, which supplied plenty of ammunition. Labour had also failed to find the themes which could have better scrutinized the Government's performance.

There was also the matter of money and the use of technology. The Conservative Party had its traditional support from business plus funds from computerized direct-mail donations, whereas Labour was left merely with support from the unions. Not surprisingly, the Tories outspent their opponents four to one. In the use of computers and electronic electioneering the Conservatives also outstripped their opponents. Both nationally and locally they led the way. The Tories' Central Office had an expensive ICL ME29 computer – a gift from a private supporter – which carried out polling analysis, direct-mail and routine work in the most streamlined operation ever seen in Europe. The tactics of using computerized direct-mail were new to British politics. Apart from helping to control CND, the right messages were mailed direct to areas that were critical to key seats in the election. Computers had been used for 'selective targeting' where the location of ethnic groups and various categories of the population, from working class to upper-income groups, were pinpointed. Half a million letters were delivered in sixty marginal constituencies to potential Conservative supporters. These were particularly important in the inner city areas where Britain's Asian and Afro-Caribbean families exercised a disproportionate influence in elections. Half of the specially targeted constituencies were designated 'ethnic marginals', where in some cases an increase of only a few percentage points either way could have decided who took the seat. The Tories coordinated their direct-mail blasts with the activities of about twenty Anglo-Asian Conservative Associations, mainly in the Midlands. The party relied on businessmen such as Asian Ugandans, who were allowed into the UK in 1972 after Amin threw them out; these were natural converts to the new, more widely appealing Tory cause. Nor did the party neglect the West Indians in the South, who in the past had traditionally voted

Labour almost exclusively. Along with selected mail hits there was some very specific and controversial advertising. One newspaper ad featured a well-dressed young black man and bore the caption: 'Labour says he's black. Tories say he's British'. This caused a stir in the media and was criticized by Labour for its racist undertones. The ad was not aimed at swaying all the nation's blacks over to the Conservatives, but a certain percentage of them who had been found by the pollsters to be concerned with their nationality status. They regarded themselves as British above all else. The Tories latched on to this in the hope of gaining enough black support to give them the edge in certain areas. They claimed success in their targeting, with response from those wishing to vote Tory for the first time in each selected constituency. Just as in the 1980 US election, the Conservative Party was learning the value of small increments in key 'swing' voting areas which could make the difference between victory and defeat in a close election.

The Tory ICL computer helped Thatcher decide quickly when to hold the election. In the three-day interval between local elections in early May 1983 and the day Thatcher chose to go to the nation, the votes of 28,000 candidates were fed into the machine which produced results from which the Tories could make speedy conclusions. The local elections acted as a massive poll guide which could be translated seat by seat across the nation to indicate how a national election would go, taking into account the fact that the mood of the nation was not likely to change in the next month or two. In addition, twenty-four local Conservative Associations had their own micro-computers which they used to maintain membership records and, in some cases, mail political propaganda to local voters. Voter lists, some already on computer tape, were obtained from registration officers, and they allowed a direct assault of the Tory hard-sell on the political market. By contrast, Labour made no progress in the use of computers from the 1979 election. It depended on an antiquated ICL 2903 bought in 1976 which was fully stretched running financial accounts, and the party was left to fight an election using traditional manual methods.

However, despite learning much from their American cousins, the Conservatives did not attempt to introduce a sophisticated simulation method which would have been invaluable in the short campaign. Instead, they relied on a suspect operation called 'Operation Fast Feedback' in which 150 people such as doctors, Rotarians, teachers, journalists, and publicans were asked nightly to gauge public reactions. It was hardly a scientific exercise and would have been useless if the election had been close. This operation demonstrated that the Tories still had much to learn about the scope of the most advanced methods. In May and June of 1983 it did not matter, for the Tories won by a huge 17 per cent of the national vote. Labour's number of seats in Parliament was decimated. The victory promised nearly a decade of continuous Tory rule and left Labour with much soul-searching to do.

Compared to the Tories they were badly organized and technologically unaware. To have any hope of challenging the Conservatives in the future, Labour had to find a strategy suitable for the television-dominated and computer-planned elections of the late 1980s and beyond. The selection of Neil Kinnock as leader, and subsequent efforts to make him appear 'presidential', were steps in the right direction if the party was serious about retaking power. But a year after the 1983 loss the party's key tacticians had still not grasped the far more important concept of strategic research and consistent unified themes which it would have to find long before the next UK election to have any hope of truly tackling the Tories. If given overall planning control, a left-leaning strategist of the stature of Caddell would find the Tories a relatively easy target to defeat. But the Labour Party of the mid-1980s did not appear ready for such a step.

CHAPTER 21

HERE COME THE DEMOCRATS

BLITZING FOR FRITZ

Bespectacled, academic-looking Peter Hart walked out of Walter Mondale's Washington HQ a happy man. With fifteen months to go before the 1984 presidential election, the forty-one year old Hart had just landed the survey business for Mondale's campaign for the Democratic nomination, and later, probably the Presidency. Hart had hedged his bets by doing survey work for four Democratic hopefuls – Senators John Glenn, Ernest Hollings, Alan Cranston and former Vice-President Mondale – and he expected to work on the campaign of one of them. The odds were in his favor, for he was regarded as the fourth most accomplished pollster in the land after Wirthlin, Teeter and Caddell, all of whom had polled for successful presidential campaigns, and Presidents. Winning the Mondale account elated Hart, because he felt that it boosted his chances of joining the other three in their 'presidential' status. Mondale had been running now for two and a half years and was still clearly the front-runner, despite a strong challenge from John Glenn who was not used to coming second at anything. Of the six or seven contenders for the Democrats who would do battle in the primaries in 1984, Hart was certain he had the best candidate.

The son of an English professor at the University of California at Berkeley, Hart went East to school at Colby College in Waterville, Maine, where he gained a BA in history. He began his polling craft in 1964 as a $75-a-week coder with Louis Harris. In 1968, Hart had his first client, John J. Gilligan, in a Senate race in Ohio and later did surveys for the Democratic National Committee. In 1970 he joined the political polling company run by the late Oliver Quayle, then returned briefly to Harris as a vice-president before founding his own company, Peter D. Hart Research Associates, in Washington. Gradually through the seventies Hart built his business and polled for many Democrats, including Senators Edward Kennedy, Henry Jackson and John Stennis, as well as former Illinois Republican, Abner Mikva. Hart polled for Kennedy in his failed attempt at the Democratic nomination for the Presidency, and in the 1982 mid-term elections his company worked on 35 senatorial, congressional and gubernatorial campaigns. By the time Mondale chose him, he was ready and willing for the Big One in 1984.

Hart always felt that Mondale was favorite to gain the

Democratic nomination because he had the best chance of winning the party's traditional constituencies such as labor and blacks. Several members of Congress had endorsed him, as had scores of local politicians and leaders of women's and Hispanic groups. Labor was also certain to back him. Mondale had crisscrossed the nation since Carter lost in 1980, building on that traditional support with the aim of creating an organization big enough to withstand any rival, yet flexible enough to swoop in on any possible endorsement or vote-catching issue. By the time Hart was on board the campaign in the late summer of 1983, Mondale had raised double the funds of the other five Democratic candidates together, and his staff consisted of the most experienced people from the 1976 and 1980 Carter campaigns. Other pluses in Mondale's résumé were that he knew Congress, having been a liberal Senator, and that he knew the White House as a very involved Vice-President. Carter made Mondale much more than a cipher, and he not only learned how the Presidency worked, but was an intimate part of it. He was in on every high-policy decision of the Carter administration, and had access to all policy decisions and meetings. Important too in his credentials was the fact that he had represented Carter abroad as a competent trouble-shooter and diplomat on such major issues as the Middle East.

Hart's first polls concerning Mondale were encouraging as he surveyed the nation's feelings about his candidate. Mondale's experience, many surveys suggested, could almost allow him to start a Presidency in 1985 as if it were his second term. When Hart passed this on to Roy Spence, the candidate's TV consultant, he came up with a possible slogan: 'A President starts from strength, not from scratch', which could have been directed at both Reagan and Glenn. However, for the moment, and right through until the summer convention of 1984, the target and main opposition would be Glenn. He still ran at 10 per cent behind Mondale in the polls, but because of his hero status and dogged determination, the balding Senator promised to remain a threat.

THE FLYING MONK

A small speck on the unremittingly blue horizon beyond Williamsport, Pennsylvania, was seen by several of the small crowd at a distant corner of the airfield.

"That's him," David Sawyer called to his cameraman. "Give him another thirty seconds, then turn over." Three minutes ahead of schedule, a twin-engined, cream-colored Beachcraft Baron began to take shape and the crowd started cheering.

"Crowd reaction?" the cameraman said.

"Nar," Sawyer said, "better when he lands, they'll get really excited then. Just stay right on his face." The face in question was circled by huge green earphones and belonged to John Glenn, Senator, authentic hero and now a Democratic candidate for the Presidency. This was the part of the job Sawyer liked best. He was a political consultant who specialized in producing commercials, and next to Joe Napolitan and David Garth was one of the leaders in his field. Sawyer himself had the image of a young, handsome politician, rather like the one Robert Redford played in the film *The Candidate*. Like Napolitan and Garth, Sawyer had recently been plying his trade as much abroad as at home. These politcal 'guns-for-hire' and others had extended their business to elections and referendums in the Philippines, Israel, Spain, Australia, Mcxico, the Sudan, Venezuela, Italy, the Dominican Republic, France, Costa Rica, Britain, Sweden, Bermuda, Canada and Mauritius. These three particularly, along with Wirthlin and Caddell, had been wielding an international influence far more important than blue jeans, Coca-Cola, rock music, Hollywood movies or even cars and computers. They had helped elect leaders and governments which decided the fate of nations.

Sawyer himself had had some mixed success until the Glenn appointment. The Senator expected to have a million dollars left in the kitty by the end of 1983, and was due another three million from the Government in matching payments, all of which was going toward making paid commercials for TV. Glenn was a believer in the media. "People buy almost everything they need through TV," he told Sawyer when he asked him to be his consultant, "and they're not going to break that pattern when it comes to electing their leaders." Sawyer was not about to argue, although critics had begun asking whether Glenn should be channeling more of that money into expert political strategy and survey work.

As Glenn climbed out of his beloved plane he gave a familiar grin to the crowd, and Sawyer's cameraman caught it all. Later the camera kept rolling during a parade and an old-fashioned political rally in a field where a Country and Western trio played their version of 'The Marine Hymn'. Sawyer's aim was to capture Glenn, subtly, in a way to remind the TV audiences that the Senator was a genuine hero. The consultant and his client had agreed he should run on an image based on his appeal as a strict Presbyterian spaceman, and a private life so blameless that his fellow astronauts looked upon him as a flying monk. In World War Two and Korea, Glenn flew 149 combat missions, and he collected five Distinguished Flying Crosses for his efforts in Korea where he shot down several MIGs. Later he set records as a totally fearless test pilot, and then blasted to fame aboard the Friendship 7 satellite as the first American to orbit the earth. Those three orbits of 20 February 1962 were seared into America's collective psyche as a great day of national reassertion after the humiliation caused by the Russian's earlier space triumphs. All this added to an image of Glenn which needed only indirect reinforcement, for much of the image-making on the hero level had been immortalized in a film version of Tom Woolfe's book about astronauts, *The Right Stuff*, which many Americans were expected to have seen by the 1984 convention. Sawyer's task was to widen the image to one which encompassed Glenn as a candidate of high technology and strong national defense. The consultant also had to conceal Glenn's dullness, for despite his exciting life he was not an exciting man, especially when he spoke. Sawyer planned to use voice-overs for the commercials which would stress Glenn's stand on issues, although this would always appear subordinate to the 'image'. This was in direct contrast to Mondale's campaign which planned to place issues and experience first. The two candidates promised to provide an alternative in campaigning method as well as a clear political choice. Mondale based his appeal on traditional Democrat liberalism, whereas Glenn offered a centrist appeal that would reach out to independents and even Republicans.

As well as having the best financed and organized campaign, Mondale was expected to widen that advantage significantly by winning the endorsements of two huge labor groups. Both the AFL-CIO and the National Education Association, with 15.4 million members between them, were expected to pledge their support to him.

THE LONG SHOTS

By September 1983 the other Democratic candidates as well as Glenn seemed determined to run vigorous campaigns. There was much talk of changing battle plans, despite their true inner feelings that it was already a two-horse race, with Mondale the best bet. Senator Alan Cranston of California, who had campaigned virtually on the one issue of a nuclear weapons freeze, was running out of money. Telegenic young Gary Hart, the Senator from Colorado, was also in debt and having trouble focusing on and articulating his 'new issues', which were intended to appeal to a more youthful, thinking America. He had different ideas about arms reductions, and the economy – expansion of the money supply; reduction of the budget deficit by defense cuts; support to stimulate failing businesses – but had failed to communicate them. Hart seemed to be falling into some of the traps of candidate McGovern in 1972, for whom Hart worked as campaign manager.

He had not learned to boil down his complex beliefs into simple themes. As Hart stumbled blindly towards failure in 1984, Pat Caddell, his political colleague from McGovern's presidential bid, was creating the blueprint for a candidate just like Hart. In a 150-page document, which Caddell had written to entice another Democrat – Senator Joseph R. Biden – to run and win the nomination, the strategist wrote: "The baby boom generation is coming to life politically . . . a division is becoming more apparent between the party's older traditional leadership and younger Democrats who come to politics through the anti-war movement and are now coming of age as elected and party leaders." Of Hart he wrote: "Hart probably comes closest to understanding and articulating the emerging generational divide in the party." Caddell recognized that despite this asset Hart had not challenged Mondale or Glenn. "His failure to rise to that level reflects what critics say is attributable to an inability to excite, to exude or stir passions, to develop a thematic message with a sharp edge." He concluded that "lacking a natural constituency, or regional base, Hart more than most needs to make the idea-thrust click, and it just hasn't."

His thesis went on to affirm that there was still a way to assure that the front-runners did not win the nomination: "There exists all the conditions for a late and successful candidacy; a compelling and invincible message as yet unarticulated by any of the current contenders. They are a weak field without a candidate who presides over a sizable natural electoral base, and a party élite-activist corps not only unmobilized but also restless and yearning."

Biden showed some interest and Caddell drafted a speech for him that drew ovations in New Jersey and Maine. It brought Biden to the brink of candidacy; but he opted out at the last moment. Then Caddell was approached by the candidate who most closely fitted the 'profile' that the strategist was seeking: Gary Hart.

THE HART OF THE MATTER

Hart came to Caddell for advice – and he got it.

"Your campaign has been a disaster," Caddell told him with brutal frankness at his home in Bethesda, Maryland. "You have the greatest potential of anyone in the field, and you are doing everything wrong."

Hart didn't like what he was told but he knew the strategist was right.

"What do you suggest I do?"

"Get a strong theme," Caddell replied. "You have the issues but nothing to hook them on." He reached into his briefcase and pulled out the original 150-page blueprint for victory in the fast looming primaries, to which he had already made minor adjustments.

"Read this," the strategist said bluntly. "It will show you how to win."

Hart was concerned about taking on Caddell for he knew he would dominate the campaign. That was his nature. Yet Hart's efforts had hit rock bottom and it was nearly 1984. He spent the night reading the report, and the next morning rang his campaign manager Oliver Henkel.

"We just have to take Pat on," Hart told him. "The document is brilliant. The guy's a genius."

CHAPTER 22
THE COMPUTER PRESIDENCY

COMPUTER FOR A CRISIS

There was an urgent spring in Richard Beal's step as he entered the Pennsylvania entrance of the Old Executive Office Building (OEB) and hurried past heavily armed guards, who did not bother to check him. His chubby face was as familiar to them as the Vice-President's, who also had his offices in the neoclassical colonial-style building. It was 8 p.m. on Wednesday 19 October and Beal had been halfway through a meal with his wife, Ruth, and their five children when he had been summoned back to the White House by National Security Adviser Robert 'Bud' McFarlane. There was a crisis in Grenada which Beal and his team of managers had been monitoring closely since 13 October when the island's Prime Minister, Maurice Bishop, had been placed under house arrest.

Beal took the elevator to the second floor and headed along the polished marble corridor toward his office in Room 200. Halfway along he stopped, acknowledged a guard and opened a solid mahogany door to a large suite. Inside was the high-security Crisis Management Center. Six computers, twenty terminals, processors and scanners were being monitored by the staff. Beal went straight to a terminal. On the TV screen was the cryptic message which had been stripped to essential words: BISHOP, CREFT, FOUR OTHERS ASSASSINATED BY GENERAL HUDSON AUSTIN. NO GOVT CONTROL. 24 HOUR CURFEW. STANDBY.

Beal did not react, but knew immediately why he had been summoned so urgently. He realized that US military action was already a considered option in Grenada, but because of the top secret nature of the crisis, he was not about to let any of the staff under him know it. Their job was to monitor data coming in and report it to him. There was every good reason that no hint be given concerning the build up of a crisis and possible military action. Nevertheless, the shocking events in Grenada had his adrenalin flowing. His system was about to have its first major test. It had been operational for only two months, and while trials had ironed out the potential 'bugs', only a real crisis would test its efficiency. The system's main function was to collect and summarize vital information from a plethora of data – a task which would normally take a score of computers and a thousand people working around the clock weeks to sift and coordinate. In the modern era decisions in situations like the Grenada crisis had to be taken in hours if they were to lead to quick action. Beal wanted to be able to pass on the right data quickly to McFarlane and allow him to advise the President of all his options.

Through the night and well into Thursday 20 October, data started building up in the crisis system from terminals linked to other areas of Government such as the CIA, State and Defense Departments, which in turn gathered data from satellite links to military, diplomatic and CIA sources, particularly in the Caribbean. The crisis computers distiled pertinent details of the tiny island of Grenada, including information about its armed forces, constitution, economic and trade conditions, culture, and – most important to the President – the number and location of American citizens. Late in the day, Reagan asked Vice-President Bush to convene a Special Situation Group which was to meet in the OEB.

Based on the intelligence at hand, the decision was made to prepare for invasion, and it was agreed that the US should let the Organization of Eastern Caribbean States (OECS) know that it was willing to use force to restore order and protect American citizens. All these states – Antigua, Dominica, St Lucia, St Kitts-Nevis, Montserrat and St Vincent – were concerned that the new extreme-leftist regime that had taken over in Grenada posed a threat to them. It was not difficult therefore to get them to agree to 'ask' the US to invade Grenada, and also to supply a token force to accompany the Americans on their mission.

On Friday evening President Reagan, Secretary of State George Shultz, Treasury Secretary Donald Regan, and McFarlane flew to Georgia's Augusta National Golf Club, ostensibly for a relaxing weekend, but in reality to await the well-staged but genuine formal request from the OECS states, and Barbados and Jamaica, who also felt threatened by events on Grenada.

The invitation came at 2.45 a.m. on Saturday 22 October, when Shultz was awakened in the Eisenhower cabin at Augusta with an urgent cable from Barbados which said that the OECS states wanted the US to invade. Shultz and McFarlane reported the request to Bush in Washington at 3.30 a.m. on a secure telephone, and two hours later the President had the request explained to him. The tightly managed events were now firmly set on a course of armed conflict.

Beal was awakened at 4 a.m. by a call from Bush's office and asked to report in person immediately. He found the OEB a hive of activity, as pressure built for action in the Caribbean. The Vice-President and the National Security Adviser wanted a wide range of intelligence regularly reported to them. McFarlane had been in the top NSC job only a week after Reagan had posted Clark to the Department of the Interior, and the forty-five year old former marine Colonel was concerned to cover all contingencies, and not let the focus on Grenada neglect potential problems elsewhere. He was well aware that an inadequate performance now could finish his promising career. McFarlane had started as a White House aide under Henry Kissinger, before becoming a State Department counselor under Al Haig, and most recently Reagan's special envoy to the Middle East. He had been a supporter of Beal's ever since he had been appointed special assistant to the President, Crisis Management and Support Planning, late in 1982. Both men made a study of international crisis, complementing each other's background, knowledge and experience in the field: where McFarlane was the combat marine with a strong political background, Beal had come to the NSC as the world's number one expert in the theory of management of international conflict. The skills of both were now on trial, along with the new system.

Although invasion of Grenada seemed inevitable, the timing was still not fixed, and there was some debate about it when a phone link with Reagan was arranged with Bush's Special Situation Group at 9 a.m. "Mr President," one White House aide said, "I feel we could get a lot of harsh political reaction over this . . ."

"I know that," a weary Reagan replied, "I accept that, but there'll be harsher reaction if those medical students of ours on the island are taken hostage . . . that's our prime concern."

Defense Secretary Weinberger, although most positive about an invasion, was still hesitant about the timing. "Mr President," he said, "perhaps we should have more intelligence on the amount of Cuban weaponry on that island. We haven't established that yet . . ."

"OK, Cap," Reagan said, "but let's not hold things back until it's too late."

Still an invasion time was not set, although a naval task force, headed by the aircraft carrier *Independence*, had been diverted to Grenada. It had been en route to Lebanon with 1900 marines scheduled for routine rotation with those there.

MINI-CRISIS

Shultz had just played a handsome stroke down the 16th fairway when the radio phone on the golf buggy rang. A security agent was on the line, wanting to speak with Reagan urgently. The President picked up the receiver.

"Sir, everything is under control", the agent began calmly, "but we have a gunman at the club's pro shop. He has taken hostages and wants to speak with you. We think he's drunk. He keeps saying something about wanting his job back . . . we have a contingent of security people on the way . . ."

Reagan could see a jeep full of security agents speeding over the fairway toward him. All were armed with submachine guns.

"Yeah," Reagan said, "they're coming. Can you put this guy on the line?"

"We'll try, sir."

"What does he want again?"

"We don't really know, but its something to do with losing his job."

The security jeep arrived and the agents suggested they escort Reagan to the 16th green which gave them a better vantage point of the area. From there Reagan waited on the line to speak with the gunman who had earlier crashed his pick-up truck through a golf course gate and driven to the pro shop. But he would not come to the phone. The nervous security agents wanted the President in the Eisenhower cabin where it would be easier to protect him. On the bumpy ride back to the cabin Reagan asked to speak with McFarlane, who was already there.

On hearing of the unexpected dramas at the pro shop, McFarlane had quickly ascertained that the 'drunken gunman' was not part of a wider disturbance. Everyone back in the Eisenhower cabin breathed a sigh of relief. "As if we didn't have enough on our hands . . ." Reagan said to McFarlane.

MACRO-CRISIS

The Mercedes pick-up truck circled the parking lot twice to increase speed and was then driven straight through a wrought-iron gate and into the US Marine Headquarters Building, Beirut, in the early morning of Sunday 23 October. The collision at the front entrance triggered the detonation of a lethal cargo which destroyed the building and killed more than 230 marines. Within minutes, the horror story was flashed to several Government Departments in Washington and the Crisis Center. Beal was woken at 2.30 a.m. at his Maryland home and told of the tragic event as it was transmitted to the Eisenhower cabin, where McFarlane had the unpleasant task of telling the stunned Commander-in-Chief of the attack on the marines and a similar suicide mission at the same time which had killed 56 French paratroopers. The next few hours were spent in urgent telephone discussions with Beirut, Paris, London and Washington. Reagan now had second thoughts about the Grenada invasion, as several of his closest aides wondered if the timing was right. "Could we be in danger of having too much blood on our hands?" one said to him.

"Let's get back to the White House," Reagan replied grimly, "then we can get a better look at this."

McFarlane could see no logical reason for not going ahead with Grenada, unless the Crisis Center, which had been fully staffed from the time of the news of the marine mass murder, found some new piece of intelligence which would deter action. As a fighting man, the National Security Adviser was not about to be put off. If anything, the slaughter of fellow marines had hardened his resolve, and that of the President, to press on.

By 9 a.m., when Reagan, McFarlane and Shultz were back in Washington for a special meeting of the NSC – this time in the Situation (or 'War') Room in the White House basement – the intelligence from Beal indicated that world conditions had been stable since the bloody massacre. The military force was prepared for the Caribbean assault. All through the night the computer system had read, rejected, sifted and synthesized intelligence from innumerable sources in Washington and worldwide, and McFarlane was confidently able to report to the Commander-in-Chief that there was no obstacle to Operation 'Urgent Fury', as the Grenada mission had been designated. In the words of the crisis experts, the events were "under control and manageable". Furthermore, intelligence reports coming through during the night and morning suggested that there had been a big build up of Cuban arms on Grenada. In the urgent NSC meetings which continued through the day, the President, McFarlane and others became more concerned with the safety of the Americans on the island, and fears about 'another Iran hostage situation' sometimes dominated conversation.

At midday during the height of the tension Beal was in the Cordell Hull Conference Room next door to the computer suite with two members of the Crisis Management System and Planning Group who had helped him set up the center. Suddenly Beal stood up. "I've got to be away for three hours," he said, "and no one will be able to contact me."

"Where are you going, Rich?" a commander of the Center and a close friend asked in surprise.

"Church with my wife and family," Beal replied as he walked out. He had designed the computer network so that at anytime he could leave it to the control of his staff. As a member of the NSC, he was forever trotting in and out of meetings all over the White House, and at no stage did he want to be left hovering over a terminal. Being Sunday, only one thing came above his commitment to his President and country, and that was worship at the gleaming white Mormon Washington Temple. Beal intended to pray hard for the good judgement of himself and his President, and the smooth operating of his new system in its first major operation.

As more timely data filtered through from the Crisis Center, Reagan edged closer to a definite date for the invasion, and by 3.30 p.m. gave his approval to proceed. At 6 p.m. he signed an order that put the invasion plans into action. Then, following the best precedents for the proper handling of such critical moments, as designated and outlined by crisis scenarios stretching back to the Cuban missile encounter in 1962, presidential aides began to schedule Reagan's time so that he could notify key congressional aides and alert allies of his decision.

Early on the morning of Tuesday 25 October, hundreds of marines stormed ashore to seize the old Pearls airport. Simultaneously, at Grenada's southernmost tip, army rangers arrived by parachute and helicopter to seize the new Cuban-built airport. But instead of lasting just a day, the fighting dragged on for several days, partly because of poor intelligence reports from the island about the number of Cubans and their ability to fight.

'Passive' or non-human spying – satellite surveillance and intercepts of radio communications – had not functioned perfectly for the crisis network. However, once the American forces were on the island, the computer again played an important role, as it had early on the Sunday when the Grenada plans could have been abandoned because of the Beirut massacre. More accurate intelligence from Grenada and all over the world flowed into the system, and succinct summaries were passed to McFarlane, the President, Weinberger, Shultz and the chairman of the Joint Chiefs of Staff, General John W. Vessey Jr, in the Situation Room. The speed and precision of the system and breadth of data, which included reaction from allies and enemies, allowed this tight clique to stay on top of events which ranged from military to diplomatic and public relations decisions. Just two days after the invasion the President was able to go on prime-time television to the nation and the world and do his now familiar, and effective, 'selling' of the operation. Reagan kept it simple. "Grenada," he said, "was a Soviet Cuban colony being readied as a major military bastion to export terror and undermine democracy." Then he added theatrically, "We got there just in time."

It was a one-liner to rank with his "There you go again" to Carter during the 1980 debate. Polls carried out on Friday 28 October, when the last of the fighting was still going on in Grenada, indicated strong support for Reagan's actions. The same day Mcfarlane visited the Crisis Center to thank Beal for the 'timely and vital' data that had come to him at the most critical times in the week of high pressure and conflict. Shaking hands with Beal, the National Security Adviser said: "That's the first time in US history that a crisis has been truly managed." Traditionally, all the heads of departments such as the CIA, Defense and State had jealously guarded their intelligence and data from one another. Now for the first time all information had been channeled to the National Security Adviser, allowing him to monitor – via the system – the whole spectrum of events on the President's behalf. This significantly increased the speed and efficiency of the operation.

Although unaware of the secret technology behind the decision making, sections of the stunned and surprised press were unconvinced when they came to review the speedily executed affair. Some saw it as too hasty, others saw it as unnecessary. The Cuban missile crisis of 1962 (when the Soviet Union had tried to place their nuclear warheads on Cuba aimed at the US) was cited warily as a conflict where decisions made too fast could have led to a deadly confrontation with the Soviet Union. Commenting on that crisis, the then Secretary of State George Ball wrote: "Had we fixed on a response during the first 48 hours we almost certainly would have made the wrong decision." Crisis planners, he said, must "carefully examine all the consequences and look far beyond the initial action." At first, the planners in 1962 assumed the US would have to take direct military action. In the early moments of that thirteen-day affair, President Kennedy described an air strike on the missiles already on Cuba as something "we're certainly going to do". But as time, discussion and diplomacy took their course, other options emerged which placed military action further down the list.

Yet despite this justified and inevitable press skepticism, the crisis computer system, which significantly helped facilitate the operation from invasion to the diplomacy afterward, was there to stay. Beal would not be satisfied until the system was running as he had dreamed it should when he first began its implementation a year earlier. He eventually wanted to have TV terminals installed in the Situation Room so that the President and others in the tight decision-making process could press a button and see the vivid computerized representation of a crisis illustrated by charts, maps and easily digested, summarized information.

The success of the Grenada exercise in the eyes of the key White House planners ushered in a new era in world international politics.

From that fateful week in October 1983 on, every conflict would be increasingly monitored and managed by machines. For better or for worse, the most important operation of the Presidency was now being greatly influenced and manipulated by computer.

WHOSE DIGIT ON THE BUTTON?

This institutionalized increase in the computer's influence over conflict was another instance of further erosion in human control over events that could lead to World War Three. The speed and advance of technology by the early eighties had taken decision making out of the hands of elected and traditional authority and placed it in the memory banks of sophisticated machines. For instance, in the event of Soviet forces attacking West Germany, the President of the US might not be in a position to stop the introduction of nuclear weapons. Decision on their use, according to Richard Beal, would already be in the field of battle with the NATO Commander. There would be no time for consultation, except possibly to inform Washington of a *fait accompli*.

"The President would have that kind of situation already defined for him by the Defense Department," Beal said in interviews in September 1981 and March 1983. "He would know what the priorities and options were."

Decisions are made in advance to save vital time. All possible scenarios which have been considered in wargames on computer, where possible developments are 'simulated' to prepare a plan of action. If such plans were to fit what was happening in the field, the Commanders – not just in Europe, but wherever in the world an incident escalated very quickly – could, under extreme circumstances, start firing nuclear weapons. Beal reiterated the President's position when he played down the chaos which ensued after the attempted assassination of President Reagan on 30 March 1981. In that incident, US Army Colonel Jose Muratti, the person carrying the black attaché case known as the 'Football', was separated from the President. The 'Football' contained the top secret 'Gold Codes' and the President's instructions to communicate with the US National Command Authority. This body would have had the power to release nuclear weapons and execute American war plans if the assassination attempt had proved to be part of a Russian plot to destroy the US.

"That incident was misunderstood," Beal said. "The 'Football' was one of four ways the President could communicate with the National Command. If he is incapacitated, he and all the others in the chain of command have successors. There are many back-ups."

When asked what would happen if Soviet Forces had attacked NATO forces in Europe at the same time as the attempted assassination, Beal repeated, "Again, as in all cases, the President does not have his finger on the button. Commanders in the field have the authority to take the necessary operational decisions."

This development makes a mockery of the claim by the UK Government that it has the right of veto over the firing of American-controlled Cruise missiles from British soil. If, in certain circumstances, not even the US President has to be consulted before the plans for war are executed, it is out of the question that a US commander in the field of battle would bother to contact a British Prime Minister and ask permission to fire Cruise or any other nuclear weapon.

Unfortunately the increased chance of war does not end with weapons escalation, or the generals taking over. Computer technology again has taken the danger of war a notch higher, not this time, because of its sophistication, but because errors can occur – and do so, not once or twice a year, but in their thousands. Some have been serious, such as blips on computer terminals indicating Soviet missiles on their way by the score to US targets. The American strike force has been put on full alert on several occasions in recent years because of the malfunction of single micro-silicon chips. The faults were detected because there was enough time – seventeen minutes – to check the computers deep in US military bunkers. A different situation arises in Europe where US and Soviet missiles face each other only six minutes' striking distance away. If an alarm were to occur it is probable that some errors could not be detected in time. Would a general in the field wait to see if Western Europe was being attacked? Or would he think that he could not afford to wait, and therefore order a retaliatory strike? The risks are more than doubled because the Soviet Union, despite its scramble to catch up with and steal US high technology, has systems even more prone to faults. The streamlining and computerizing of the Presidency by 1984 has meant that the planet has been brought closer to the brink of destruction than ever before, whether or not the art of crisis management has been transformed into a brilliant new science.

CHAPTER 23

THE PROGRAMMING OF THE PRESIDENT 1984

THE BLACK BOOK

Wirthlin handed the President a 120-page black bound folder embossed with the title: 'Strategy for Re-election of President Ronald W. Reagan, 1984'. The timing – early October 1983 – and the place – the Oval Office – were both significant, because throughout the summer Wirthlin had been locked in an internecine battle for control of Reagan's re-election bid. Wirthlin's rival, James A. Baker III, Reagan's chief of staff, had increased his reputation and power since 1981 by expert handling of his White House job. Baker would have preferred the veteran Californian political consultant Stu Spencer to be nominated as Campaign '84 strategist, because this would have left Baker himself overall planning and decision making. Spencer was highly regarded for his legendary skills as a tactician, which had been enhanced by his ability to direct Reagan to 'stick to the script' during the 1980 campaign. And this was how Baker wanted to use Spencer again in 1984, while the former Houston lawyer plotted the main strategy. Baker had managed Bush's campaign against Reagan in 1980 and felt he was well qualified for his role as overall planner in 1984. Some of the old, respectful rivalry remained from the 1980 Reagan-Bush battles in which the Reagan-Wirthlin combination had out-foxed and out-strategized the Bush-Baker team. On the one hand, Baker had increased his status since 1981 as chief White House architect of Reagan policy, especially on domestic issues. On the other hand, Wirthlin had maintained his position as a trusted outside adviser and friend for fifteen years. In addition, he had also proved his value by masterminding the PINS-based strategy in 1980. It seemed at the end of the summer of 1983 as if Reagan was attempting to accommodate both parties, as he had with Sears and his rivals in 1980. But Wirthlin decided to move swiftly to cover his position, for as the White House outsider he did not have the power or access to Reagan that Baker and his supporters did.

Apart from his personal link with Reagan, Wirthlin's main asset was his great command of and experience with the 'numbers' – the intelligence on the electorate. This allowed him to create a finely honed first strategy document for winning the 1984 election. While Baker, Spencer and others jockeyed for special titles, the strategist put together a blue-print for victory more than a year before the nation would go to the polls and make their decision as to who would lead the nation from 1985 to 1988. The basic strategy document would be modified dynamically according to indications from Wirthlin's updated PINS system, which would guide broad planning and tactics right through to election day. The document told Reagan where he stood with all the voting groups and where he would have to be in a year if he was to win. Wirthlin pointed out the problems Reagan would face, particularly with the Gender Gap and the lack of support from women's groups, the Jackson-inspired black voter resurgence, and the softness of support from blue-collar workers and others in the coalition which had backed Reagan in 1980. Yet for each problem raised, Wirthlin had a strategic path to overcome in order to align a coalition based on the Republican Party's traditional base of conservative support, voters attracted to Reagan personally regardless of party, white conservative Democrats, moderate Democrats and Hispanics.

Overall, the document was an optimistic stratagem for victory. Reagan's popularity was fairly high compared to other presidents at the same point of their first administrations, and Wirthlin expected it to climb gradually over the next twelve months. Allied to this was the progress of the economy. Reagan would probably be able to base his campaign's general themes on improved economic conditions. Inflation had been squeezed out of the system, interest rates and unemployment figures were continuing to decline. Apart from the huge budget deficit (which showed signs of diminishing in the 'out years' or near future) most indicators, it would be argued, were pointing to a complete economic recovery – even boom conditions – in 1984.

The Black Book also contained the basic themes for 1984. These were a continuation of the developments and trends in the 1970s which had helped create the watershed changes in 1980. According to Wirthlin, America was being nudged towards more conservative views and values, and he planned to use the same themes to form the framework of the 1984 strategy. A key Reagan theme to emerge directly from DMI's surveys of 125,000 Americans was based on the discovery that there was a 'pool of patience' in the US. A high proportion of the electorate was prepared to give Reagan more time to carry through his economic policies, especially as they seemed to be working well. Lines such as 'stay the course', 'no turning back' and 'give Reagan a chance' would be proposed as standard Republican text. The campaign would stress that Reagan was on the right track and that he must have four more years to put right the economic wrongs of previous misguided administrations. Passionate appeals would again be made to the amorphous, yet most useful, 'American Dream'. Wirthlin claimed: "Americans are going to eagerly pursue the

Dream – from owning a house to getting the kids a good education and buying a new car – but more diligently and more wisely." The vision was not quite the two-car family of past American reverie, but still it was a hope, a challenge and part of the optimism that Reagan addressed so well.

The Black Book also outlined the plans for handling the likely problems posed by certain Democrats. Mondale's involvement in the Carter years, which he saw as a strength, were seen as a weakness by the Republicans. Instead of the line, "Are you better off now than you were four years ago?", Republicans would now ask the nation: "Do you really want to return to all that? – the years of high inflation, recession, uncertainty in foreign affairs and weak leadership?" Wirthlin had tracked all the Democratic presidential contenders for years and had fat computer files on all of them, but particularly Mondale, Glenn and Jackson. He had respect for Mondale as a strong candidate and thought him most likely to gain the nomination. Yet he feared Glenn in a run against Reagan, because of his "visibility as an astronaut and Senator, his political base in Ohio [a crucial Midwest state] and his relative lack of association with politics of the past." Glenn had come late to Congress and could not be labeled as a 'free spending' Democrat who had assisted in making the US economy weaker. Another problem for the strategist was that in contrast to Mondale's more liberal outlook – which Reagan found easier to run against – Glenn's politics were safely in the center, and he was more hard line on defense than Mondale. This put Glenn closer to Reagan and therefore more difficult to attack. The electorate would not be given such a clear choice on defense issues if Glenn was the Democratic candidate. However, Wirthlin saw some chinks in the astronaut's protective spacesuit. He was "well known but not known well". In other words people knew who he was, but not what he stood for. It was a problem Wirthlin knew a lot about, for it had been Reagan's in 1976 and 1980. The strategist had had to fight hard and long to sell Reagan's record. With just weeks to go in the 1980 campaign, 70 per cent of the electorate claimed they knew what candidate Reagan stood for. Wirthlin's polls now were saying that Glenn had a long way to go before his positions were clearly and definitively understood. Also, the Glenn strategic themes – if any – did not seem to be bent on improving this weakness. The concentration on image – whether or not *The Right Stuff* proved a box office success – would not be enough. In the end people were inclined to vote on leadership qualities, capacity for the job and policies, rather than image and character alone.

Like his old rival Caddell, Wirthlin had been tracking the resurgence of black interest in politics – long before any other

Republican had begun to acknowledge it as a problem for Reagan. Wirthlin pointed out that in 1980 Reagan had captured the 47 electoral votes of Alabama, Louisiana, Mississippi, North and South Carolina by a combined total of 174,147 votes. By 1984, the Atlanta-based black drive to enlist new voters, the Voter Education Project, expected to have registered more than twice that number of new black voters in those states and Georgia. But now, in mid-1983, none of these states could be considered safe for Reagan in 1984. Nor was California. It would have 47 electoral votes in the coming election – the largest bloc in the nation, and 17 per cent of the 270 needed to win the Presidency. Increasing numbers of black and Hispanic voters could tip the balance against Reagan, although he had never lost an election in his home state. Wirthlin's strategy, which had begun early in 1983, was partly to offset the heavy black opposition influenced by Caddell by making inroads into the strong Hispanic voting bloc. Reagan would be wooing them for the better part of 1983 and 1984. The Republicans were also quietly registering more than two million more white voters likely to support Reagan.

The inspiration for the black revival at the polling booth was Jesse Jackson, and the influence of the so-called 'Jackson Factor' would be monitored by PINS throughout 1984, as would the entrance of John Anderson into the race as an Independent, and a myriad other 'factors' which could affect Reagan's chances for re-election.

STRATEGY FOR A STRATEGIST

When the Black Book was completed in September 1983, Wirthlin decided on a shrewd move. He flew to California to show it to Stu Spencer, his rival for the job of planning Reagan's bid for re-election. Spencer had not thought deeply about 1984, for as a tactician he was not a great believer in too much early planning. He gave his approval to the Black Book, while suggesting four minor changes. On the way back to Washington Wirthlin reviewed the document and the suggested adjustments, and allowed himself the briefest smile of satisfaction. In the initial contest to wrest control of the basic thrust of the planning for 1984, he had already outflanked his opponents. However, he appreciated that there was still a long way to go until the National Campaign, and that there would be many attempts to influence the Reagan drive, especially now that great prestige was involved in climbing aboard a presidential bandwagon which would look stronger as the months rolled on.

Soon after seeing Spencer, Wirthlin had his appointment with Reagan who gave his full approval to the plan. The President appointed him Director of Planning, Policy and Research, and the strategist immediately set up a PINS team in the Reagan-Bush '84 HQ on First Street NW, Washington DC. Grayling Achui, Beal's original assistant on the computer strategy in 1980, was appointed PINS coordinator. In mid-October he and a squad of five Mormons, including two interns from Brigham Young University, started writing the updated PINS program using the PLI software language. By mid-November survey, demographic, historic and economic data from the US Census, DMI and other sources on all sub-groupings of the population in every county had been incorporated into the system. PINS was well prepared for the next twelve months which would decide who would rule the nation, and effectively the Western world, for the rest of the 1980s – potentially the most dangerous period in the history of the human race.

1984 AND ALL THAT

By 29 January when Reagan formally announced his decision to run for a second term, the PINS system had been operating smoothly for several months. It was silently giving direction to every move and utterance the President made. Strategy was aimed squarely at improving the 1984 vote with battlefield groups such as blue-collar workers, Catholics, Hispanics, Independents and 'soft' Democrats. The increments needed for victory had been calibrated down to decimal points in each county and within each of Wirthlin's more than one hundred subcategories of the population. In raw numbers the Reagan camp was allowing for a very high turnout of voters at the 1984 presidential election, perhaps as high as one hundred million. In rough figures this meant they had to score fifty million. Forty four million voters were already considered Reagan's, and in February the question was how the Republicans could collect another seven million. They had support from one in four Democrats, and at least 50 per cent of the Independent voters – those not necessarily supporting either party. However, even more important than the popular vote in a presidential election was the state-by-state breakdown in the contest, which was really a fifty-state battle. Wirthlin was reading from PINS that Reagan was doing better in this than in the popular vote where the strategist had him easily clear of Mondale. PINS gave Reagan a 'lock' on 157 electoral votes at that stage, with 270 needed for nomination. In the ten most populous states PINS indicated that only Massachusetts was unwinnable. It put California, Florida and probably Texas strongly in the Reagan column. The computer also suggested that leadership was going to be the key issue. This could be seen as a referendum on Reagan himself –

a situation that made Wirthlin very comfortable. He told the press in February: "In 1980 the country rejected one kind of leadership, and Walter Mondale is still very much part of it. Ronald Reagan offered a new direction. The first key question is how well he accomplished the goals he set for himself, and the second is whether the voters will give him a mandate for a second term to continue that leadership." Clearly the PINS strategy of making leadership the main issue was working well for Reagan. This too kept the focus off foreign policy, where Reagan was more vulnerable – although he had scored well in that direction with Grenada, which was also largely responsible for his high rating as a leader. Much to the chargin of the Republican 'moderates' led by James Baker in the White House, Wirthlin's polls gave the President some flexibility in handling the Lebanon crisis. This gave Reagan the confidence to keep the US marine peace-keeping force there until late February despite the weight of press and Democratic opinion against such a stance.

Again, as in the second half of 1980, Reagan was flying on automatic pilot, but this time from the news-dominating Oval Office. His TV deliveries on arms control, the State of the Union and his re-election were all upbeat and positive, and easily the best stage-managed of any presidential election in history. The prevailing theme of 'America is back, standing tall' was simple yet solid, and was perceived as credible in view of current economic recovery. The President was making much of this and the fact that he had overseen the biggest arms build-up in history, which he now claimed put him in a position to drive for 'peace' with the Soviets. In the opening months of the year it seemed that this was going to be marketed strongly, if not to the Soviet Union, then definitely to the American people. Such a drive would be an attempt to prevent the Democrats from making Reagan's cold war tactics in 1981 to 1983 too big an issue against the President.

In contrast to the confident-looking Reagan, the Democratic challengers seemed lackluster, even lost. The political advantage the President enjoyed against them as an incumbent unopposed for renomination was seen vividly on US television on 23 January. Early morning network news repeatedly showed the highlight of the previous afternoon's Democratic presidential candidates' forum in Hanover, New Hampshire – the shouting, finger-pointing exchange of insults between Mondale and Glenn. An hour later, the nation's screens were filled with Reagan standing alone in the East Room of the White House before his administration and colleagues and Senators of both parties. He spoke in convincing tones about war and peace and invited the Soviets to resume negotiations on nuclear arms control. "Nineteen eighty-four is a year of opportunity for peace," he said. Wirthlin considered the two TV news items the biggest contrast in electronic imagery for Reagan since early 1980, also in New Hampshire in the last hours of his battle for the primary in that state against Bush. Then Reagan had been seen in a TV news item shaking hands with factory workers in the bitterly cold snow, followed immediately by a shot of Bush jogging in the Texas sunshine.

Apart from the demeaning Democratic bun-fight, Mondale was taking a long time to focus his campaign on a big theme. "I still have to end up with some overarching something," he told Elizabeth Drew of the *New Yorker* magazine, 30 January 1984. "We still don't have that yet – it'll come." Such thoughts must have been more wishful thinking than fact at that stage, for the contrast between the two campaigns was being reflected in the polls. Wirthlin's data – the only polling information to which Reagan paid any attention – had the President twenty points ahead of Mondale by February. Mondale himself, however, held a handy lead over his nearest challenger for the Democratic nomination, John Glenn. The latter's far more serious lack of theme, direction and strategy based on hard research had taken its toll, and he was a beaten candidate even before the primaries got under way. Glenn had slipped to about 14 per cent, equal with Jesse Jackson – the latter having boosted his support noticeably after his coup in unofficial diplomacy of winning the release from Syria of Navy Lieutenant Robert Goodman, the airman who had been shot down during an American bombing raid over Syrian-held Lebanese territory on 4 December 1983.

After a slow start in the primaries Jackson campaigned successfully and looked set to make good his promise of controlling an impressive bloc of delegates to the convention. Yet like Glenn, he had to make way for Gary Hart who emerged as the only real hope of challenging Mondale.

THE CONJURING OF GARY HART

"I love New Hampshire," said Gary Hart in a husky voice, staring triumphantly at thirty TV cameras as he made his victory speech full of the now familiar catchphrases of the primary season: ". . . promise, hope, excitement . . . idealism without illusion . . . fresh ideas . . ." A week earlier he had been campaigning in a light plane. Now he needed a Boeing 727.

Not far from the man of the moment was the person who had made similar moments for scores of politicians, including a president, over the past sixteen years. The brooding, serious Pat Caddell seemed for a few minutes like a well-fed cat who has just devoured the cream. Once again the Democrat's leading electioneering brain was exerting his great influence on presidential primaries. Since early in the year he had dominated the thinking behind Hart's campaign.

Caddell had distilled the themes from Hart's so-called new ideas which until now had inspired but a few. He had instructed the candidate on when and where to say the right slogans which would sell him to the electorate. And they were buying.

As the strategist watched Hart's suddenly more confident performance, a journalist edged close. He had a vague idea that this large man who looked for all the world like an unkempt Irish poet might have had something to do with the transformation of the handsome Kennedyesque candidate's campaign.

"Do you think the Senator can really overcome Mondale" the journalist asked.

"Oh, I always thought the Mondale campaign was the Maginot Line," Caddell said, drawing on one of his favorite war analogies. "What looked like the greatest political organization a week ago, now looks like a wreck."

This sounded as if Caddell was just another onlooker caught up in the excitement, and the journalist scribbled on, oblivious of the comment's double edge. In acting as Hart's top tactician, Caddell had been mainly responsible for Mondale's early shock defeat. It had given him some satisfaction, for there had been much bad feeling between the strategist and the former Vice-President, which stretched back to Carter's 'malaise' speech of 1979. This Caddell invention had emphasized a spiritual crisis in America. Mondale had opposed the speech and felt that it went a long way towards helping defeat Carter in the 1980 election. It caused a split with Caddell which meant that two of the most powerful forces in the Democrats' ranks were set on a collision course.

Mondale had always insisted on steering his own vehicle after watching Caddell with Carter. Of course, Mondale would have a pollster, but he would be just part of the strong organization behind the biggest election juggernaut ever seen in US politics. It was enough, Mondale was convinced, to speed him steadily towards the Democratic nomination, with himself alone in the driving seat. Consequently he decided not to campaign in New Hampshire for the last three days when it appeared that the other candidates were beaten. Peter Hart, his own pollster, had stopped polling after the shaky Glenn tank had been driven into a ditch. Yet the failure to campaign was the most visible early blunder by Mondale. Like Reagan against Ford in 1976 and Bush against Reagan in 1980, the front-running candidate had not remained in the state right up until election day. At the very least Caddell had assured that Hart, against all odds, would provide the Mondale machine with a real contest.

CHAPTER 24

TOMORROW THE WORLD

"We [the strategists] are the pre-selectors," Caddell told journalist Edwin Graham. "We determine who shall run for office."

Caddell did not wish to associate himself with just any Democratic candidate who offered to put him under contract for the 1984 elections. He wanted to choose the person whom he felt could best take advantage of the way the majority of the nation was heading, according to the reading of his polling research. Caddell had worked for Ted Kennedy in senatorial campaigns, and had polled for him again in late 1982. After Kennedy decided not to run for the Presidency, Caddell spear-headed the sensational election of several black candidates to city and state office. As the official Democratic pollster he also advised Jesse Jackson, although he did not work directly for him as he did not feel that the time was right for a minority leader like Jackson to win the Presidency. Caddell did encourage Senator Dale Bumpers of Arkansas, but this was a mild flirtation, for Bumpers, like Senator Biden, did not really believe he could make it. In his attempt to 'pre-select' Biden, Caddell had gone to New Hampshire to find out what the people of the state wanted in a presidential contender. Without giving names, Caddell's researchers asked a random sample to select one profile from several, and they found that Colorado Senator Gary Hart came nearest to the ideal. Caddell found the same thing in many other surveys elsewhere in the nation, but he had to be cautious about approaching Hart with this information. He knew that Hart was reluctant to be under the thumb of a dominating strategist, or be too closely linked with the failure of the McGovern campaign, on which they had both worked closely.

But now, with his campaign in trouble, Hart at last sought Caddell's advice, and was presented by the strategist with his blueprint for victory. The new Caddell-Hart alliance worked from the moment it began. The candidate with the "boring issue-oriented news ideas", as Caddell called them, sharpened his themes about "new Leadership". He began appearing in new Caddell-inspired TV ads that had a Star Wars, computer age look. Speaking direct to camera he said: "The politicians of yesterday are trading away our future by asking our price instead of challenging our idealism . . . my candidacy is for those who still dream dreams . . . who will stand together even more to build an American future . . ." Finally a narrator intoned: "Gary Hart . . .

a new generation of leadership." The themes were meant to help Hart avoid the left-right tag and take advantage of the generation gap detected by Caddell. As Caddell had said in his memorandum: "There's a fault line in the Democratic Party, and it isn't artificial. This campaign has broken right through that fault line. Mondale is the agent of restoration. Gary is the agent of change."

The cliché parroted by Hart supporters went: "Mondale understands the politics of this country, but Gary Hart understands the rhythms of the country, the way history is moving. And history always beats politics." It was a Caddell hyperbole that, however banal, contained a grain of truth. Hart was now benefiting from his new strategist's deep understanding of the trends in voter thinking and articulating it in tight, easily digested one-line capsules for voter consumption.

Like Wirthlin, Caddell had been carefully 'reading' the electorate's mind since the 1980 presidential election. Such a long view of trends allowed these two great strategists to develop the right messages for their respective candidates in 1984. The tactics for defeating opponents in the primaries had also been developed from razor-sharp computerized polling analysis. In 1980, Wirthlin had a computer-backed strategy which allowed Reagan to come from behind and run down a field of powerful candidates. Two of them, George Bush and John Connolly, had strong organizations and powerful financial backing behind them. Yet neither one had a strategist to match the soft-spoken, affable Mormon.

As Senator McGovern's campaign manager, Gary Hart had watched Caddell – the emotional, at times explosive pollster – defeat such notable opponents as Hubert Humphrey and Edmund Muskie. In 1972 and 1980 Caddell had knocked out George Wallace, Henry Jackson and Ted Kennedy for Carter. In 1983, Caddell had been the key strategist behind Harold Washington's victory as Mayor of Chicago, although Washington's opponents out-spent him by ten to one. Gart Hart's campaign in 1984 was laboring under identical restrictions when Caddell took on the Mondale machine. Hart's emergence was due entirely to Caddell's guerrilla tactics: he destroyed opponents with lethal attacks on their weakest points, and then promoted his man with direct appeals to disaffected, alienated voters, who were inclined to vote for change, if only for change's sake. For the fourth presidential primary season in succession, Caddell found a healthy market for such a candidate against more traditional Democrats, who were typically conservative in cultural and foreign affairs, but willing to spend money domesticaly. Since McGovern in 1972, traditionalists had suffered from the problem that in the affluent US, more and more voters saw themselves as those who paid for generous

Government programs, rather than those who benefited from them. An increasing number of voters – particularly those under forty-five and in Caddell's baby-boom-come-of-age category – were interested in liberating themselves from the restraints of traditional values rather than honoring them. This was what Caddell called his six o'clock evening news show audience and he directed Hart to play to it with well-rehearsed lines in different states.

Elections in the US today are as much about bringing down opponents as promoting candidates. In 1980, Caddell had concentrated on accentuating Reagan's 'warmonger' image while Wirthlin had sought to destroy Carter as a 'nice guy'. Both strategists kept extensive computer files on all candidates which were updated continuously to probe every possible weakness. In the 1984 primaries and caucuses, Mondale proved a vulnerable target for Caddell who had files on him going back to 1975. The former Vice-President was tagged as 'the captive of special interests', a stinging reference to Mondale's efforts to gain support from a wide range of groups with binding promises. Gary Hart, in contrast, was portrayed as being above such things.

If Hart's challenge to Mondale ensured that the battle for the Democratic nomination would extend longer than the Party had hoped, it also shortened the time available for a united campaign by the Democrats to remove Ronald Reagan from office. The prolonged struggle would inevitably expose all the strengths and weaknesses of the challenger. Each personal issue and characteristic that emerged would be filed and analyzed by PINS and Wirthlin. As his system ticked over and adjusted to the new Democratic contender, it would indicate the course that Reagan must take to have the best chance of winning in November.

The ferocious contest between the two brilliant political adversaries, Wirthlin and Caddell, was now entering its sixteenth year. Each man continued to use the new computer technology in an effort to perfect his methods and gain victory for their opposite ideologies through the United States' democratic process. Their epic battle has ensured that from today all candidates for high office will have to rely upon the new strategists with their computer simulation technology to gain high office. The great pollsters have already moved into pre-eminent positions of power in elections and running government. With their control over politicians and their understanding of the new technology, it is the strategists who, more and more, will dictate the direction of nations and the world.